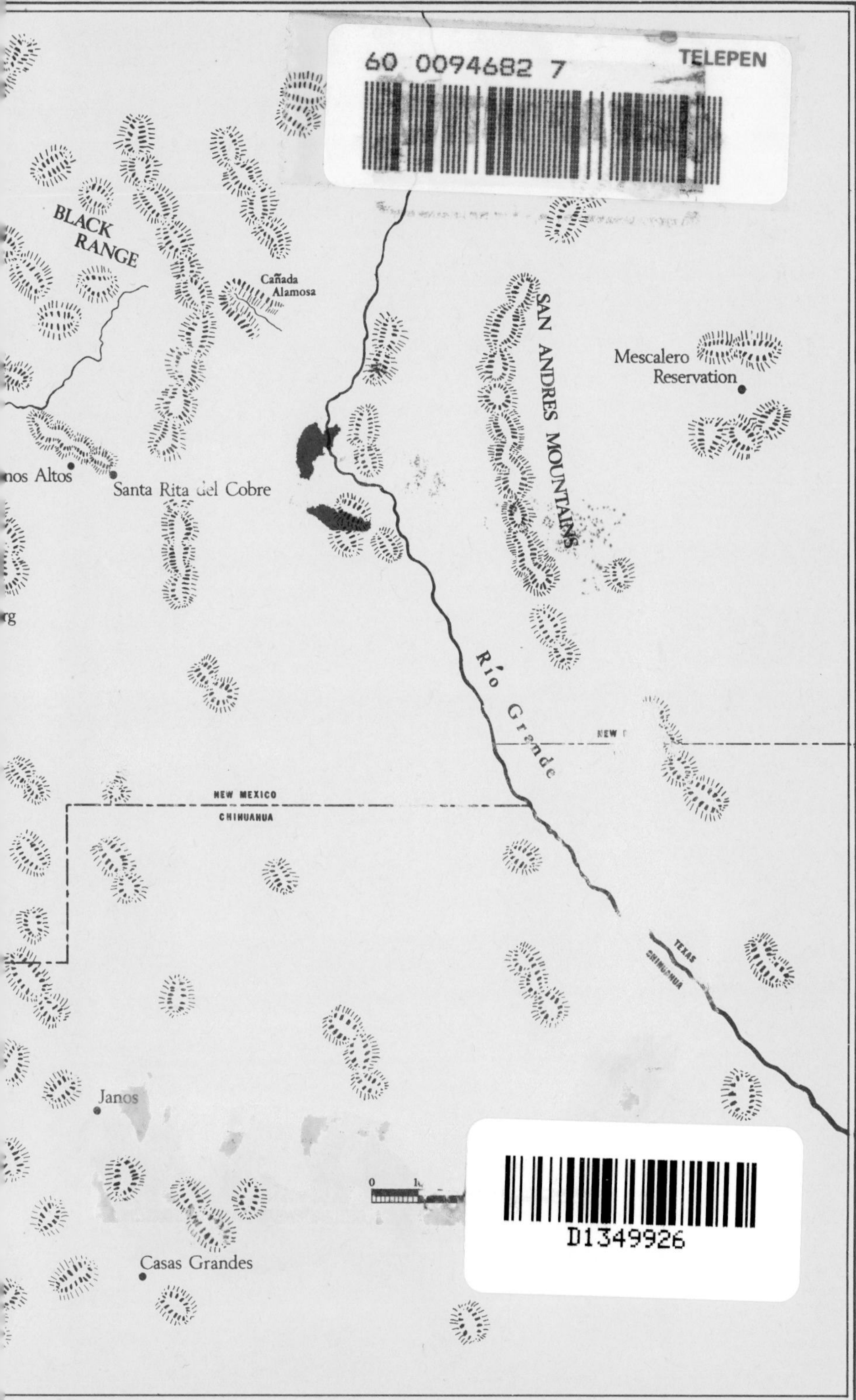
BLACK RANGE
Cañada Alamosa
SAN ANDRES MOUNTAINS
Mescalero Reservation
nos Altos
Santa Rita del Cobre
rg
Río Grande
NEW MEXICO
CHIHUAHUA
TEXAS
CHIHUAHUA
Janos
Casas Grandes

Geronimo

BY ALEXANDER B. ADAMS:

Thoreau's Guide to Cape Cod

First World Conference on National Parks
(EDITOR)

John James Audubon: A BIOGRAPHY

A Handbook of Practical Public Relations

Eternal Quest: THE STORY OF THE GREAT NATURALISTS

Eleventh Hour: A HARD LOOK AT CONSERVATION

Geronimo. The best known of all the Apache war leaders, Geronimo waged war against the Americans for many years. His final surrender brought peace to the United States.

Geronimo

A BIOGRAPHY

ALEXANDER B. ADAMS

NEW ENGLISH LIBRARY
TIMES MIRROR

First published in the United States of America by G. P. Putnams Sons and simultaneously in Canada by Longmans Canada Ltd, Toronto.

First published in Great Britain by New English Library, Barnard's Inn, Holborn, London E.C.1. in 1973

Printed in Great Britain by C. Tinling & Co. Ltd, London and Prescot.

All of the photographs in this book are copied from the collection of the Arizona Pioneers' Historical Society. Grateful thanks are hereby expressed by the author and publisher to Miss Margaret Sparks and the Arizona Pioneers' Historical Society.

0450016277

To

Harriet and Jacques Transue

Because this book contains much about
personal courage, it belongs to you

Contents

This report shows plainly that . . . the Apache Indians were the friends of the Americans when they first knew them; . . . that their ill-will and constant war with the Mexicans arose from the fact that the Mexicans denied them any rights to the soil as original occupants, and waged a war of extermination against them; that the peaceable relations of the Apaches with the Americans continued until the latter adopted the Mexican theory of "extermination," and by acts of inhuman treachery and cruelty made them our implacable foes; that this policy has resulted in a war which, in the last ten years, has cost a thousand lives and over forty million dollars, and the country is no quieter nor the Indians any nearer extermination than they were at the time of the Gadsden Purchase. . . .

—REPORT OF VINCENT COLYER TO THE BOARD OF INDIAN COMMISSIONERS, 1871

About Some of the Names

APACHES—The term "Apache" is applied to all Southwestern Athapascan Indians with the exception of the Navajos. This includes a large group: the Jicarillas, the Lipans, the Kiowas, the Mescaleros, the Chiricahuas and their related tribes, and the Western Apaches. Aside from their common language and descent, many of these Indians had little to do with each other, and sometimes they were enemies. Many of these larger divisions can be broken down into numerous smaller ones, some twenty for the Western Apaches alone. Each of these subdivisions formed a distinct unit that might or might not act in concert with the others. To confound the subject even further, the Spanish sometimes applied the term "Apache" to non-Athapascan Indians, particularly to those who were effective in resisting the Europeans' invasion of their lands.

This book deals primarily with the Indians who can be loosely gathered together under the term "Southern Apaches." While there were many Apache tribes that fought—and fought well—against the white men, these carried on the war the longest. When they finally surrendered, the Southwest at last knew peace for the first time since the arrival of the white men, a span of time covering many hundreds of years.

For purposes of simplification, I have, therefore, applied the word "Apache," standing by itself and without a modifier, only to the Southern Apaches or, with the exception of some of the Plains Apaches, to all the Apaches taken together. Thus, for example, when mentioning the Mescaleros, I have called them either Mescaleros or Mescalero Apaches and not merely Apaches. I do this, acknowledging the slight injustice but believing this practice will make the subject easier for the reader to follow.

Warm Springs Apaches—This name was originally applied to the Apaches living near Ojo Caliente in New Mexico but soon came to encompass the Apaches to whom they were most closely related, such as the Mimbreños and the Bedonkohes. (Geronimo belonged to the Bedonkohes.) I have used the term throughout the book in its later sense.

Chiricahuas—This is the name of the mountain range that, along with the Dragoons and the Dos Cabezas Mountains, served as a stronghold for the Chikonens, who lived in southeastern Arizona. The name came to be applied to the Indians themselves and was later extended to include the Warm Springs Apaches and the Nednis, with whom they were closely associated. I have used the word in its original sense except toward the end. By that time, the tribes had combined and were fighting as one unit. Both the military and civilians, as well as many Apaches, then referred to them all as Chiricahuas, and so do I.

Geronimo—This is the Spanish for Jerome. Americans who do not speak Spanish generally used a hard "g," but this is incorrect. The "g" is pronounced like an "h"—just as it is in Gila River or Gila monster. The accent, which is written out in Spanish, falls on the second syllable. In dealing with white men, the Indians were unlikely to use their Indian names for several reasons: They were difficult to pronounce; they often changed as an Apache attained maturity; and they sometimes described personal characteristics that the Indians did not wish to expose to the white men. In the early days of the Southwest, Spanish was the most widely used of the European languages. Therefore, it was customary to call Indians by their Mexican nicknames.

Juh—The chief of the Nedni Apaches was one of the few exceptions to the use of Spanish nicknames. His name was spelled in various ways by the whites, one version being "Whoa." Although this closely approximated the pronunciation of his name, the spelling "Juh" was more commonly employed.

AMERICANS—Oblivious to the feelings of the many other nationalities who also share the Western Hemisphere, the people of the United States apply the word "American" only to themselves, and unfortunately there is no adequate substitute. In Mexico, we are officially known as *norteamericanos,* but this ignores the Canadians and sounds awkward to our ears. The word "Anglo," used by many early writers, sounds equally awkward and fails to recognize the many people—soldiers and civilians—who were not of British descent. So I have fallen back on "Americans," but do so with apologies to the Mexicans and all others equally entitled to the name.

WHITE MEN—The Apaches did not use the term "white men." Their name for the Americans was "white eyes." Again, this is so unfamiliar that I have not employed it but have used the more conventional "white men" to designate both Americans and Mexicans, even though, I regret to say, many Americans in the Southwest did not include Mexicans in the term.

Geronimo

Before the Rocks Were Hard

A white man lived near an Apache reservation. One of his friends wondered that he dared do so, because Apaches were so dangerous. So he invited his friend to come and see for himself that it was safe.

They got in his truck and drove to the reservation, where they stopped to talk to an Apache, one who remembered the old days.

"Are you an Indian?" asked the white man, getting out of the truck.

"Yes," replied the Apache simply. (Unlike white men, Indians do not think silly questions deserve lengthy answers.)

"What tribe do you belong to?"

"I am an Apache."

"And how long have you been here?"

"My people," said the Apache, "were here before the rocks were hard. Your people came afterward."

The white man said nothing more. He got back in his truck and drove away.

The Apache to whom this happened was telling me about it. We were sitting on a wooden bench in the shade of the ramada outside his house. In the direct sunlight, the day was hot; but here, protected from the sun by the roof of brush laid over the open wooden framework, we were cool. A few feet away, under another ramada, his family was preparing food for a party—Indian *tortillas,* lima beans, frijoles, corn on the cob, and other favorites of the Apaches. Because he was an old man, his family was numerous—gentle-spoken men and women and quiet, gay children and their friends. Two dogs wandered among the tables, hoping for scraps. And a duck, followed by her duckling, roamed here and there.

It was a quiet scene, but there was no quiet in the Apache's heart. "I don't tell stories anymore," he said. "People only tell lies."

We sat in silence for a few moments. He was staring straight ahead with eyes that looked into the past. The two dogs gave up their search for food and lay down under one of the tables. I told him it would be a sorry day if the history of the Apaches was ever lost.

"Let it be lost," he said. "The white man has already forgotten the Apaches, so let their history be forgotten also."

We sat again in silence. Then, with an Apache's courtesy, he began to explain his meaning. There are many lies, he said. People talk of Geronimo as a bad man. They do not mention that he was fighting for his own land. They call the Apaches mean, but they were not. The Apaches were taught to respect the lives of all "two-legged beings." Then the white men came and said, "Those are wild Indians" and began killing them.

He told how, many years ago, twelve Apaches had been arrested at the San Carlos Agency for breaking into a store and stealing some money. An Indian asked the Army officer who made the arrest if he knew the Indians had actually stolen the money. The officer said, "Yes."

"Did you see them?"

"No."

"Did someone else see them?"

"No."

The Indians asked the soldiers to accompany them. They followed the trail from the store, telling the soldiers to stay back some distance. The trail led north and looked as though it had been made by reservation Indians. Then it began to circle around until it led back to one of the white settlements near Safford, Arizona. They came to a cabin and a corral, which held two horses.

One of the Indians said to the soldiers, "If that horse has a broken shoe, these will be the people."

He raised the horse's hoof, and the shoe was broken in half.

The Indians told the soldiers to station themselves out of sight at the four corners of the cabin. Then they walked up to the cabin. The white men came out.

"Don't shoot," said the soldiers.

The white men asked, "What are these Indians doing here?"

The soldiers again said, "Don't shoot."

Then they arrested the white men.

Later the leader of the Indians told the soldiers that it was evil to always suspect Indians of wrongdoing and that it had been foolish in the first place to suspect Indians of having broken into the store. There was no place where they could have spent the money that had been taken.

The Apache had said to me that he no longer told stories, but he told many of them as he sat in the cool of his ramada. He talked about the troubles at Cibicue when the soldiers, misunderstanding an Indian ceremony, caused needless arrests and death. He recalled the massacre at Camp Grant, when citizens from Tucson led an attack on a camp of peaceful Indians living under the protection of the Army. "Their camp was surrounded and attacked at daybreak," wrote the commanding officer. "So sudden and unexpected was it that no one was awake to give the alarm, and I found quite a number of women shot while asleep. . . . The wounded who were unable to get away had their brains beaten out with clubs or stones. . . . Of the whole number killed and missing, about one hundred and twenty-five, only eight were men."

With such memories and thoughts, no wonder the Apache was bitter. The white men's war against the Apaches was not honorable.

Of course, the horrors and the betrayals were not all on one side. As the outnumbered Apaches fought desperately to retain possession of their lands or at least to compel the white men to live up to their own agreements, they became more and more fierce and vengeful. "The Adobe walls are there, but bare and blackened," wrote a reporter about the results of an Apache raid. ". . . Around the corner of the ruined house is the stalwart ranchero, stretched upon the ground. A big, rough stake, split from his own wagon, is driven through his abdomen and deep into the hard earth." And in the cemetery near Fort Bowie, where they often buried the casualties of Apache attacks, the hand-lettered wooden markers sometimes bore this inscription:

In Memory of
[name]
[date]
Supposed to Be

The final three words told much.

But it is these atrocities, usually committed after the victim was already dead, that are best remembered, not the many instances in which white men used a flag of truce to set a trap or the times they massacred peaceful Apaches, killing women and children as indiscriminately as warriors. For white men's newspapers and books, and later their movies and television sets, have recorded their side of the story; but the Apaches' was rarely heard, because they had no written language, no historians, and few spokesmen. Even today in the Southwest, the words "marauding Apaches" are commonly used, but not often "invading Mexicans and Americans." Yet that is what the white men's presence amounted to: an invasion.

Ever since they came to the Southwest from their original home in Alaska, the Apaches were known as warlike people who took what they wanted whenever they liked. But the ferocity for which they are now famous was not aroused until the coming of the Spanish. It was then that they began attacking even the Pueblo Indians, with whom they had often previously traded. They rightly regarded the pueblos as strongholds of

Spanish influence and believed they must dislodge that influence before they could drive the Spanish out. Because the Mexicans, after they gained independence, did not relent in their efforts to gain control of the Apaches' land, the Apaches did not relent in their efforts to defend it. When the Mexicans were replaced by Americans, the Apaches at first greeted them with a friendly, if somewhat suspicious, attitude that did not change until they became convinced that the Americans, too, planned to stay. Then, once more, their warriors started on the warpath.

When the Apaches did go to war, they were among the best of fighters. I have talked to a retired Army colonel who once commanded Apache scouts. He described them as "the greatest infantry soldier the United States has ever known." They could march incredible distances, suffer unbelievable deprivations, and fight with unequaled tenacity and skill. Always poorly equipped and short of ammunition and guns, they held off the troops of technologically advanced nations. And the use they made of their terrain put the best officers to the test.

There were many tribes of Apaches, so many that anthropologists have devoted years of work to an attempt to untangle their relationships. This account is largely limited to those who comprised the Warm Springs Apaches, the Chiricahuas, and the Nednis, not because their exploits were necessarily greater, but because the story of their struggle is enough to fill an entire book. It is a story of a small group of men, women, and children holding at bay a large and powerful nation. It is a story of courage and tenacity and of a battle fought bravely against overwhelming odds.

The war followed an American pattern that has continued into at least the last half of the twentieth century, a pattern that does little credit to our nation or its people and reveals an astounding inability to learn from the past. The Army, always inflexible, simply could not cope with the guerrilla tactics used by the Apaches. Although greatly outnumbered and fighting with inferior equipment and no regular sources of supply, tiny bands of warriors held off thousands of troops. Not until an

American general was wise enough to enlist Apaches to fight Apaches did the tide of battle start to change. It might almost be said that, in the end, it was really an Apache victory over Apaches.

As with too many wars waged by this country, many people gained an economic advantage from it. Because of their dependence on the government's expenditures, they supported an unsuccessful military strategy and an ineffective Indian policy. As for the government itself, faced with a problem it could not understand, much less solve, it vacillated from one extreme to another, breeding distrust and confusion. At least one general tried to direct the war from Washington with no comprehension of the actual difficulties. Like so many generals, he remembered too well his younger days and believed this war was like the others in which he had fought. As a consequence, he made impossible demands of the men in the field and did not appreciate their successes. And, as so often in America's history, red tape, protocol, and interdepartmental bickering also did their damage. Because of them, many lives were lost.

The Americans' contempt for an alien culture was as conspicuous then as it is today. Only a handful of people made an attempt to learn about the Apaches, and when they did, the rewards were numerous. If they were Army officers, they found themselves more effective than their fellows, and whether they were in the military or not, they gained respect for a remarkable people. To most Americans, however, the Apaches remained "gooks"—alive but scarcely human, objects it would be better to annihilate.

Most serious of all was the debilitating effect of the war on the American spirit. True, many individuals remained courageous and honorable, a credit to our nation. But others, in their frustrations, fell victims to the basest passions and allowed their actions to be governed by hate and fear. Murder—and even genocide—was openly advocated by people who considered themselves normal, law-abiding citizens. Patriotism was expressed not in noble acts but in lies and distortions. And honor was given not to those who earned it but to those who claimed it.

This deterioration of character while under stress has been evidenced by us too many times. The failing seems to be rooted in several causes. One of these is a myopia that makes us expect the facts to turn out according to a pattern that we have predetermined. When they do not, we bend the truth to fit our expectations. This has created a mythology that obstructs our thinking. Even now, for example, many of us believe we have never fought a war that was not justified on moral principles. The reader of this book can judge for himself whether this is true. Another myth we continually reiterate is that we have never fought a war we did not win. Some of the wars we have won were fought against antagonists so much weaker militarily that defeat for us would have been impossible. The Mexican War and the Spanish-American War are two of them. And one war was never won at all. For that example, we have only to look at another tribe of Indians, the Seminoles. No historian, as far as I know, has been able to produce evidence of the Seminoles' surrender, either orally or in writing. Our avowed purpose in fighting was to remove every Seminole from Florida to Indian Territory. Yet there are still Seminoles living in Florida.

These myths permit us to live in a cloud of self-righteousness. We keep repeating that we are honorable and peace-loving. And we are—until we cannot have what we want. Then we are prepared to go to any ends to get it. We will prop up dictatorships, engage in wars of aggression, and even kill civilians, as we did so freely in the Apache wars. But if we finally get what we want, we can be extremely pretentious. After a highly competitive struggle in which we sacrificed billions of dollars and several lives, we finally landed two men on the moon and, being ahead, made the self-righteous comment: "We come in peace."

That is precisely what we told the Apaches.

As long as we cannot face ourselves realistically, we cannot be a real people.

Greed also lies at the base of our deterioration of character. Many of us are greedy, and more than most nations, we respect greed. The Mexican War came about, not because Mexico posed a military threat to the United States, but because the United States wanted New Mexico, Arizona, and California; and since we could not get that land by peaceful means, we resorted to force—plain, brute force. We did the same with the Apaches. The demands of the ranchers and miners were practically insatiable, and they resulted in numerous violations of America's word—and honor. As for the war contractors? We have always had people who have been willing to benefit personally by other people's deaths.

In addition, we are from time to time the victims of a peculiar type of paranoia. Ever since the passage of the Alien and Sedition Acts, the nation has gone through recurring periods of hysteria, when its hate, springing out of fear, has been directed at classes of people, whether they were friendly or not. Anyone who doubts this has only to think of loyal Germans in World War I, loyal West Coast Japanese in World War II, hippies today, or anyone that can be labeled a Communist, and, in the 1880's, anyone who was an Apache. In a frenzy, the Americans turned on them all, even those who fought valiantly on the American side in the war and without whose help the Americans could not have won, or at least as soon as they did.

Among the poltroons, the vain, the greedy, and the shortsighted who were involved in the wars with the Apaches, there were also heroes, men of understanding and courage. Their lot was often unhappy. One was relieved of his command, one was repeatedly court-martialed, one was retired on the half pay of a first lieutenant, and another was killed by a bullet from the Mexicans he was supposedly helping. Some of them fared better, but none of them fared well. Yet these were the men who represented what we consider the best of our tradition—honesty, bravery, and consideration for others. For along with our faults, we have always had some men who exhibited these traits to an unusual degree, and I hope that, in the end, it is these qualities that will prevail.

As I sat with the old Apache in the shade of his ramada, I thought of these things. Even if the Apaches themselves desired their story to be lost, we should not let it be. It tells us too much about ourselves.

Today much of their land is laced with highways, and much of it is crowded with real estate developments. The smoke from the smelters rises in the air, and the silence is often broken by the sound of jet airplanes flying overhead. Yet much of the land remains the same. The faint haze of the desert cloaks the foothills of the Dragoon Mountains in the daytime, and the winter snows fall on the high peaks of the Chiricahuas. In New Mexico, in the land of Mangas Coloradas and Victorio, enormous machines remove the ore at Santa Rita del Cobre; but farther north, in the heart of the Black Mountains, little has changed. The white oaks and the piñons put forth their nuts each season, and the Gila River flows through the deep canyons it has dug for itself over the centuries. The Sierra Madres of Mexico are still almost as inaccessible as in the days when Juh was alive and Geronimo sought refuge in their wilderness.

In places such as these, the spirit of the Apaches still exists, but it is not limited to them alone. It lives wherever men and women are struggling against overwhelming odds for freedom and justice. We, as Americans, should be proud that the Apaches' story is part of our country's heritage.

I

Treachery at Santa Rita del Cobre

THE war had gone on for several hundred years. Yet neither side had been able to win a decisive victory. The Apaches, with their small population and primitive weapons, could not muster the strength to expel the invaders. On the other hand, the Spanish, and then the Mexicans, had never been able to control the Apaches. No matter how many troops they garrisoned in their towns and no matter how many presidios they built, the Apaches came and went almost as they pleased, attacking when and where they wanted to.

At last, the war reached a virtual stalemate in what is now Mexico. The Apaches continued to make raids in present Sonora and Chihuahua, but aside from their refuge high in the Sierra Madres, the range that divides those two states, they had no territory left they could claim as their own. Farther north, however, they had prevented the invaders from taking over large sections of the country, driving their enemies from such establishments as the mission and pueblo at Quaraí, which stood a few miles south of the present town of Manzano. The ancient church and fortification, unable to withstand the constant attacks of the Apaches, lay in ruins, its adobe walls dissolving back into the soil from which their bricks had been formed. In the arroyo near the former church, the cottonwoods bloomed each spring; grass grew again where the ground had been trodden bare by the feet of Spanish soldiers and priests and the hooves of Spanish horses. No one lived there anymore; and the nights at Quaraí were silent and black, the candles of the Spanish priests extinguished forever.

A similar fate had befallen Gran Quivira. Situated on a rise of ground some miles farther south, its ruins represented the failure of a Spanish dream. Once the buildings of the immense pueblo had stood in testimony to the Pueblo Indians' industry. And the great church, with its elegant decorations, had symbolized the religious and political dominance of Spain. Each day in the growing season, the Indians had gone out to the nearby fields to tend their crops; the priests had chanted their masses before the altar; the soldiers had lounged in the shade or fed and watered their horses; and the women had cared for the children, swept out the quarters of the clergy, and prepared the meals for their husbands' return. Now Gran Quivira, too, was deserted. The fields were untended, and the furrows had long since been flattened by the wind and rain. If a courageous traveler had ventured to the highest point and looked at the view that extends for miles around, he would not have seen a single Mexican or Pueblo Indian. They had long since fled, and the land belonged to the Apaches once again.

On the other hand, the Apaches had never been able to mass the forces necessary to dislodge the Mexicans from such centers in northern Chihuahua as Santa Fe. In cities like this, the men could finish their day's work and, in the evenings, join their friends in the plaza, knowing they could have a quiet conversation without being interrupted by an Apache attack. Occasionally the Apaches would steal some horses from a rancher or a party of trappers who had wandered too far, and the white man who attempted to penetrate too deep into their territory would probably never return. But in much of the land an unspoken truce prevailed. As long as the Mexicans did not expand their activities and as long as they remained within the areas they already controlled, they were relatively free from danger.

Among those who had taken advantage of this lull in the fighting were the residents of Santa Rita del Cobre, a town that was a few miles east of present Silver City, New Mexico. Situated in the foothills at the entrance to the Black Range, the town was low enough in elevation to be free of the heavy snows that swept across the mountains farther north during the winter months, yet it was high enough to be spared the heat of the desert plains to the south and the dust storms that blinded men and horses during the early spring. Life at Santa Rita was comfortable and prosperous, even though the town was far from the more cosmopolitan pleasures of Chihuahua and Santa Fe.

The sources of the community's wealth were its extensive deposits of copper. These had been discovered in 1804, but no one had dared to mine them because of the Apaches. Any settlement would have been immediately attacked, and the profits from the copper could not have paid the costs of a garrison large enough to protect it. The local chief was Juan José, a great fighter. No white man knew much about him, but it was rumored that a priest had taught him how to read and write. Instead of leading him into the ways of Christianity, this skill had been useful to him in war. According to the rumors among the soldiers and merchants, Juan José's warriors intercepted the Mexicans' messengers and carried their dispatches to the chief. He in turn read them and used the information they contained in planning his attacks and ambushes. Nothing else could account for the sagacity with which he carried on his war with the Mexicans, preventing them from entering his country or mining the copper.

As time went on, however, and relations between the people of northern Chihuahua and the Apaches became somewhat more peaceful, a Mexican businessman, Don Francisco Manuel Elguea, saw an opportunity to make money. Because the Mexican government needed copper for coinage, Elguea purchased the Mexican rights to the deposits and proceeded to make an agreement with Juan José. In return for gifts of horses, bolts of cloth, and other articles the Apaches liked, he secured permission to found a town and open a mining operation. Juan José insisted on several conditions. The activities of the Mexicans were to be limited solely to mining. They could not establish farms or ranches or engage in trading. Also, they could come and leave only by two designated routes, one to Chihuahua and one to Sonora. But these restrictions did not affect the efficiency of Elguea's enterprise. The miners went to work; the copper ore came out of the ground; the Mexicans grew wealthy; and the Apaches benefited from the presents the Mexicans gave them.

Santa Rita del Cobre never became self-sufficient because the terms laid down by Juan José prevented the development of large-scale farming on the outskirts of the town or the establishment of trade with other communities. But this was of no concern to the inhabitants. On a regular schedule, the *conducta,* or armed convoy of wagons, came north from the city of Chihuahua, lumbering over the mountain passes and across the plains, past Janos and other settlements in the valleys. The dust rose from the creaking wheels of the wagons. The guards rode ahead on the flanks, exchanging jokes with each other, for the Apaches kept their word and never attacked. The *conducta*'s route took it near the Florida Mountains in present New Mexico and over the flat, arid stretches that cover part of the southwestern section of that state. Finally, it entered the foothills near Santa Rita del Cobre, the men thankful to escape the heat, and arrived at the plaza. In the wagons were everything the town needed to survive: guns, ammunition, supplies of food and clothing, trade goods for the Indians, and all the liquor the Mexicans could drink.

For a while, everyone seemed happy with the arrangement worked out by Elguea and Juan José. Considering the long enmity between the two peoples, the truce was an unnatural one, but it survived despite the protests of some of the Apaches. One leader, Cuchillo Negro, or Black Knife, was concerned about the growing numbers of Mexicans. But he lived northeast of Santa Rita del Cobre in the area around Ojo Caliente, or Warm Springs, and it was not his right to interfere with Juan José's decision.

Another dissident was Mangas Coloradas, or Red Sleeves. Among the Apaches he was unusual for his height, six feet or more, and for his great strength. No man who saw him ever forgot him. His physical stature was impressive, and so was his intelligence. Yet he, too, followed the policies decided on by Juan José and the majority of his warriors. A delicate balance had been struck that was dependent on the good faith of both the Mexicans and the Apaches, and it might have gone on for years if the government of the state of Chihuahua had not upset it.

In 1835, Sonora, weary of continued Apache attacks on its settlements and unable to halt them, passed a law setting up a bounty for any Apache scalp. The measure was vigorous, vicious, and cruel, one of several instances in which genocide has been practiced on this continent. The most obvious stupidity in the law was the government's inability to distinguish between the scalps of friendly Apaches and those who were enemies. In fact, the authorities could not even be certain that a scalp was an Apache's, and probably some Mexicans were killed as well as Indians. In Ures, the capital of the state, the government paid bounties on all scalps.

Two years later, the state of Chihuahua decided to follow a similar course. It promulgated a law requiring the authorities to pay one hundred pesos for every Apache warrior's scalp, fifty for a woman's, and twenty-five for a child's. Again there was no means of proving whether the scalped Indian had been an enemy; the scalp of a friend was worth a hundred pesos, too. And so the stage was set for bloodshed and treachery.

In the mountains near Santa Rita del Cobre, Juan José continued his peaceful way, unaware that he and every warrior in his band were now valued at a hundred pesos each—dead. He still freely visited Santa Rita del Cobre, talked to his Mexican friends, and accepted presents from them for himself and his people. He had not relaxed his vigilance, however, and from time to time his scouts still intercepted the Mexican mails and brought him their contents. Among the letters he was reading one day was a dispatch from the Chihuahuan government to an American trader, James Johnson, notifying Johnson of the new bounty policy and inviting him to take advantage of it. The news came as a complete surprise to Juan José, and he had difficulty believing it, for he knew Johnson well, having met him several times while the American was trapping near the Gila River. Juan José had liked him and had permitted him to pass through the country unharmed. Learning that Johnson was camped nearby, he decided to talk to him and find out the truth.

Feeling more curiosity than fear, he entered his friend's camp and found with him a group of Missouri mule traders led by a man named Eames and accompanied by a personal friend, Gleason. With them they had a mule train of supplies. And for all Juan José could tell, they were traveling on a normal trading expedition. This belief was reinforced by everything that Johnson said. He assured Juan José that, regardless of the policies of the Chihuahuan government, he and the chief were friends; and to prove this, he invited Juan José to come back for a party, bringing with him as many Apaches as he pleased. There would be plenty to eat and drink, Johnson promised, and presents for everyone.

Such an invitation was not unusual from a white man who wished to be friends with the Apaches, and Juan José accepted. Returning to his own people, he spread the word that they were to assemble at Johnson's camp on the day agreed upon. Mangas Coloradas, although he distrusted the white men, decided to go, too, and take his two wives and his infant son. When the Apaches arrived, they found Johnson true to his word. Just as he had said he would, he laid out a feast for them and provided enough liquor to satisfy even the hard-drinking Apaches. The Indians set about helping themselves to the food and drink, thankful for the white men's generosity; and as he looked at the peaceful scene, Juan José had reason to congratulate himself on the success of his policy of moderation.

Toward the end of the party, when the Apaches were filled with liquor and food, Gleason came up to Juan José and asked him to step aside for a private conversation. At the same time, Johnson announced that the Apaches were to help themselves to some meal he had now placed out for them. With much laughter and joking, the Indians gathered in a group around the pile, each trying to make sure he got his share, while Juan José and Gleason stood talking. Johnson himself looked on for a moment and then, lighting a *cigarrito,* left the party and moved behind a screen of brush that had been gathered near the camp. The Apaches, who were normally alert, had not paid any particular attention to this brush pile because they had been too anxious to get to the liquor. Now they had drunk too much to be suspicious of Johnson's quiet departure from the camp.

While they were happily scooping up the meal, a loud roar resounded through the camp. The mules jerked frantically at their tethers. The laughter of the Apaches turned to moans of pain, as a shower of deadly slugs, nails, and bullets rained into their midst from the howitzer Johnson had concealed behind the brush screen and had aimed directly at the spot where he had placed the meal.

Before the Indians could recover from the shock, the traders leaped on those who remained alive, guns firing and knives flashing. Each Apache child, woman, or warrior was worth from twenty-five to a hundred pesos, and the scalp-hunters did not discriminate among them in their killing.

At the sound of the howitzer, the signal for the white assault, Gleason fired his gun at Juan José, wounding him but not fatally. The old Apache may have made peace with the white men, but he was still a capable warrior. Although blood was streaming from his wound, he drew his knife and refused to give up. The struggle that followed was uneven. Gleason was no match for the powerful chief. The two men tumbled to the ground, with Juan José on top and Gleason completely at his mercy. At least this part of the white men's plan had failed, for the chief, who had been specially marked for death, was still alive. What is more, he had a hostage.

But Juan José was still bewildered by the sudden turn of events and unable to grasp what had happened. Instead of plunging his knife into Gleason's throat, freeing himself, and fleeing to safety, he hesitated to kill a man whom he knew to be a friend of his own good friend. While he hesitated, Johnson came running toward them. Juan José called out to him in Spanish, saying he did not want to kill Gleason but that he needed Johnson's help. Johnson did not even reply. Pressing the trigger of his gun, he sent the final, fatal bullet into Juan José's wounded body. The muscles of the chief relaxed; his hand opened; the knife slid to the ground; and he lay there dead.

A few of the Apaches had escaped the blast of the howitzer and the first onslaught of the traders. They fought back as best they could. In fierce hand-to-hand combat, they managed to inflict a few casualties on the white men, broke free, and made their escape. One of these was Mangas Coloradas. Both his wives were killed, but as he turned to run, he stooped down, picked up a baby lying on the ground, and carried it with him to safety. Only later did he learn that he had rescued his own son.

When the battle was over, Johnson and his severely frightened friend, Gleason, tended to their own wounded. Then they and the men from Missouri drew their knives and started the bloody task of removing the scalps of the dead Indians. These were hung in the sun to dry so they could be shipped to Chihuahua, while the bodies were left to rot.

Counting up their trophies, Johnson and Gleason figured out their profits. For a few hours of work and the price of some supplies, they had earned hundreds of pesos. They had also reignited the war between the Apaches and the Mexicans near the Black Mountain Range.

Juan José had been a reasonable man, one with whom the whites could deal. When James Johnson murdered him for a hundred pesos, he did the people of Mexico a disservice. Never was government money more badly spent, because Mangas Coloradas succeeded to the leadership of the Apaches. He was a different type of person. He hated the Mexicans bitterly, he was an intelligent fighter, and he had an unusual capacity for persuading the Apaches to coordinate their warfare.

Many stories have been told about him. According to one, he

had had two wives when he captured a particularly beautiful Mexican girl, married her, and made her his favorite. The relatives of the two earlier wives complained about this treatment of their kinswomen, whereupon Mangas Coloradas challenged them to fight him with knives. He killed two men and established his right to live as he wanted to. Another story told how he had three beautiful daughters by this same woman and married them to the chiefs of three important tribes, thus establishing significant alliances. These tales, related by white settlers around their campfires, have a European overtone to them, but their existence signifies the special respect in which the whites held this chief.

Under his direction, the Apaches mobilized their strength and began taking revenge for the recent slaughter. A company of fifteen white trappers had been permitted to camp unmolested on the Gila River. Not knowing of Johnson's treachery and not realizing that the Indians were no longer friends, they continued to follow their lines and collect their furs. One day, when they were together in their camp, the Apaches struck. After the Indians had finished their work, the fifteen trappers were dead. Another party of three white men was also attacked and overcome, although one man was finally set free, probably through the intercession of Mangas Coloradas.

But these were minor activities compared with the major objective of dislodging the people who lived at Santa Rita del Cobre. In view of Johnson's treachery and the new policy of the Chihuahuan government, the agreement made by Juan José could no longer hold force. Furthermore, the Apaches suspected that the inhabitants of the town knew of Johnson's plan and may even have supported it.

Although the Apaches were excellent warriors, they were neither equipped nor trained for attacks on fortified places. Often the white men's guns had a longer range than their own weapons, so they could not get inside the ring of fire that their enemy could lay down. The individualism that made them so successful at raiding was a further handicap, because they could not conduct formal military maneuvers. And their respect for their own lives prevented them from making massed charges in the European tradition. When they had driven the Spanish from such establishments as Gran Quivira and Quaraí, they had done so by continuous, prolonged harassment. In major engagements, the Spanish might rout them and claim a victory; but the Apaches continued to attack small parties of travelers or workers who strayed too far from the guards. Stretched out over many years, these minor victories made the retention of the churches and forts so costly that the Spanish finally abandoned them.

These tactics might have worked against Santa Rita del Cobre, which was protected by a permanent garrison and a fort, but they would not have satisfied the Apaches' desire for immediate revenge. Infuriated by Johnson's treachery, they wanted to drive the men, women, and children of the town to their deaths and do so without delay. So they searched for some means of making the people desert their fortifications and come into the open. Because of their many visits to Santa Rita del Cobre, the Apaches knew about the *conducta*. They had often seen it arrive and had watched the sweating men unload the supplies, handing the crates, boxes, and bags from the wagons to the men waiting in the street to receive them. The vast pile of goods was in itself enough to tell the Apaches that the town could not survive without the *conducta*.

In the wilderness south of Santa Rita del Cobre, along the route that wound its way from Chihuahua, they laid an ambush. None but the most experienced soldier could have noticed where they were hidden, for the Apaches were marvels at concealing themselves. The *conducta* came lumbering along the trail, the mules straining at their harnesses and the soldiers still exchanging jokes, not realizing that the new policy of their government had endangered their lives. Suddenly, the Apaches struck, their lances raised, their guns filling the air with puffs of smoke, and their arrows striking the astonished men and mules. The Mexican guns went off, but too late. The deadly net of Apache warriors had trapped its prey. The wagons of the *conducta* were overturned and destroyed; and as far as anyone knows, not a prisoner was taken. No messenger remained to carry news of the disaster to the city of Chihuahua or Santa Rita del Cobre. It was as though the *conducta* and the men accompanying it had suddenly vanished in a mire of quicksand at some ford.

At Santa Rita del Cobre, the inhabitants, unaware of the drastic change in their relationships with the Apaches, expected the *conducta*'s arrival on the scheduled day. When it did not appear, they were slightly inconvenienced but completely unconcerned. No discernible change had occurred at Santa Rita del Cobre. The miners went out each day and dug the ore; the businessmen went about their affairs as usual; and the women washed the clothes, cared for their babies, and cooked the meals. As for an Indian attack, no one expected one; there was not an Indian in sight. The peaks surrounding Santa Rita del Cobre were empty of people, red or white.

Slowly the inhabitants sensed that something had gone wrong. The *conducta* was now many days late, and the town was running short of supplies. A party of men climbed one of the tallest of the neighboring mountains that gave a view over the plains north of what is now Deming, New Mexico. In the bright, clear air of the Southwestern desert, they could see for many miles. The wheels of the wagons churning in the dirt would raise a cloud of dust visible from a great distance. But there was no cloud.

With the growing realization that something had happened to the *conducta* and that the Indians were no longer friendly, fear struck the town, and with it came dissension. Some argued that a small armed force should be sent to Chihuahua to spread the alarm and ask for reinforcements while the remaining men guarded Santa Rita del Cobre. Others said they should not divide either their men or their dwindling supplies. To do so would be fatal to both parties.

The argument swept the town; but in the end the second view prevailed, and the authorities decided to evacuate Santa Rita del Cobre. The men herded the mules and horses together and collected every usable wagon or other means of transportation. The women wept at the thought of the possessions they would have to leave behind to the mercy of the Apaches and the mountain winds and rains. The soldiers cleaned and oiled their guns. This time there was no joking about the trip to Chihuahua, no cheerful boasts about the pleasures they would enjoy when they reached civilization. Many of them were not certain they would ever see the capital again. The able-bodied men, especially those who were good shots, received their allotments of ammunition. And the convoy was ready to start.

The drivers cracked their whips; the riders struck the flanks of their horses with their spurs; and the convoy moved forward, headed for the safety of Chihuahua, hundreds of miles to the south. Even if they could reach one of the smaller towns, like Janos, they might be secure from an Apache attack. But the attainment of that goal required a long journey over the plains and through the passes. Few of the inhabitants of Santa Rita del Cobre were optimistic, and most of them foresaw days of misery and fighting, if not death.

The convoy left the relative cool of the foothills and entered the heat of the desert. The sun burned fiercely, and the anxious men urged the animals forward as quickly as possible. Speed was as essential to their security as well-armed, alert outriders. The Mexicans could not have remained in Santa Rita del Cobre without additional supplies. But once the Apaches' tactics had forced them to leave the shelter of its adobe walls, they were vulnerable to the type of warfare at which the Apaches were experts. In the open desert and the mountain passes they knew so well, the Indians were difficult to defeat without greatly superior forces.

The Apaches had been waiting for this moment and now vented their pent-up hatred. The attacks were relentless. If the Mexicans succeeded in driving them off, the Apaches returned. If the Mexicans killed an Apache, another warrior appeared to take his place. If the Apaches ran short of ammunition, they used their bows and their lances, charging down on the Mexicans or crawling through the grass until they were within bowshot. One after another, the soldiers fell dead or wounded. The ranks of the miners were shattered, and the Apaches, remembering the deaths of their own wives and children at Johnson's hands, did not spare the Mexican women or babies. This was not a military campaign conducted by some rule of polite European conduct. This was a war of vengeance, with no possibility that the entrapped Mexicans could make a truce or surrender. The Apaches were not interested in prisoners or further agreements with the Mexicans; they only wanted dead bodies to repay the memory of those left rotting in the sun by Johnson.

So the convoy continued across the desert toward Chihuahua, its numbers growing less and less with every mile it traveled. There was little hope of relief. No one in the city of Chihuahua knew about its predicament, and no one could ride ahead to carry the word. Out of the three or four hundred people who had left Santa Rita del Cobre, only a handful, perhaps ten or twenty, reached safety. The rest lay along the trail that led from the foothills of the Black Range.

At Santa Rita del Cobre the rains poured down on the deserted buildings, leaching in between the bricks of the adobe buildings. With no one there to make repairs, the clay gave way. Some of the walls collapsed, roofs fell in, weeds sprang up in the streets that had once been kept clear by the constant pounding of horses' hooves. The town was as dead as its pact with Juan José.

II

In a Fortress of Mountains and Deserts

ALTHOUGH they had no means of regular communication, news spread quickly among the Apaches. One traveler told another, and within a short time after the destruction of Santa Rita del Cobre most Apaches had heard of Mangas Coloradas's brilliant and rapid succession of victories. Because his tactics had proved so successful against the enemy, the Apaches heeded his advice, and lesser chiefs like Cuchillo Negro demonstrated their willingness to serve under him. In this manner and without any special ceremony, Mangas Coloradas became chief of all the Warm Springs Apaches.

This did not mean he controlled every band or even wanted to. But on questions affecting all the groups jointly and demanding common leadership, the others would turn to him. This included all the Apaches living in the southwestern portion of present-day New Mexico and those living near the headwaters of the Gila River in Arizona.

But while Mangas Coloradas was successfully fighting the Mexicans, new enemies were establishing a base of attack from the East, too far away for Mangas Coloradas to know about them but close enough so that their westward movement was inevitable. These were the people of the United States, the one power on the North American Continent with the resources to conquer both the Indians and the Mexicans.

The Spanish had been well aware of the threat from the North. For many years their attitude toward their neighbors had been suspicious and hostile. As best it could, the government had maintained a ring of defenses around its empire and refused admittance to any but its own citizens. Although this prevented commerce and impeded settlement, Spain saw it as the only policy that would protect its lands against the aggressive *norteamericanos.* In 1819, however, the tensions between the two countries were somewhat relaxed by the signing of the Adams-Onís Treaty, which provided for the cession of East Florida and disposed of any Spanish rights in West Florida. For in return for these unfavorable provisions, the United States agreed to renounce any future claims to present-day Texas. Believing in this assurance, Spain shortly after passed an extremely liberal law that permitted Americans to obtain generous allotments of land in Texas.

By 1830, at least 20,000 Americans had come to Texas, but frictions inevitably developed between them and the Mexicans. The Mexicans were slow-moving, respectful of tradition, and in their government extraordinarily inefficient and chaotic. The Americans, on the other hand, were brash, aggressive, and independent. If they did not like a particular law, they simply disobeyed it. Above all, they considered themselves and their customs greatly superior to anything Mexico could offer.

Regretting the mistake it had made in permitting the Americans to enter, Mexico passed a new law in 1830 that established a stiff tariff on trade with the United States and prohibited further immigration by Americans. The troops the government later sent out to enforce the law were inadequate and poorly commanded, and instead of restoring Mexican control over Texas, they merely created greater controversy. Therefore, the dictator, General Santa Anna, decided to take personal command of the army. A short, paunchy man with heavy-lidded eyes and the stupidity that comes from vanity, he placed himself at the head of 4,000 troops and marched to San Antonio, where a band of Texans had defeated a contingent of Mexican soldiers and taken possession of the city. By the time Santa

Anna arrived, most of the Texans had gone home, leaving only about 180 men to guard the city; but they took over the mission of San Antonio, turned it into a fort, called it the Alamo, and prepared to defend it to the last. Santa Anna ordered a direct assault on the former mission and succeeded in killing every one of its occupants, but in the process he lost a third of his army and the last possible chance for peace in Texas. For the defenders of the Alamo became martyrs and the Americans rallied to their memory.

After his apparent victory, Santa Anna set out in pursuit of the remainder of the Texans' armed forces. But instead of catching them, they caught him. On April 21, 1836, he was camped on the banks of the San Jacinto River near the modern city of Houston. At noon, he retired to his tent with his mulatto mistress and for some reason, probably overconfidence, failed to post adequate guards. The Americans, under Sam Houston, attacked and caught the Mexicans by surprise. In fifteen minutes the Battle of San Jacinto was over. The Americans had killed more than 600 Mexicans, captured more than 700, including Santa Anna himself, and set the remainder into retreat toward the Río Grande. Texas had won its independence, and so just about the time that Mangas Coloradas was driving the Mexicans from Santa Rita del Cobre, the Apaches were being flanked on the east by a new and potentially more dangerous enemy.

One band of Apaches, however, was unaffected by the tumult raging through the Southwest. They lived at the headwaters of the Gila River near the present city of Clifton, Arizona, an area well suited to the Apaches' way of life. To the south, the land, with its sparse covering of mesquite trees, may seem barren to a white man, but it provided adequate grazing for the Apaches' livestock. The Gila River itself offered water, that most precious of all desert commodities. And the deep arroyos that run from the mountains into the plains were a sanctuary in which an Indian could move unobserved by a white enemy. To the north, the mountains rise higher and higher in a great maze of canyons and tumbled rocks. Arizona cypress, with its strangely shaped nuts, grows in this region. And in the summer, the agave plants burst from yellow buds to red blossoms, the colors creeping up the giant stems in a succession of change. Piñons, silver leaf oaks, Douglas firs, and ponderosa pines appear as the land rises higher, and in those days the deep forests were always full of game. In the distance, mountain ridge follows mountain ridge, deep blue and hazy in the falling light at sundown, creating an impregnable fortress in which the Apaches could hide if they were outnumbered. In the winter, when the mountains were covered by deep snows, the Indians could move down to the warmth of the foothills and plains. In the summer, when the desert heat became unbearable, they could work their way back into the mountains, where even in the dead of summer the winds are cool and fresh. Everything they needed was within the compass of a few miles—food, water, a change of climate that kept them comfortable as the seasons came and went, and, above all, natural protection from their enemies. No Mexican would be foolhardy enough to lead a raid against them in this land they knew so well and that was so unfamiliar to any white man.

Among the Apaches in this remote band was a young boy named Goyakla, or One Who Yawns, a name that the white men would have found most inappropriate. Later the Mexicans gave him another by which he became known to thousands of troops and settlers and newspaper readers throughout the United States. It was the Spanish for Jerome: Geronimo.

He was born, he recalled later, in June, 1829, the year when Andrew Jackson was inaugurated President of the United States and began his effort to deal with the delicate problem of states' rights.

Geronimo's father was a member of the fiercest of all the Apache tribes, the Nednis, who made their home in the Sierra Madres, the mountain range that divides Sonora from Chihuahua. But in spite of the remote character of their native region, the Nednis were not isolated from the other Apaches. Much to the dismay of the white men, who built forts, garrisoned towns, and sent out armed scouting parties, the Apaches were able to travel freely from south to north, sometimes for purely social reasons, sometimes to combine their forces for a major war party. On one of these trips, Geronimo's father had met the boy's mother and married her. According to Apache custom, he was then required to leave his own family and join that of his bride. For in this way, Apache parents replaced the help and support they lost when their own sons married.

By moving to the headwaters of the Gila River, Geronimo's father forfeited his right to succeed his own father as hereditary chief of the Nednis. This sacrifice, however, was not as great as a white man might have supposed. The Apaches had a highly democratic society, and the worth of an hereditary chieftainship depended entirely on the performance of the man who held it. The title might or might not be significant. On the other hand, there were many outstanding warriors who were not formally chiefs but whose influence was even greater. So although Geronimo's father had given up his title, he had not lost the respect of the other Apaches.

Other changes had also taken place in his life as a result of his marriage to Geronimo's mother. Although the Nednis were the most warlike of the Apaches, many of the tribe into which he married were farmers. So, faithful to the traditions of his wife's family, he took up farming. His fields were not extensive. Like other Indians in that area, he cultivated about two acres of land, growing small crops of melons, pumpkins, beans, and maize. But although he had become a man of peace, he did not neglect to train Geronimo properly in the ways of war.

He told his son about his grandfather, a man of great strength and wisdom who had been a leader in fighting the Mexicans. And he encouraged Geronimo and his brothers to play the warlike games of Apache children. "Sometimes we played that we were warriors," Geronimo said later. "We would practice stealing up on some object that represented the enemy, and in our childish imitation often performed the feats of war. Sometimes we would hide from our mother to see if she could find us, and often when thus concealed go to sleep and perhaps remain hidden for many hours."

As a child, Geronimo was also expected to help the women find nuts and berries in the forests around the Gila River. Sometimes when they were to be gone all day, the women would bring ponies with them to help carry the baskets home. These trips, like everything else in the world of the Apaches, had their dangers. Once a woman named Cho-ko-le became separated from the others in the berry-picking party. While she was searching for them, a bear jumped out of the underbrush and attacked her pony. She quickly dismounted and drew her knife, while the pony galloped off, the baskets dangling at its sides. Fortunately she had a small dog with her, and the dog kept biting at the bear's heels, distracting its attention and permitting the woman to stay at a distance. But the bear was finally able to come close and with one swipe of its paw tore off a large piece of her scalp.

Cho-ko-le fell to the ground, but like a good Apache of either sex, she kept on fighting. Desperately wounded and bleeding badly, she struck four severe blows with her knife. These did not kill the bear, but they discouraged it from attacking anymore; and it lumbered off into the forest, leaving the wounded woman on the ground. As best she could, she replaced her scalp and staunched the bleeding, but she could not move. That night her pony arrived at Geronimo's ranchería—the Spanish name for the temporary settlements of the Apaches—without her, and a search party finally located her and brought her back. With the help of the medicine man, she recovered and was able to continue leading a useful life.

Such an example of self-reliance was not unusual among the Apaches. Unlike the Pueblo Indians, who lived in large communities, Apache men and women were more dependent on their individual capabilities for survival, whether they were driving off a bear, fighting an enemy, or making their way through the deserts and mountains. Knowing this, the parents made every effort to develop in their children the skills and strengths they would need.

As soon as he was old enough, therefore, Geronimo's parents permitted him to play with their horses. Wandering down the canyon to where they were grazing, he would pick out one of the gentler ones and try to ride it. Later his father and uncles gave him more formal instruction, and by the time he was in his teens, he was an expert horseman. They also taught him how to use a bow and arrow and an Apache lance. Above all, they made him run. As one Apache father explained to his son, an Apache's best friends were not his relatives, but his brain, eyesight, hands, and legs. Of these, his legs were perhaps the most important. From an early age every boy was made to run long distances; and more than one Indian in later life was grateful for this training that helped him outstrip his enemies either on the attack or in retreat. Some fathers, to toughen their offspring, went even further. On occasion, they would order their boys to fight a tree, striking the rough bark of its trunk with their hands and breaking its branches to develop their strength. A common exercise was to pull young saplings up by the roots. Many children were also forced to stay awake for long periods of time so they would learn to conquer sleepiness, and they were sent out in the snow without clothes to become accustomed to the cold.

They were also expected to work. "When we were old enough to be of real service we went to the field with our parents: not to play, but to toil," Geronimo said later. "When the crops were to be planted we broke the ground with wooden hoes. We planted the corn in straight rows, the beans among the corn, and the melons and pumpkins in irregular order over the field. We cultivated these crops as there was need. . . .

"Melons were gathered as they were consumed. In the autumn pumpkins and beans were gathered and placed in bags or baskets; ears of corn were tied together by the husks, and then the harvest was carried on the backs of ponies up to our homes. Here the corn was shelled, and the harvest stored away in caves or other secluded places to be used in the winter."

Even when they became old enough to share in the adults' labors, all was not work for Apache boys, and they were allowed to watch their elders' games and learn how to play them. One of Geronimo's favorites was called Kah, meaning "foot," which was played only at night. By firelight, one team hid a bone in one of several moccasins placed on the ground, and the other team tried to guess which one, while they reenacted an old Apache legend. There were many other games and festivities. A ceremony that Geronimo, like most Apaches, especially liked was one announcing that a girl had come of marriageable age. At nightfall the masked dancers came down from the mountains, and the shaman sang the old song:

"Thus speaks the earth's thunder,
Because of it there is good about you.
Because of it your body is well.
Thus speaks the earth's thunder."

The ceremony ended in social dancing that lasted most of the night, and it was repeated four successive times, because to the Apaches four was a number with magical qualities. When the sun appeared on the fifth day, the happy, sated Indians would return to their homes, content with their period of feasting, playing, and visiting one another.

Although Geronimo's father had moved to the land near the Gila River, he had not forgotten his relatives in the Sierra Madres, and in spite of the great distance separating them, he either saw them or received word about them from time to time. At least once while Geronimo was still a boy, a group of his Nedni relatives made the long journey from their mountain fortress to pay a visit. Among them was Geronimo's young cousin, Juh, a wild boy of whom the elders in the ranchería did not entirely approve. He and Geronimo, however, became fast friends, spending as much time as they could together, hunting, riding horses, wrestling, and playing war games.

Geronimo's family thought that perhaps the Nedni was leading their child astray, for Juh was a rough-handed, practical joker. When the girls went into the woods to gather acorns, Juh would collect a gang of boys, sneak up on the girls, and jump out at them. Sometimes when the girls had gathered an especially large store of nuts, Juh and his gang would forcibly take them away and, with much laughter, scatter them on the ground. Geronimo's grandmother heard about this and resorted to one of the means that Apaches sometimes used to discipline wayward children. She ordered Geronimo to form another band and go into the woods after Juh. When he stole acorns from the girls again, Geronimo and his friends were to beat him up. Being an Apache boy, Geronimo had to carry out his grandmother's instructions. He gave Juh a beating. Although it may have kept Juh from bothering the girls again, it did not affect the friendship between the two boys, and when the Nednis later departed for their home in the Sierra Madres, Geronimo was sad to see his cousin go.

It was a happy boyhood, safe from the white men and attacking Indians but marred by one tragedy—the death of Geronimo's father. He fell sick while Geronimo was still a boy, and the medicine man could not save him.

The Apaches believed in a life hereafter that took place in an underworld whose entrance was concealed by bushes. Down below, men and women lived just as they had on earth, following the same practices and customs. At the opening to the underworld was a huge pile of sand. Sometimes those who had died tried to come back, but they could not climb up the sandy slope. Because life was the same in the hereafter, the dead needed their belongings. Therefore, most of an Apache's personal possessions were buried with him and the remainder destroyed. This also removed from the ranchería any sad reminder of the deceased man or woman and it meant that no one could inherit, so there was no reason to wish anyone dead. Nothing could be gained by deserting the sick or abandoning a relative in time of battle.

After his death, they wrapped Geronimo's father in a blanket and collected his belongings, including his favorite horses. Those who had loved him put on their oldest clothes. As the funeral procession passed the other wickiups, the occupants cried out in grief, for Geronimo's father had been a good man.

The funeral party came at last to a small cave—caves being one of the Apaches' favorite burying places—and reverently laid the body inside with the face toward the west, where the sun goes down. Then they slew his favorite horses, laid their bodies and his possessions alongside him, and sealed up the entrance with stones and clay to make it appear as though it were merely part of the natural side of the canyon wall. On their return to the ranchería, they destroyed the remainder of his belongings and burned the wickiup. When they were finished nothing was left, not even his name, for the Apaches never spoke the name of a dead person. To do so would only cause sorrow to those who loved him.

After that Geronimo and his mother moved some distance off to build a new wickiup. For in spite of their sadness, it was time to start life over again.

III

The Appearance of a New Enemy

WHILE Geronimo was playing with Juh and learning the skills that would soon make him an Apache warrior, the white men's politicians were debating the annexation of Texas by the United States. Southerners and Northerners were divided over the issue because of the question of slavery; but if they could dispose of that problem, they both would be glad to see that large area added to the United States. The Mexicans regarded the discussion as further evidence of American expansionism at the expense of its neighbors and as a threat to Mexican security. They said they would fight if the United States annexed Texas.

War between the two countries became almost inevitable in 1844 when James K. Polk campaigned for the Presidency on a platform that specifically called for annexation. This was in direct violation of the Adams-Onís Treaty signed just a few years before. But Polk cared nothing for America's honor, and neither did the people, for they elected him. Since the United States had now become well established in the areas it had gained under the pact, there was little point in continuing to abide by its other provisions. Almost immediately Polk set in motion the procedures that would lead to Texas's admission on December 31, 1845, and sent troops south to protect it against a possible Mexican attack. In a further display of arrogance, he dispatched an envoy to Mexico City to settle some legitimate claims and also to negotiate the purchase of much of California and what is now the American Southwest. The Mexicans were as affronted by this action as the Americans would have been, and any illusions they may have held about their powerful northern neighbor were dispelled. They refused to treat with the envoy; Polk moved his troops farther south; and the Mexicans advanced across the Río Grande. A clash occurred, and Congress had the excuse it wanted to declare war.

The United States then launched a three-pronged attack against its neighbor. Troops under Zachary Taylor marched southward from the Río Grande; troops under Winfield Scott landed successfully at Vera Cruz and proceeded to Mexico City; and the Army of the West under Colonel Stephen Kearny was instructed to march to Santa Fe and from there to California—straight through the heart of the Apaches' land.

Kearny captured Santa Fe with ease. There is some reason to believe he may have used bribery; in any case, the corrupt Mexican government did not resist him. Then he moved south and west toward the territory of Mangas Coloradas. Shortly after he left Santa Fe, the Pueblo Indians at Taos rose up in bloody revolt against the Americans, killed the civil governor, and were put down only after several weeks of fierce struggling. The Apaches, on the other hand, welcomed the new arrivals. Obsessed with his warfare with the Mexicans, Mangas Coloradas thought they might prove to be useful allies against the common enemy. He offered to join forces with Kearny and was puzzled by Kearny's reaction. Instead of taking advantage of the opportunity to move south and win a major victory over the Mexicans, the American colonel refused the Apache's offer of help and insisted on marching west as he had been ordered to do. Furthermore, he seemed determined to protect the now subdued Mexicans that remained in that part of the country. Although Mangas Coloradas was bewildered by Kearny's response, he was not alarmed. The Americans seemed determined to continue west, and he thought it unlikely they would ever return. Therefore, he let them pass safely.

In February, 1848, the United States and Mexico ended their war with the signing of the Treaty of Guadalupe Hidalgo. By its terms, the United States acquired for $15,000,000 the white man's title to most of present-day New Mexico, Arizona, and California. The United States also agreed to protect Mexico from Indian attacks that might originate from this territory.

Mangas Coloradas did not learn about this disposal of the Apaches' lands until 1851, when he heard that a small party of Americans was advancing toward Santa Rita del Cobre. The treaty had provided that each nation would appoint a commissioner and a surveyor to survey the new boundary line, and the commission had decided to make its temporary headquarters at the old mining town. These first arrivals were to prepare it for the others.

The old presidio, which the Mexicans had been forced to evacuate, was still standing. The military force accompanying the party repaired it and used it for their headquarters and for storing their supplies. Approximately fifty other buildings remained, some of them in ruins and all of them without roofs; but the better ones were fixed up to accommodate the white men. The Indians, concerned about all this activity, asked how long the strangers intended to stay. After seeing all the work being done, they could hardly believe it when they were told this was only a temporary camp.

Yet they did not try to dislodge the Americans, and by May, 1851, when the American commissioner, John Russell Bartlett, had arrived, the white population of the town had reached 250 to 300 men, more than the Indians cared to attack.

Mangas Coloradas kept track of all this activity with interest, although he himself did not appear. When Bartlett soon left for Arizpe, Mexico, to check on his supplies, Mangas Coloradas followed him closely. He even knew that Bartlett was riding in a carriage, instead of being mounted on a horse or a mule like the rest of the party. (Bartlett had recently broken his arm; he had been thrown by a mule and then kicked.) Sometimes Mangas Coloradas camped near the commissioner's own resting place, but the white men never saw him. When they returned from Mexico a few weeks later, he again picked up their trail but remained out of sight. In true Apache fashion, he did not want to expose himself until he knew more about what these men were up to.

On his return to Santa Rita del Cobre, he went with twelve or fifteen of his people to talk with Bartlett. He warned the commissioner he had been foolish to go to Mexico with so small an escort and explained how he himself had followed the Americans without their ever seeing him. His people, he said, wished to be friends with the new white men, but they were not the only Indians.

Bartlett in turn told the chief about the outcome of the war with Mexico and how the Americans would protect the Apaches as long as they remained at peace and refrained from stealing livestock. This was agreeable to Mangas Coloradas, who had no desire for war with these newcomers. He replied that the Americans were safe from the Indians. If their horses or mules strayed away, he would even send out men to search for them.

But the next words of the commissioner made no sense to the chief. For Bartlett began talking about the provision of the Treaty of Guadalupe Hidalgo that required the Americans to protect the Mexicans from Indian raids. To Mangas Coloradas this provision was ridiculous. Why, he wondered, should the Americans want to help the Mexicans after having conquered them? And why did the Americans think their victories over the Mexicans gave them any right to dictate to the Apaches, whom they had not defeated? But he did not argue, knowing that argument would be futile. White men rarely tried to understand the Apaches' point of view.

In return for the chief's promise of cooperation, Bartlett distributed presents of shirts, cotton, and beads to Mangas Coloradas and the other Apaches. The Apaches then asked for whiskey, too, but Bartlett positively refused to give them any. He said there was none in camp, a statement the Indians did not believe. To prove his point, Bartlett later let them taste the contents of a bottle of catsup and one of vinegar; but the

Apaches were still unconvinced and finally obtained whiskey from the whites, probably from the sutler, until Bartlett confiscated all hard liquor.

The Apaches made their camps only a few miles from Santa Rita del Cobre and showed their confidence in the Americans by settling down with their women and children and letting their horses and mules graze nearby. They were so trusting they even brought with them two Mexican boys whom they had captured earlier during raids on Sonora.

From what they overheard the Apaches say, the boys decided they might gain their freedom if they could reach the Americans. Like most Apache prisoners, they were not well guarded; and one hot afternoon, while many of the Indians were visiting at Santa Rita del Cobre, they saw their chance, slipped away, and headed for the tent of one of the white men, John C. Cremony. This tent was about 600 yards distant from the others and hidden from their sight by a hillock. Cremony had chosen this location because he thought it especially attractive and because a stream passed through a small basin nearby. By damming the stream at this point, he had been able to create a small pool for bathing. The isolated site made an ideal refuge for the boys, for they could approach it without meeting the main body of Apaches going to and from Santa Rita del Cobre.

Belatedly, the Apaches saw the boys and started in pursuit, but they failed to catch them before they entered Cremony's tent. By the time the Indians arrived, Cremony had emerged. On his belt he had two six-shooters and held two more in his hands, and he was accompanied by his Mexican companion, who was armed with a carbine. The two men had the boys with them and were headed for the commissioner's.

The Apaches surrounded the small party and made signs to Cremony to give the boys up. But Cremony cocked both his revolvers and told his Mexican companion to cock his carbine. The white men then stood back to back, circling around and at the same time moving forward with the two boys in their custody. There was no way the Apaches could recapture their prisoners without the risk that some of them would be killed. The strange procession, therefore, continued on its way, the white men and the two captives in the center, the Apaches, frustrated and angry, gathered around them. They had covered about 200 yards in this fashion, when they came in sight of the main campground. Other members of the commission noticed them and formed a bodyguard to help escort the boys to Bartlett.

As soon as they heard what had happened, Mangas Coloradas and another chief, Delgadito, went to Bartlett. They proposed what they thought was a simple solution. If Bartlett wanted the two boys so much, why did he not buy them instead of stealing them? That was the way the Apaches dealt with each other and with the Mexicans. In vain, Bartlett tried to explain the terms of the treaty with Mexico and the merits of the white men's laws. Neither Mangas Coloradas nor Delgadito could understand what Bartlett meant. The two boys were property, taken by an Apache warrior at the risk of his life, and they belonged to him. Because the difference in the points of view could not be resolved, Mangas Coloradas and Delgadito left, although Mangas Coloradas said he would return the following day and continue the discussion. He failed to do so, however; there was so little point in arguing with a white man. Because of rumors regarding the future safety of the boys, Bartlett sent them under heavy guard to the camp of the Mexican commissioner, many miles away. This alleviated his immediate problem, but it reinforced the Apaches' opinion that the Americans were thieves.

Annoyed by Bartlett's action, which he considered dishonest, Mangas Coloradas allowed several days to pass before he came back to see the commissioner. This time he was accompanied by the boys' captor and owner. But nothing came of this or a number of subsequent meetings. Finally Mangas Coloradas asked again, "Why did you take our captives from us?"

Bartlett replied, "Your captives came to us and demanded our protection."

"You came to our country," Mangas Coloradas said, reiterating the Apaches' case. "Your lives, your property, your animals were safe. You passed by ones, by twos, and by threes through our country; you went and came in peace. Your strayed animals were brought home to you again. Our wives, our children, and our women came here and visited your houses. We were friends! We were brothers! Believing this, we came among you and brought our captives, relying on it that we were brothers and that you would feel as we feel. We concealed nothing. We came not here secretly or in the night. We came in open day and before your faces, and we showed our captives to you. We believed your assurances of friendship, and we trusted them."

Mangas Coloradas then repeated his earlier question. "Why," he asked, "did you take our captives from us?"

Bartlett again explained the terms of the treaty with Mexico and the obligation of the United States to protect Mexican citizens.

Another chief spoke up. "Yes," he said, "but you took our captives from us without beforehand cautioning us. We were ignorant of this promise to restore captives. They were made prisoners in lawful warfare. They belong to us. They are our property. Our people have also been made captives by the Mexicans. If we had known of this thing, we should not have come here. We should not have placed that confidence in you."

Bartlett again tried to explain the Americans' position to the Apaches, and again he failed to make sense to them.

Another chief joined the discussion. "But the owner of these captives is a poor man. He cannot lose his captives, who were obtained at the risk of his life and purchased by the blood of his relatives. He justly demands his captives. We are his friends, and we wish to see this demand complied with. It is just, and as justice we demand it."

The Apaches were growing angry. For many years, they had been fighting the Mexicans, and for many years it had been the custom on both sides to take and sell prisoners. Now the Americans were suddenly trying to enforce a new law. On the other hand, Bartlett was caught in a dilemma. He had to abide by the treaty, but he could not afford to antagonize the Apaches. If they became more irate than they were, they could destroy the commission. Finally he came up with a solution. Under American law, neither the commission nor any American could buy the boys, but a Mexican could, and there were Mexicans on the commission's payroll. Bartlett would put up the money for a Mexican to make the purchase.

But one of the chiefs replied, "The owner does not wish to sell. He wants his captives."

"I have already told my brother that this cannot be," Bartlett said. "I speak not with two tongues. Make up your minds."

The chief replied that, at the least, the owner would want twenty horses. And when Bartlett laughed at this price, he went on, "The brave who owns these captives does not wish to sell. He has had one of those boys six years. He grew up under him. His heartstrings are bound around him. He is as a son to his old age. He speaks our language, and he cannot sell him. Money cannot buy affection. His heart cannot be sold. He taught him to string and shoot the bow, and to wield the lance. He loves the boy and cannot sell him."

Part of what the chief said was undoubtedly for the purpose of bargaining, but much of it was likely true. The Apaches often became fond of the boys they captured and considered them members of their own families. But Bartlett remained adamant. At last, the Apaches gave in. Without open warfare, which they wished to avoid, they could not regain the two boys, so the only thing to do was to settle on a price.

Bartlett took them to the commissary. There he laid out goods worth about $250 and asked the Apaches if they would accept them. They did, and the affair was ended, but it left the Indians with a strange impression of what constituted American justice.

At Santa Rita del Cobre, the Apaches had the Americans almost completely at their mercy. Mangas Coloradas was camped about four miles to the west, and Delgadito made his camp about eight miles away in the finest pasture land in the vicinity. That was where the Americans kept the greater part of their horses and mules, and it would have been easy for the Indians to have driven them off. Instead, they helped protect the livestock. Several times when horses or mules strayed away, and once when some were captured by another tribe, the Apaches retrieved them.

Although Mangas Coloradas did not understand the Americans' behavior over the captives, he still went to Santa Rita del Cobre every day, often bringing one of his children with him. Usually he would first visit the commander of the military force, who always received him well, and then Bartlett, who generally had some small present ready for the chief or for his children. Sometimes Bartlett would ask Mangas Coloradas or one of the other chiefs to dine with him. Although they were curious about the food and afraid they might inadvertently eat something that was taboo, they accepted. The speed with which they caught on to the white men's customs impressed Bartlett, who later commented on their "decorum." But he was annoyed by a practice they soon developed. They would eat until they were full and then ask to have their plate replenished. When this was done, they would get up from the table and beckon to a friend to come and finish the meal. In this way, they shared with the other Indians the benefits of the commissioner's hospitality. Bartlett finally told them he would not feed them if they did this any longer.

One day, in a further effort to gain his friendship, Bartlett asked Mangas Coloradas if he would like to have a suit made for him. The chief, of course, said yes. The tailor assigned to the commission selected blue broadcloth and created a frock coat with a scarlet lining and gilt buttons. For trousers, he made a pair of pantaloons designed, at Mangas Coloradas's request, in the Mexican fashion with slits from the knee down. They were decorated with strips of scarlet cloth and small buttons. While the suit was being made, Mangas Coloradas visited the tailor every day. When it was finished, the Americans gave him a white shirt and a red silk sash. Mangas Coloradas was delighted, although he could not understand why the Americans insisted that he wear the shirt inside the trousers. It was less comfortable, and he refused to do it.

In spite of the disagreement over the two Mexican boys, the

Apaches continued to adhere strictly to their policy of peace with the Americans. Bartlett later testified to this when he wrote: "During this time the members of the Commission went about freely in small parties or alone, for twenty or thirty miles around our camp, and were on no occasion molested. They also visited the Apache camps, where they were well received. Our wagons with stores went unprotected to and from the Surveyors, and their attendants, who were scattered for fifty miles along the line, where the escort could afford them little protection." As the Mexicans knew, this was an unusual development. At any time, Mangas Coloradas could have cut the commission apart, but he did not do so.

In July, however, the peace was broken by a Mexican teamster, Jesús Lopez, who worked for the commission. Mangas Coloradas was in Santa Rita del Cobre visiting the Americans when he heard that an Apache had been shot. Panic overtook the town. The Indians, afraid they might be massacred, were milling around in an effort to escape. Mangas Coloradas, Delgadito, and another chief quickly mounted their horses and rode to the top of a small hill a few hundred yards away. There they stopped briefly to see whether they were being pursued. The white men, too, were frightened, not knowing whether the Apaches would attack them.

While he waited on the hill, Mangas Coloradas saw the commander of the military force come toward him, unarmed and alone. Because he regarded the officer as a friend, Mangas Coloradas agreed to listen to what he had to say. The officer explained that if Mangas Coloradas would come with him, he would show him that the culprit had already been taken a prisoner. Mangas Coloradas and some of the other Apaches returned to Santa Rita del Cobre, and the soldiers brought out the Mexican, Jesús Lopez. He was already in chains.

In front of the Indians, Bartlett tried to find out what had happened. By questioning Lopez and the single other eyewitness to the shooting, he learned that one of the Apaches had wanted to buy a whip owned by Lopez. Lopez had refused to sell it. The Indian had grabbed for it. Lopez had pushed him away, picked up a stone, thought better of that as a weapon, and had grabbed his rifle. While the Apache stood so close that the muzzle almost touched him, Lopez deliberately pulled the trigger and shot him just above the heart.

As a result of Bartlett's interrogation, Mangas Coloradas and the other Apaches were satisfied that the fight had been between a single Apache and a single Mexican and that the commission as a whole was not involved. But although they would continue to be friendly, they laid down their terms. If the Apache died, they would demand Lopez's life. If he lived, they would expect that Lopez's earnings would be given to the Apache's family to recompense them for the loss of the Indian's services.

The wounded Apache was immediately taken to the commission's hospital, where his friends were allowed to visit him and where he received the best care the commission could provide. But nothing could be done to save him. After lingering on for a month, he died. Bartlett ordered a coffin made for the body, but the Apaches would have none of that. They did not want a white man's burial for their friend. They carried the body off on a mule and treated it according to the Apache custom. Then they visited Bartlett and demanded that Lopez be turned over to them.

Once again, Bartlett attempted to explain the Americans' law. "The great chief of the American people," he said, "lives far, very far, towards the rising sun. From him I receive my orders, and those orders I must obey. I cannot interfere in punishing any man, whether an Indian, a Mexican, or an American. There is another great chief who lives in Santa Fe. He is the governor of all New Mexico. This great chief administers the laws of the Americans. He holds court wherein all persons charged with crimes are judged. He alone can inflict punishment when a man has been found guilty. To this great chief, this governor, I will send the murderer of our Apache brother. He will try him, and, if found guilty, will have him punished according to the American laws. Such is all I can do. Such is the disposition I will make of this man. It is all I have a right to do."

The Indians were astounded by this interpretation of justice. One of the chiefs immediately replied, "This is all very good. The Apaches know that the Americans are their friends. The Apaches believe what the Americans say is true. . . . But the Apaches will not be satisfied to know that the murderer is punished in Santa Fe. They want him punished here, . . . where the band of the dead brave may see him put to death—where all the Apaches may see him put to death. Then the Apaches will see and know that their American brothers will do justice to them."

They listened while Bartlett made another proposal. Instead of sending Lopez to Santa Fe for trial, he would keep him in chains, make him work, and give whatever he earned to the dead warrior's family. This would amount to twenty dollars a month, which Bartlett would pay in goods of the family's own choosing.

The Apaches were not pleased by this offer, and one of the chiefs replied, "But money will not satisfy an Apache for the murder of a brave! No! Thousands will not drown the grief of this poor woman for her son. Would money satisfy an American for the murder of his people? Would money pay you, Señor Commissioner, for the loss of your child? No! Money would not bury your grief. It will not bury ours. The mother of this brave demands the life of the murderer. Nothing else will satisfy her. She wants no goods. She wants no corn. Would money . . . satisfy me for the death of my son? No! I would demand the blood of the murderer. Then I would be satisfied. Then would I be willing to die myself. I would not wish to live and bear the grief which the loss of my son would cause me."

Bartlett was willing to pay the warrior's family, but he would not hang Lopez without an American trial. Although the Apaches were irritated by what they considered another grave injustice, there was little they could do about it without waging war. Bartlett had possession of Lopez, and the Apaches could not take him away from the Americans except by force. Finally they told Bartlett they would discuss the problem with the warrior's widow. When they returned, they reported that she would be content with nothing less than Lopez's life.

Bartlett, however, continued to refuse the Apaches' demands and settled the affair in his own way by paying the woman for the life of her husband. He and the other members of the commission thought he had placated the Apaches, but he had not.

In the Apache camps concern was steadily growing. The Indians had not forgotten the loss of their two Mexican captives; they were not satisfied with the protection given to Lopez; and they were worried about the increasing numbers of Americans who were coming into their territory. Gold had been found near Santa Rita del Cobre, and the miners who arrived in search of it appeared to be planning to stay. The original policy of Mangas Coloradas had been based on the premise that the Americans were enemies of the Mexicans and thus helpful to the Apaches in their centuries-old war. He had also not believed that the Americans, once the Mexicans were conquered, would remain in that part of the country. Events were proving both these premises wrong.

The Apaches had been protecting the Americans' livestock, but toward the end of July, 1851, the commander of the military force discovered that several of his mules were missing. Certain the Apaches had stolen them, he rode with some of his men into the Apaches' camp and demanded their return. The Indians were alarmed at his arrival, promised they would hunt for the mules, and did nothing. Mangas Coloradas was no longer insisting on adherence to his earlier agreements with the commission. A few days later, a band of Indians crept toward a small valley where some of the commission's mules were grazing. Three or four men were on guard, but they did not notice the Indians approaching through the surrounding pine trees and scrub oaks. Suddenly, with a loud whoop, the Indians descended on them, and the frightened mules began to run. Before the guards were able to mount their horses, both the Indians and the livestock were gone. Knowing pursuit would be useless and dangerous, the guards returned as quickly as possible to the town. A party of soldiers hunted for the livestock without success, and no assistance was forthcoming from Mangas Coloradas.

Other raids occurred. Bartlett was not sure whether they were carried out by Apaches or by other tribes. (On one occasion, when the commission lost many of its best mules, the Indians may have been Navajos.) Mangas Coloradas denied any knowledge of the raids, but it was apparent that his once effective protection had been withdrawn.

The commission was worried. It was now short of livestock and unable to mount its soldiers adequately. Bartlett sent out a hurried call to the military for more soldiers. In August, Mangas Coloradas permitted another raid. This time the Indians went off with 150 head, including cattle. One of the Indians stopped beyond rifleshot and spoke with one of the Americans. He was Delgadito of the Apaches. There remained little doubt that the commission had lost the friendship of Mangas Coloradas.

In August, 1851, Bartlett, his work in the area completed, gave orders to break camp. The men collected their supplies and loaded their mules. The soldiers gave their guns a final cleaning and put their equipment in order. Soon the procession of men and animals left the mountains, entered the plains, and headed westward. With relief, Mangas Coloradas watched them disappear in the distance, but he was alarmed by the number of Americans that still remained. For the miners who had followed the commission into the country did not leave with it.

IV

The Training of a Warrior

THE difficulties with the white men gave added significance to the skills Geronimo developed in preparation for becoming a warrior. His mother knew this, and as part of this training, she decided to take him with her on a visit to her husband's Nedni relatives. This would make him familiar with the territory through which the Apaches roamed. The distance was several hundred miles across dangerous country—dangerous because of the Mexican bounty for scalps. But she knew the chances of being seen were slight, for she would travel in the Apache fashion, taking full advantage of the geographic peculiarities of that part of the Southwest.

This is an unusual region, and its topography provided the Apaches with one of their great strengths—their ability to move about freely. Just to the north of Geronimo's homeland, the relatively flat Colorado Plateau ends in a tangle of mountains that marks the Mogollon Rim. To the south, in the land where the Apaches roamed, lies the basin-and-range area. This extraordinary part of the country is characterized by relatively short, independent mountain ranges, usually some twenty to fifty miles in length and generally running north and south. Some of them are sufficiently high to be snow-covered for much of the year, and many of them contain thick forests and deep canyons into which the Indians could vanish. Practically all of them also have water—the most valuable commodity in the desert.

The passes that divide the ranges from north to south are unlike customary mountain passes. They are usually composed of eroded particles from both ranges and consist merely of a ridge that is higher than the surrounding country. Most of them can be crossed quite easily, but few of them offer either cover or water. So there is no place to hide and nothing to drink.

From east to west, the ranges are separated by basins, locally called valleys. To the casual observer they appear to be broad, flat plains. Actually, most of them are depressed toward the center and rise gradually on either side as they approach the mountains. They are deserts and almost devoid of water except in the rainy season, when their arroyos carry the overflow of rain water from the mountains.

Much of the Apaches' war strategy was based on their knowledge of these mountains. They knew every water hole, every canyon and summit, every trail that ran through them. If they were pursued by enemies, they would disappear into one range or another, where no one dared follow them. For it was almost impossible to find them and the opportunities for an ambush were many. The Apaches also used these mountains as safe north-south travel routes. Only when they crossed the divides or the valleys were they exposed to attack, and they usually made this part of a journey at night. Thus they could travel freely and unobserved throughout thousands of square miles of territory, and no number of Mexican presidios could check their movements.

On their journey, Geronimo and his mother were probably accompanied by other women and children, as well as some warriors, for on a friendly visit of this sort it was customary for ten or twenty people to go together. From the area around present-day Clifton, they went south, following the mountains on the west side of the Gila River. The party crossed the narrow divide and entered the Peloncillo Mountains. Off to the west across the San Simon and San Bernardino valleys are the

Chiricahuas. They rise so high from the hot, arid floor of the desert that their ridges are covered with forests; and in the winter, the snows are deep. Access to the mountains is through winding canyons guarded by strange formations of rock, huge columns that look as though they were carved by human hands rather than by nature. This land was part of the territory of the Chiricahuas, a tribe closely related to the Warm Springs Apaches of Mangas Coloradas.

To the east of the Peloncillo Mountains on the other side of Animas Valley are the Animas Mountains, a smaller and lower range than the Chiricahuas. The Continental Divide runs along their crest, and they, too, go north and south. If, for some reason, the route down the Peloncillo Mountains was blocked by an enemy, the Indians had only to move east or west a few miles and follow the corridors provided by either the Chiricahua or Animas mountains.

In spite of the protection offered by the mountains, the journey was not a comfortable one by a white man's standards. The Apaches could cover a greater distance in a day on foot than the best mounted cavalry units—seventy miles or even more. On a social trip, the women and children were not expected to equal this pace, but they were required to walk much faster and farther than any white woman or child normally could, for the warriors could not be asked to protect laggards.

Moving quickly down the range, the Apaches reached the point, just north of the present border between Mexico and the United States, where the Penocillos end and the Guadalupes begin. From there, they pushed farther south and entered the wilderness of the Sierra Madres, the mountains that divide the states of Chihuahua and Sonora. As these mountains climb southward from San Luis Pass in New Mexico, they rise higher and higher, reaching elevations of 12,000 feet. Because of the moist winds blowing across the continent from the Pacific Ocean, more rain falls on the western side than the eastern, helping to create an intricate drainage pattern. Often the headwaters of the rivers flowing toward the Pacific lie more to the east than those flowing toward the Gulf of Mexico. The confused traveler finds his progress further impeded by the depths of some of the canyons. At Barranca del Cobre, for example, a tributary of the Río del Fuerte has cut a steep-sided cleft that plunges downward for 6,000 feet.

Like the land at the headwaters of the Gila River, the Sierra Madres provided an ideal dwelling place for the Apaches. The mountains have no real crest. (The absence of a clear divide helps cause the complicated drainage.) Instead, there are many flat uplands on which the Apaches could live comfortably, surrounded by ample supplies of water, game, trees to provide firewood and building materials, and an abundance of plant life for food.

Few enemies could find their way into that labyrinth of mountains and canyons, and those who did had little chance of emerging alive. Yet the Apaches, whenever they wished, could descend from the range to raid the nearby towns in Sonora or Chihuahua, gather up their booty of cattle, horses, guns, and ammunition, and disappear once more into their refuge. Once they reached the shelter of the mountains, they were secure from pursuit. No small company of ranchers or soldiers dared follow their trail and run the risk of being ambushed in unfamiliar territory. No large army could move in that rugged wilderness, much less conduct a formal campaign against a highly mobile and aggressive foe.

In these mountains, the visiting Apaches soon found the Nednis, and Geronimo lost no time in renewing his friendship with Juh. The two boys were now older, but they found they still shared many interests. Both of them wanted more than anything else to become warriors, and they vied with each other in hunting and playing war games. Juh was still something of a wild boy even among the children of the Nednis, but Geronimo's mother did not object to her son's playing with him. The life of an Apache was a hard one, and perhaps a little touch of wildness in a boy's spirit would help his chances to survive.

When her visit was over, she returned with Geronimo to her home at the headwaters of the Gila River, and his training as a warrior continued. His male relatives and the other men in the settlement took a part in it, teaching him all he should know to become a warrior. If an Apache was traveling in unfamiliar country and became thirsty, he climbed to a height of land and looked for green foliage. If he saw some, he would discover water nearby, but he was never to drink during the day. That was the time when other men went to the water holes, including enemies, so he should always wait until dark. During the daylight hours, he should not travel across the plains or along the passes; he would be too visible. If he was hot, he should not seek out shade, for shady places were where Mexicans and other Indians went to rest. An Apache should search for some small bush that others might overlook and use it for shelter from the sun.

He also learned the Apache art of hiding. One American who later became friendly with the Apaches described this skill. "While crossing an extensive prairie, dotted here and there by a few shrubs and diminutive bushes," he wrote, "Quick Killer [an Apache he knew] volunteered, while resting at noon, to show me with what dexterity an Apache could conceal himself, even where no special opportunity existed for such concealment. The offer was readily accepted, and we proceeded a short distance until we came to a small bush, hardly sufficient to hide a hare. Taking his stand behind this bush, he said: 'Turn your back and wait until I give the signal.' This proposition did not exactly suit my ideas of Apache character, and I said: 'No, I will walk forward until you tell me to stop.' This was agreed upon, and quietly drawing my pistol, keeping a furtive glance over my shoulder, I advanced; but had not gone ten steps, when Quick Killer hailed me to stop and find him. I returned to the bush, went around it three or four times, looked in every direction—there was no possible covert in sight; the prairie was smooth and unbroken, and it seemed as if the earth had opened and swallowed up the man. Being unable to discover him, I called and bade him come forth, when, to my extreme surprise, he rose laughing and rejoiced, within two feet of the position I then occupied. With incredible activity and skill he had buried himself under the thick gamma grass, within six feet of the bush, and had covered himself with such dexterity that one might have trodden upon him without discovering his person." This skill was essential to an Apache, for it enabled him both to ambush his enemies and to escape from them.

Contrary to what many Mexicans and Americans believed, Geronimo and the other young warriors were not taught to take scalps. On the few occasions when they did, it was only after they had learned the bloody act from the white men. Nor did they usually make a practice of torturing their captives. Sometimes, when they were extremely angry, they would mutilate the bodies of their dead enemies. White men, coming on the corpses and seeing their condition, would believe they had been tortured. But Apaches respected what they termed a clean death, and they usually tried to give one to the game they hunted and the enemies they killed. They had a practical reason for this: The ghosts of whatever they had killed, game or man, were less likely to haunt them.

Geronimo also had to learn the Apaches' basic strategy of warfare, based on their native caution. When they were cornered, they fought ferociously, and no man was more dangerous than a wounded Apache who knew he was going to die. At such a time, there were no limits to his bravery or the lengths he would go to kill as many enemies as he could. But ordinarily they had little respect for heroics. The same American who watched Quick Killer hide himself said, "This is a distinguishing feature of the Apache. If fifty of them were to approach a single armed traveler they would do so with caution. Like all other savages they highly prize physical strength and personal courage, but are severe critics in reference to the latter quality. . . . The Apache regards our reckless onsets as vain and foolish. He is in the habit of saying: 'The Americans are brave, but they lack astuteness. They build a great fire which throws out so much heat that they cannot approach it to warm themselves, and when they hear a gun fired they are absurd enough to rush to the spot. But it is not so with us; we build small fires in secluded nooks which cannot be seen, and we gather near them so as to obtain the warmth, and when we hear a gun fired we get away as soon as possible to some place from which we can observe the possible cause.' They regard our daring as folly, and think 'discretion the better part of valor.' I am not so sure," the American added—and he had fought the Apaches often—"but that they are correct in this idea, as well as in several others." So, except when they were trapped, the Apaches did not attack unless they were certain of victory, and they avoided last-ditch engagements whenever they could. If they found themselves being overpowered, they made every effort to retreat to safety. This irritated military commanders trained in the classic warfare of Europe and imbued with European traditions. They had difficulty understanding an enemy who would not stand up and fight but simply melted away in the face of superior forces, only to reappear when the forces were removed.

As Geronimo also learned, trickery was more highly prized than bravery. A warrior who could fool the Mexicans and steal twenty-five horses without a shot being fired was more respected than a warrior who stole even more but lost a man or two in an ensuing battle. To the Apaches, unnecessary deaths were senseless.

So, from his earliest days, Geronimo was trained against rashness. Every one of his relatives, every man at the ranchería, repeated the same lesson: The best warrior is one who does not take excessive risks. Only by following this strategy could they survive in their fight against enemies who so greatly outnumbered them.

Geronimo also learned about the one occasion when the Apaches would forget to be cautious. That was when they were drinking. Long before the appearance of the first white man, the Apaches had made their own liquor. They roasted the roots of mescal plants, steeped them in water, allowed the mixture to ferment, which it did rapidly, and boiled it down. Those, like Geronimo's father, who grew corn set aside part of their crop for making tiswin, which was much liked by the Apaches, although American soldiers thought it had no more potency than weak beer. The Apaches made up for the low alcoholic content by fasting for several days before a tiswin party. With their stomachs empty, it affected them as stronger liquor affected heavy drinkers among white men. Of course, when the Apaches could obtain the white men's drinks, they preferred them to their own.

An Army officer who spent much time among the Western Indians said, "To drink liquor as a beverage, for the gratification of taste, or for the sake of pleasurable conviviality, is something of which the Indian can form no conception. His idea of pleasure in the use of strong drink is to get drunk, and the quicker and more complete that effect, the better he likes it. He is very easily affected, a few tablespoons setting him roaring and half an ordinary tumbler putting him in his paradise for hours."

As a boy training to be a warrior, Geronimo shared in the mood of excitement that came over the ranchería when a tiswin party was planned. He watched the men as they grew quarrelsome from the liquor or passed out. But he did not understand that this was a weakness. He only wanted to grow up and be able to join them.

During this period of training, he had little use for girls, partly because he was leading so vigorous a life and partly because the traditions of the Apaches strongly discouraged relations between the sexes when they were young. Chastity in girls was highly prized, and an unchaste girl was not permitted to go through the puberty rite and often forfeited her chances of marriage. Therefore, the girls did not encourage lovemaking. Sometimes the young men would find an older woman, who, having nothing to lose, would engage in intercourse with them; but they were warned by their parents that such indulgences could shorten their lives, because they were giving up some of their vital spirit to an older woman who could give them nothing in return. Even such mild forms of affection as hand-holding were scorned, and those who did it were greeted with laughter and jeering.

No one ever told an Apache boy when it was time for him to

become a warrior. That decision was left entirely up to each individual. When Geronimo thought he had all the training he needed, he asked to accompany the next raiding party as a novice, and the older warriors granted him permission.

No comments, either favorable or unfavorable, were made about his performance. When the next war or raiding party went out, he again asked permission to join it. The warriors could rebuke him by telling him no, which meant he would have to wait longer. But the warriors agreed he could come with them, and he served again in the same capacity. Geronimo successfully completed the required four raids as a novice. At the conclusion of his fourth expedition, he asked to join the next one and was accepted. This meant he was now regarded as a warrior and could marry.

Already he had picked out the woman he wanted for his bride, a girl named Alope. He was deeply in love with her and asked her father for permission to marry her. The father's response puzzled him, because he requested an unusually large number of horses. Perhaps, Geronimo thought, he did not regard their love for each other as important, or perhaps she was such a dutiful daughter that he did not want to part with her. But whatever the father's reasons, Geronimo met the price, took Alope, and built his wickiup in the land near his father-in-law's at the headwaters of the Gila. He was now a responsible member of the Apache settlement, caring for his wife and his widowed mother.

To add to his pleasure, Juh came north from the Sierra Madres and fell in love with one of the girls in Geronimo's group. He married her and therefore had to live near his wife's family. This meant the two good friends were together again, which each of them enjoyed.

The moon and sun rose over the mountains to the east. The piñon nuts appeared on the trees. The crops of corn and beans and melons grew and were harvested. The women made tiswin, and the men drank it. And, on pleasant evenings, they played the moccasin game. All seemed to be well for the Apaches living at the headwaters of the Gila River, but there were disturbing rumors. Many Americans were coming into the land of the Apaches, and Mangas Coloradas, who had fought the Mexicans so successfully, had not found the means of driving them out.

V

Massacre at Janos

ALTHOUGH Mangas Coloradas continued to dislike the Americans, he realized they were different from the Mexicans—more aggressive and more determined. They also seemed to have an endless quantity of supplies. An American who lost his gun in a battle could easily get another, but an Indian who lost his had to wait until he found a trader willing to sell him one or until he could participate in a raid in which guns were captured. The American soldiers, too, were better equipped and trained than the poorly fed, underpaid Mexicans. Therefore, unless the American population showed signs of growing much greater, Mangas Coloradas was not disposed to fight them.

But the Apaches had not lost the struggle. Their threat lay over the land, and the price they could obviously demand for further invasion of their territory was so high the Americans were reluctant to pay it. So each side made concessions to the other, and an uneasy, informal truce prevailed. Parties of travelers, working their way west from the Río Grande, did not spend the nights in fearful waiting for an attack at dawn, and they entered the mountain passes believing they had a reasonable chance of emerging on the other side unscathed.

But the Americans, although they had made their own adjustment with the Indians, could not control the north-south movement of the Apaches, and so the people of northern Mexico were left as defenseless as before. As they had done for so many years, each of the two northern Mexican states determined its own policy. At Ures, the authorities did not believe peace could ever be made with the Apaches; and the government of Sonora continued to wage active war against them, sending out troops with orders to engage them and destroy as many as possible. West of the Sierra Madres no Apache was safe, and few wandered into that desert area except when they were on the warpath or were members of a raiding party.

On the other side of the mountains, however, the situation was reversed. The government of Chihuahua had decided that continued warfare was senseless. It was expensive and had brought little safety to the inhabitants. Therefore, the government had rescinded its previous policy of extermination and was now seeking to make friends of the Apaches. The soldiers were instructed to let them pass freely. And at stated times of the year, the government issued rations to them, giving away what it knew the Apaches might take by force. The Apaches responded to these overtures in the spirit in which they were made. They knew that the Mexicans would never be truly friendly and did not trust them. But the gains from this temporary peace were sufficiently great to induce the chiefs to restrain their warriors. Undoubtedly some ranchers living in remote areas close to the Sierra Madres continued to lose cattle to hungry Apaches, but this activity was more in the nature of stealing than of fighting, and the lives of the ranchers were relatively safe. The price of a few head of stolen stock, in addition to the official gifts, was a low one in return for security.

Therefore, when Mangas Coloradas proposed they make a trip south to Chihuahua, the Apaches regarded the journey as a pleasure trip. They would, of course, follow their mountain route, for they never believed in taking unnecessary risks by exposing themselves on the plains. (They also needed the water that could be found only in the higher land.) But they had no worries about the visit to Mexico.

Because this was not a war party, the entire group would go —men, women, and children. Geronimo decided that he, too, would make the trip and take with him Alope, their three children, and his mother. He was too young yet to have won any distinction for himself as a warrior, but he was already showing signs of ambition and a desire to lead.

About five feet eight inches in height, he was powerfully built. He had a square, full jaw, and his eyes, as one white man later remarked, were "like two bits of obsidian with lights behind them." His most unusual feature was his mouth—a sharp long gash in his face without a single softening curve. Although he had a good sense of humor and was affectionate toward his family and friends, he could be short-tempered and cruel when he was annoyed. There was a latent power, a wildness that he shared with Juh, that was making others respect him. On this trip, however, he was merely one of the younger warriors, with no special standing among the older men. He had the right to speak in council, but he was not one of those to whom the other Apaches paid particular attention. Where Mangas Coloradas led, he followed.

Just as they had done so many years ago on Geronimo's first visit to his relatives among the Nednis, the Apaches moved southward along the line of the mountains, camping at their usual water holes. The warriors kept up an alert guard for unknown white men or Indians who might prove to be enemies, but they did not expect to see any. To the west across the San Simon Valley, they could watch the high peaks of the Chiricahua Mountains. In the early morning, they stood bright and clear in the fresh light. As the day progressed, a slight blue haze crept up their lower slopes, and the sharp outlines of the rock formations began to disappear. When the sun sank behind them, they became more mysterious and less distinct in the changing light, but the Apaches had no fear from that direction. In that wilderness lived their close relatives, the Chiricahuas, under their great chief, Cochise. If any danger threatened, Cochise and his warriors would come to their aid.

The band continued southward across the Mexican-

American border and into the foothills at the northern edge of the Sierra Madres. Once they had passed the lower land separating the two ranges, they felt safe from any treachery. They were at peace with the people of Chihuahua, and the high mountain ranges separated them from the more militant, angry people of Sonora. If an attack came, it would be from the west, and the Apaches were certain their scouts would notice a detachment of soldiers in time to plan a defense or permit the Indians to escape.

Their ultimate destination was the old town of Casas Grandes, located near ancient Indian ruins that had once been the home of a large and highly civilized tribe. Years ago they had been driven out and destroyed, perhaps by the Aztecs or some other warlike Indians. Later the Spanish had built a town at the same spot, and here the Apaches expected to do some trading and to visit with some of the Mexicans whom they already knew. But on the way they planned to stop farther north at Janos, where the government was making its quarterly presentation of gifts to the Apaches.

Janos had been founded by the Spaniards in 1685 as one of a line of presidios stretching from Tubac in the west to El Paso in the east, designed to ward off Indian attacks from the north. The Spanish had garrisoned the town with their own soldiers as well as with contingents of Opata Indians, who were notable fighters. Together they marched out in pursuit of the attackers. But, by 1710, the campaign waged by the Spanish still had not been successful. The northern tribes were pressing the Spanish settlements just as vigorously as ever, and Janos itself had been sacked. But the Spaniards did not abandon it, and it became a stopping point on the road from Chihuahua to Santa Rita del Cobre. When the *conducta* came up the old trail from the south and arrived at Janos, the drivers and soldiers knew they had reached the edge of the frontier. From there north the Apaches remained in control, and the Mexicans were able to travel through the country only with the consent of chiefs like Juan José or because they were accompanied by large groups of armed men.

The city was situated on the Janos River. Like many rivers in that part of the country, it was hardly recognizable as one to anyone unfamiliar with the desert. When it rained in the mountains, the Janos River ran; when the mountains were dry, so was the riverbed, its sandy channel exposed and bare in the sun. But under the sand was enough water for a settlement. Janos would never grow rich, but white men could live there, do some farming and ranching, and try to protect their more fortunate neighbors to the south from the raids of the Apaches.

On their arrival at Janos, the Apaches, in spite of the Mexicans' protestations of friendship, remained cautious and made their camp outside the city limits. Although Janos is far from the sanctuary of the Sierra Madres, some small foothills lie just to the north. These swing eastward in the shape of a fishhook, growing in size as they do, until far off in the east they form a large range standing high against the sky. The foothills were close enough to the city to provide shelter for the Apaches, and there they picked out a location for their camp. Once they had done this, they selected another site where they agreed to reassemble in case disaster struck them. Even in friendly territory this was a normal precaution for them to take whenever they were away from their own ranchería. With the approval of Mangas Coloradas and the other leading warriors, they chose a large thicket on the Janos River.

The next morning, the men were ready to enter the town. Because the women and children were to stay at the camp, a few warriors remained behind to guard them. The rest walked toward Janos. The sun was already beating down on the dusty streets. A few women were gathered at the wells, working the heavy wooden windlasses to draw water for their families. Sometimes a man passing by would stop to help them lift the dripping bucket to the stone edge of the well, where they could pour its contents into their *ollas*. Every so often a wagon moved slowly through the streets; and when the driver was a young man and noticed the girl he most admired, he would snap his whip and force his burros into a half-gallop in order to impress her. Once he had rounded the corner, he would slow them down again and hope that his father had not seen him wasting the strength of their animals. At the church the bells hung mute, suspended on the giant wooden frame to the side of the church door. They were rung for services and to raise an alarm, but the presence of the Apaches was expected, and there was no need to alert the inhabitants. A slight uneasiness pervaded the community, as it always did when the enemy entered in such numbers. But the Mexicans greeted the Apaches with smiles, for the purpose of the government's expenditures was to gain their friendship, not to anger them and set them on the war-path again.

The officials had some of the presents ready, but neither the Mexicans nor the Apaches were in a hurry. Unlike the Americans, these people did not rush to transact their business but made an occasion of it; and although the Mexicans would be relieved when the Apaches finally left the vicinity of Janos, they still enjoyed the ceremony of the distribution. They spoke a few elegant words about the new friendship between themselves and the Indians, and the Apaches responded. Then, in addition to the bags of meal and other supplies, they opened bottles of liquor, which the Apaches immediately drank. To do this was dangerous for the Mexicans, for a drunken Apache might become quarrelsome and take offense at some slight remark, thus setting off a battle. But the risk was worth taking, for the liquor made the Apaches doubly happy and thankful for the generosity of the people of Chihuahua. At the end of the day, the presentation of the gifts and the accompanying festivities were not finished, but the Apaches returned to their camp in the mountains for the night. They did not want to stay in the city after dark, nor did the Mexicans care to have them stay. In spite of the demonstrations of friendliness, suspicion lingered on both sides.

Many of the Apaches were drunk and staggered from the effects of the liquor as well as from the bulkiness of the presents they carried. The warriors who had been left on guard saw them approach and signaled to the women that their men were arriving. Then they came forward to receive their share of the gifts, most especially the bottles of liquor the Apaches had brought back to the camp. Geronimo was singled out by his mother, Alope, and his three children, to whom he gave the presents he carried. Then he ate the meal Alope had prepared for him, joked for a while with the other warriors, and rolled up in his blankets to sleep, while the camp continued to resound with the laughter of the happy Apaches.

The next day was a repetition of the first. The Apaches left the foothills of the mountains in the early morning and walked to Janos, where the authorities were again ready to receive them. As they strolled through the town, the women, both curious and afraid, watched from the windows. As before, the Mexicans and Indians continued the formalities they so much enjoyed; but at the end of the day, when the sun was dropping over the western mountains, the distribution of the presents had still not been completed. Both sides, however, were pleased with themselves. The Apaches had gained many of the supplies they needed without the hardships and dangers of raids; the Mexicans had purchased at relatively low cost the peace their soldiers could not win for them in battle. Each group believed it had gained the better of the bargain.

One evening the Apaches were returning from another happy day spent at Janos. Slightly confused by the liquor they had drunk, they were following their trail to the foothills, when they were met by a small number of women and children, who came running in their direction, dodging behind bushes and rocks to escape detection. They warned the warriors that the Mexicans had launched an attack on the camp and now occupied it. While most of the men had been in town and the few guards had again been sitting in the sun drinking, a detachment of Mexican soldiers had crept up on them. The warnings of the guards came too late. Surprised, greatly outnumbered, and partially stupefied by the liquor, they tried to fight back, but their resistance had been futile. The soldiers fired fusilade after fusilade into the unsuspecting camp. The women screamed in horror; the children attempted to hide behind them; but for many there was no way to escape, because the bullets came from every side. One moment, a woman had been peaceably cooking; the next, her body lay dead beside her fire. Another had been nursing her baby in the shade; now both mother and baby were corpses, the blood softly seeping from their wounds and staining the desert soil.

The campground was littered with the dead and dying when the Mexicans charged. They ran forward, leaping over the bodies on the ground, firing their guns, and sparing the lives only of those whom they could take prisoners. In the confusion that followed, a few of the women and children were able to escape, slipping through the Mexicans' lines and disappearing among the brush and rocks of the foothills. Some headed toward Janos to warn the returning warriors; others went directly to the thicket the Apaches had chosen earlier as a meeting place in case of disaster; still others hid as best they could, waiting motionless until darkness would make their escape possible. The Apaches' casualties were enormous. More than a hundred had been killed, and an almost equal number had been taken captive. At the expense of betrayal, the Mexicans had won a major victory over their enemies.

Because the camp was completely occupied by the soldiers and there was no hope of retaking it, Mangas Coloradas led his men to the thicket by the river. All night long, they discussed what they should do next. From time to time, the guards they had posted would hear a rustling in the brush and a faint call, perhaps the howl of a wolf, a favorite Apache signal. Cautiously the guard would let the person come forward, and it would prove to be one more woman or child who had somehow managed to escape the massacre, but the total was pitifully small. Each warrior waited expectantly for those whom he loved. Wives rejoined their husbands, and children found their parents, but there was always the sad emptiness occasioned by those who did not return. ". . . and, when all were counted," Geronimo said later, "I found that my aged mother, my young wife, and my three small children were among the slain. There were no lights in camp, so without being noticed I silently turned away and stood by the river. How long I stood there I do not know. . . ."

As chief, Mangas Coloradas presided over the meeting of warriors to decide what they should do next. They had no way of knowing that the soldiers had come from Sonora, which was still at war with them, and not from Chihuahua. The governor of Sonora, annoyed at a policy that fed the Indians in Chihuahua while he was fighting them in his own state, had decided to act on his own. Without consulting either the federal government or the governor of Chihuahua, he had led his troops in a forced march over the Sierra Madres. Knowing the date set for the quarterly distribution of presents in Janos, he had arrived in time to attack the unsuspecting Apaches in their camp. Like the scalp-hunter Johnson, he did not care whether the Indians he killed were old or young, male or female. He simply regarded every dead body and every prisoner as a personal triumph.

Although the Apaches did not understand the contradictory policies of the two Mexican states and the inability of the federal government to control its officers, they were realistic in appraising their own situation. They were outnumbered by the nearby troops, who were now firmly entrenched in the Indians' former campground. They had lost most of their arms and horses and were deep in their enemy's territory, far from the protection of the mountains. Even if they had known about the conflict between Sonora and Chihuahua, they would not have appealed to the Chihuahuans for help. The officials of Chihuahua might—and actually did—protest Sonora's intervention in their affairs, but they were not likely to muster their troops to protect the Indians. Under the circumstances, a white man might have yielded to the instinct to launch an immediate counterattack, however hopeless, in an attempt to free some of the prisoners; but Mangas Coloradas was wise enough not to encourage such rash action. The chance of success was too slight; the chance of heavy losses too great. With the restraint that is part of the Indians' character, the Apaches decided they could only retreat.

Geronimo did not take part in the discussion, although as a warrior he was entitled to express his views. Overcome with sadness, he stood to one side, heedless of the outcome. None of the Indians, including him, made any attempt to recover the bodies of their relatives or friends, for that was not part of their code. They did not believe the rescue of a corpse was worth the risk of lives. So as soon as they had reached their decision and made certain there were no more stragglers trying to reach the security of the thicket, they set out on their sad way north.

"I stood until all had passed," Geronimo said later, "hardly knowing what I would do—I had no weapon, nor hardly did I wish to fight, neither did I contemplate recovering the bodies of my loved ones, for that was forbidden. I did not pray, nor did I resolve to do anything in particular, for I had no purpose left. I finally followed the tribe silently, keeping just within hearing distance of the soft noise of the feet of the retreating Apaches."

That morning some of the Indians killed a little game and stopped to eat, but Geronimo did not join them. Keeping his sadness to himself, he stood apart from the others in mournful loneliness. After two days and three nights, during which they paused only briefly, the Indians reached the Mexican-American border, where they rested for two days. Everyone respected Geronimo for his losses, because no other family had been completely destroyed; and as they went about their camp duties, men, women, and children fell silent at his approach.

After their rest, they started north again, taking their route along the Peloncillo Mountains, and finally reached their home at the headwaters of the Gila River. By Apache custom, Geronimo was required to burn everything that had belonged to his mother and Alope, and this he did. But he went further than custom demanded. He burned, too, all the playthings that had been owned by his three children, and he also burned his own wickiup. Nothing was left to remind him of his family except the deep hatred in his heart. That could be extinguished only by the deaths of many Mexicans.

VI

Revenge at Arizpe

ALTHOUGH the Apaches had had the wisdom not to risk certain defeat by counterattacking after the massacre at their campground, they never forgot the horror of those hours at Janos, the desperate wait in the thicket, and the sad retreat homeward. The governor of Sonora, sitting comfortably in his mansion in Ures and bowing to the *señoras* as he walked across the plaza to Sunday mass, might congratulate himself on the resounding defeat he had given his enemies. But far to the north, in the deep forests of the mountains, the Apaches were plotting their revenge.

Mangas Coloradas called a council of war; and the Indians decided to form a major war party, not a minor raiding party. If he had known what was happening, the governor would have called on the federal government for aid, added to the garrisons of every presidio, and braced himself for the attack. An apparent lull had occurred in the war between his people and the Apaches, but to the Indians, time meant little. For the large-scale attack they wanted to make, they needed allies; and while they were gathering their supporters together, they remained peacefully in the mountains.

Because of the personal losses he had suffered, the warriors chose Geronimo as their emissary to the other tribes, being certain he would be driven to speak eloquently of the Mexicans' treachery. First, he went south to visit the Chiricahuas, and somewhere in the Dragoon or Chiricahua mountains, he met Cochise. Of all the Apaches, Cochise was the closest to the white men's conception of a chief. A giant, more than six feet tall, strong and straight, he had even features and a quick intellect. The Chiricahuas respected his opinions and were afraid of him personally. He could quiet the wildest of the tribe with merely a glance. But even his authority was not great enough to commit his people to take to the warpath without first consulting them. Therefore, he called a council of war at which Geronimo was to talk.

In a remote valley in the mountains, the warriors assembled at dawn. As the eastern sky slowly brightened, they took their seats on the ground, sitting in rows according to their rank, the younger warriors in the rear, the older, more experienced men in front. At a signal from Cochise, Geronimo stepped in front of them, his black hair tumbling to his shoulders and held firmly in place with a headband. As he started talking, the bitter memory of those hours in Janos welled up within him and gave power to his words. His eyes, "two bits of obsidian with lights behind them," grew gentle with grief as he briefly reviewed the disaster and recounted the losses the Apaches had suffered. Then they flashed with anger as he told about the war party that Mangas Coloradas was forming and appealed to them to join it. He promised that he himself would fight in the forefront and take as many risks as any other warrior; but if their kinsmen fell, they should remember that every man had come of his own free will. The decision would be theirs, not his. Having ended his speech, he waited while the Chiricahuas consulted among themselves. The decision was not to be made lightly, for the possibility of heavy losses was great. On the other hand, the Mexicans could not be allowed to go unpunished. If they slaughtered the Warm Springs Apaches at Janos with impunity, they might slaughter any Apache anywhere. This was a common cause, and they decided to join it.

The meeting over, Geronimo returned to Mangas Coloradas

and reported his success. His next assignment was to visit his boyhood friend, Juh, who had become the hereditary chief of the Nednis, and persuade his tribe to take part. Again he traveled south, following the trail to Mexico. And in the depths of the Sierra Madres, far from any Mexican settlement and without the news reaching the governor of Sonora, he met with Juh. Still as wild as he had been as a boy and always anxious for war, he was personally ready to join Mangas Coloradas in an attack on the Mexicans. But, like Cochise, Juh was compelled by Apache custom to call a council. Word went out to the warriors, and they quietly assembled to hear what Geronimo had to say. Geronimo made the same speech to the Nednis that he had given to the Chiricahuas. Once more the Apaches debated what he had said and came to the same decision. They, too, would join the attack on Mexico. Mangas Coloradas now had three tribes to help him avenge the dead at Janos.

The tribes met in a mountain wilderness near the Mexican-American border, where no white man could learn what they were doing. When they had gathered, they began discussing their war plans. The first consideration of the chiefs was to select a campground where the women and children would be safe from retaliatory attacks while the warriors were away. Next, they chose the small number of men who would stay behind as guards, and then they decided on a number of places where they could meet in case of disaster. This was their usual precaution, the one that had saved lives at Janos.

When these arrangements were completed, the Indians were ready for their war dance, a ceremony held only before the Apaches went on the warpath, not when just a few of them formed a raiding party. As darkness fell over the mountains, they lit a fire. The flames rose and cast their light on the faces of the waiting warriors, one of whom began beating a drum. The sound echoed in the night, and four dancers, marching abreast, appeared from the east. While the drummer continued to beat, the singers began chanting. The dancers circled the fire four times and then divided into two pairs, one standing on the south side and one on the north. They danced in these positions and then changed places, repeating this routine four times. After that, they joined in the singing. The time had now come for the individual warriors to signify whether they wished to be members of the war party. If they did, they stepped forward one by one and joined in the dancing or simply walked around the fire. This was the sign that they would fight.

From time to time, some of the men dropped out of the dancing and joined other groups to pray, not for personal safety, but for many Mexican deaths and success in punishing the enemy. Thus the ceremony continued throughout the night until, before dawn, all the warriors reassembled around the fire, and everyone danced at once. The flames blazed up again as the Indians added fresh wood. The singers' voices gained a new intensity, and the women chanted their approval ever louder. Then the dance came to an end; and the war party, now sanctified and carrying the blessing of the Indians' spirits, was ready to depart.

They went on foot, because the care of horses would only have imposed an additional burden on them. Each warrior wore his breechclout and high-topped moccasins and carried his weapons and a few day's supply of food. Some had fire drills placed in their quivers. and many of them carried bags of pollen, intended to bring them success in fighting. The three tribes moved through the mountains under their own chiefs, for the time had not yet come to select the war chief who would lead them into battle under a common leader. Yet all knew their purpose, and there was no division among them.

The knowledge that Geronimo had gained on his trips to Mexico now served him in good stead, for although he was still a young warrior, the chiefs asked him to act as the guide. He led them along the western flanks of the Sierra Madres, where they were unlikely to meet any Mexicans who might give the alarm, and quietly past the soldiers at Fronteras, who would have spread the warning if they had known the Apaches were near. Even in that mountainous country, they covered some forty to forty-five miles a day, often traveling fourteen hours with only slight pauses to eat or rest.

Quickly the war party wound its way through the mountains and down the canyons of Sonora. It slipped past Nacozari on the Yaqui River without being observed and then turned westward to the mountains on the other side of the river valley. Up these the Apaches climbed, following the canyons and staying out of sight of the few ranchers and farmers who sometimes ventured into the lower slopes. The higher they rose toward the crest of the ridge, the safer they were from observation, because few Mexicans traveled that far into the mountains. Finally the Apaches crossed the top and began the descent into the valley of the Sonora River, which empties finally into the Gulf of California.

Toward the south, this valley is broad and fertile and easily reached from Hermosillo. Farther north, it enters a steep-sided canyon, where travel becomes difficult. The riverbed provided only a partial roadway, especially during the rainy season, and the walls of the canyon are so sheer that in many places it was impractical to cut a road along them. The traveler, therefore, had to follow the higher ridges to the west. As the river emerges from the canyon, it is joined by another and again becomes more accessible. At this juncture is located the lovely town of Arizpe, the former capital of Sonora, which the Apaches had selected as their goal.

Their choice was based on sound tactics. The fertile fields of the Sonora River made Arizpe a wealthy community with a large population for a Sonoran town, thus an object worthy of attack. The narrow canyon cut it off from rapid reinforcement from the settlements to the south. To the north, the population was slight. The land to the west is somewhat flatter, although it, too, is bounded by mountains. But to the east, the direction from which the Apaches were approaching, the mountains are high and rugged and close to the town. Thus the Apaches could come near to Arizpe without being detected, and they also had a nearby refuge for retreat in the event of defeat. Few Mexican troops would be foolhardy enough to pursue them into that wilderness, where every canyon offered an opportunity for an ambush. On the other hand, the people of Arizpe were militarily isolated from the rest of Sonora because of its location. When the Apaches attacked, the town could only rely on the troops already stationed there for its defense. No others could arrive in time to be of help.

Staying to the east of the river with the mountains at their rear, some of the Apaches ventured far enough into the open so they could be seen from the town, which rests on high ground along the slope of the western bank. In Arizpe, the alarm quickly spread. Some men carried warnings to those who were working in the fields, while others gathered in the public buildings on the square to decide what to do. In the handsome church, some of the women knelt on the floor, offering prayers for the safety of their men and their children. If, as everyone hoped, this was only a raiding party, the Apaches might be persuaded to leave by a demonstration of superior strength or by giving them presents. As the latter course was less likely to start the Indians fighting, the Mexicans decided to follow it first. They chose eight men to ride out and treat with them, a force small enough to show they desired peace but large enough so it could not easily be overcome. The eight Mexicans saddled their horses, crossed the river, and rode over the fields toward the waiting Apaches, their silver bits flashing in the sunlight and their large-roweled spurs jingling. There was no laughter or joking among them; they all realized this was a dangerous mission; and they knew that the safety of their fellow citizens depended on their making reasonable terms with the Indians.

Smiling and with protestations of friendship, they drew near the small band of Apaches, who, serving as decoys to lure them closer to the main body, made no move to come forward. The distance between the two groups of men became smaller and smaller, and still the Mexicans could not determine the Apaches' intentions. Finally the gap closed. The Apaches, assisted by those who had been hiding, seized the Mexicans and immediately killed them.

Their purpose in taking this abrupt action was simple. As a war party, they had no desire to spare lives; and cruelty, after the massacre at Janos, was no consideration. All that the warriors wanted were dead Mexicans to avenge their own dead. By slaughtering the eight men in full view of the town, they knew they would lure the troops out of Arizpe. For the honor of their commander would compel them to take to the field, thus saving the necessity of storming a fixed position, a tactic that would have placed the Apaches at a disadvantage.

That night, leaving the Mexican bodies unburied, the Apaches made their camp near Arizpe, being careful to post guards so they would not be surprised while they slept. In the town, terror and confusion reigned. The people now knew they were being attacked by a full-fledged war party that would give no quarter. Yet they saw no hope of the Apaches making a direct attack on their fortified positions.

The commander of the garrison recognized his duty, although he did not relish the idea of carrying it out. That night he laid his plans; and the following morning, being unwilling to commit his men fully, he left his cavalry in the town to protect it from a flank assault, while he led his infantry across the river and through the fields to where the Apaches were waiting. Although he would not be far from Arizpe, he brought with him a supply train loaded with rations and ammunition, for one of the whites' greatest advantages was their ability to maintain superior gunfire.

The subsequent fighting continued all day, but it was sporadic and indecisive. Occasionally a Mexican would fire at an Apache; occasionally an Apache would shoot and kill a Mexican or bring one down with a well-aimed arrow. But each side realized this was only a preliminary skirmish before the real battle, a first testing of each other's skill and determination. Sooner or later, the Mexicans would have to deploy larger forces if they hoped to drive the Apaches away. And the Apaches, anxious for blood, were willing to wait until that moment came.

The Mexican commander, however, had made a grave tactical error in bringing the supply train onto the field and would have been far better off if he had carried ammunition from Arizpe to his men only as they needed it. All day long, the

Apaches' attention had been focused on those mules and their packs, but they had been frustrated in their attempts to capture them. As dusk was falling, they made a final effort to seize the supply train, and this time they succeeded. This was a major victory for them and a serious setback for the Mexicans. There was now no chance of the Apaches ending their attack because they had run out of ammunition, a circumstance that often forced them to cease fighting. Nor would they have to pause and go in search of food. The prospect of an intensive battle, therefore, had become greater than ever before, and both the Apaches and the Mexicans knew it.

Dissatisfied with the day's inconclusive results, the soldiers withdrew that night to the comparative safety of Arizpe to prepare for the following morning, while the Apaches again rested in their camp. Around dawn, they woke up and began praying, once more not for their personal security, as white men might have done, but solely for victory over the enemy. In Arizpe, the Mexican commander had decided on a different course of action from the one he had followed the previous day. Having failed to dislodge the Indians and having lost his supply train to them, he decided he would confront them with his entire force, holding nothing in reserve, and attempt to overwhelm them.

About ten o'clock in the morning, the Apaches saw the Mexican soldiers leave the buildings at Arizpe and come down the slope toward the river. They estimated there were two companies of infantry and two of cavalry. As the soldiers crossed the riverbed and came nearer, the Indians recognized the cavalry as the men who had massacred their relatives and friends at Janos. As soon as this became known, Geronimo spoke to Cochise, Mangas Coloradas, and Juh and asked for the privilege of serving as war chief during the coming battle. Although he was young and relatively inexperienced, no one doubted his courage or his hatred of the Mexicans. For these reasons and because he had suffered the greatest personal losses at Janos, they granted his request.

He formed some of the Apaches in a semicircle under the

cover of trees, while others moved to the flanks so they could later attack the advancing soldiers from the rear. Then they waited for the Mexicans' next move. Stationing his calvary as reserves, the commander ordered his infantry into lines and began to advance toward the waiting Apaches. When his men were within a few hundred yards of the Indians, they opened fire, and the Apaches charged.

Almost immediately, they broke the Mexicans' lines; and the action in the field became so confused that the people watching from Arizpe could not tell what was happening—whether their men were losing or winning. Much of the fighting was between individuals or isolated groups of soldiers and Apaches. Geronimo, the memory of his murdered family constantly in his mind, was in the forefront of the struggle, dashing here and there whenever he saw an opportunity to kill a Mexican. Sweating with exertion, using his bow until he had exhausted his supply of arrows and then turning to his spear, he so distinguished himself that the Mexicans picked him out as an individual. One of them nicknamed him Geronimo, the Spanish for "Jerome"; and the word passed from soldier to soldier—"Geronimo, Geronimo," they called to each other in their fear of this hate-ridden warrior who seemed so heedless of danger. From that time, this was the name by which he was known to both Indians and whites.

After two hours of fighting, Geronimo and three other Indians remained alone at the edge of the river, for the majority of the Mexicans had retreated to Arizpe to escape the Apaches' fury. The other Indians had pulled back toward the east. The ground was covered with the dead and dying. Here lay a Mexican soldier, the broken shaft of an Apache lance sticking in his chest. There was another with the feathered end of an arrow protruding from his dead body. In another spot, the brains of an Apache warrior were spattered on the ground. On both sides the casualties were heavy, but the Mexicans had suffered by far the greater losses.

Except for their knives, the four remaining Indians were now weaponless. All the arms they had possessed had been lost in the fierce fighting. Two Mexican soldiers, more courageous than their fellows, came within firing distance and killed two of them instantly. Geronimo and his remaining companion turned and ran toward the woods where the other Apaches were waiting. Even in battle, the Apaches' individualism prevailed and no man was required to come to the aid of another unless called upon to do so by name. This, therefore, was Geronimo's personal struggle with the two soldiers. One of the Mexicans drew his saber and, overtaking Geronimo's companion, struck him down with a slash of the blade. As there was nothing Geronimo could do to help his fallen friend, he kept on running, reached the other Apaches, and grabbed a spear from one of them. He then turned to face his nearest pursuer. The odds were now changed, and the Mexican, with his relatively short saber, no longer enjoyed the advantage. Geronimo plunged the lance into his body and brought him to the ground.

Bending over the dead soldier, Geronimo seized the saber and faced the remaining Mexican, who managed to elude the sharp blade and began grappling with the Indian. The two struggling men dropped to the ground, but the Mexican was no match for the powerful, angry Apache in hand-to-hand combat. Geronimo let the saber slip from his hand. It was of no use to him at such close quarters, and he drew his knife, a favorite weapon of the Apaches. The fight was short. The Mexican, bleeding from his wounds, relaxed his grip and fell limp.

Geronimo, still with the fury of the battle in his heart, rose from the dirt and looked around for more Mexicans to kill, but none appeared. Except for the dead and dying, the field was empty. All the soldiers able to do so had fled to Arizpe and taken shelter behind its walls. The Apaches' victory was complete.

VII

Raiding into Mexico

MOST of the Apaches were content with the results of the battle at Arizpe and saw no reason to press their attack further. The field on which they had fought was covered with enough Mexican bodies to avenge the massacre at Janos. And although an onslaught against the town itself might add to the total of enemy dead, storming the adobe walls of the buildings could also cost many Apache lives. As they did not believe in taking unnecessary risks, further fighting was not worthwhile. So they quietly disappeared into the mountains, leaving Arizpe to mourn its losses.

Once in the wilderness and certain they were not being followed, the Apaches turned toward the secret campground where they had left their women and children. As they approached, they announced their coming by lighting smoke signals. Noticing the columns rising in the clear air, the women made ready to receive their men, and when the warriors entered the camp, there was mourning for those who had died and great rejoicing over the successful outcome of the expedition. Then the three tribes under their chiefs went back to their homes.

But Geronimo did not return to the headwaters of the Gila. After the death of Alope, he had fallen in love with a Chiricahua woman and married her. Following the usual custom, he had joined her family and had gone to live in the Dragoon and Chiricahua mountains of southeastern Arizona. This placed him under the leadership of Cochise.

Unusually tall for an Apache—he was a giant standing some six feet two inches—Cochise's prestige was as great as his physical stature. Among the Chiricahuas, his counsel was almost always accepted, and he carried great influence with the other Apaches as well. The lands of his tribe included the Dragoon and Chiricahua mountains, the broad Sulphur Springs Valley that lay between them, and, most important to the Americans, Apache Pass. This pass divided the Chiricahua Mountains to the south from the Dos Cabezas Mountains to the north and provided the best route from the east into the Sulphur Springs Valley and on to Tucson and California.

It was tortuous, difficult country for the traveler, with high mountains flanking much of the passageway, snarls of canyons, and a windswept summit more than 5,000 feet high. In many respects, the terrain at the northern limits of the Dos Cabezas Mountains was better, because it was more gradual and open and thus far less suited to an Indian ambush. But Apache Pass offered what the more northern pass did not—water. Part way through, a spring opened at the foot of a grove of green-leaved trees. Water gushed from it by the gallons and ran into a pool in the sandy riverbed just below it. Even in the dry season, when the rest of the riverbed was dry, the pool was full. No matter how thirsty the travelers or their livestock, they could obtain in Apache Pass more than enough water—the first and last for miles on the east-west route through that part of the country. And water was worth even the risk of an Indian attack.

Cochise never attempted to close the pass completely. If he had wished to do so, he could have delayed the settlement of southern Arizona until the federal government constructed a fort. Instead, he permitted travelers to go through his land and to drink at his spring and even allowed the construction of a crude military road. But he did not guarantee a safe passage.

On at least one occasion, more than thirty men and women, who were accompanying a wagon train, entered Apache Pass and found—not water—but death. A band of Indians swept down on them while they were following the winding, rough road; and except for a few women taken captive, they were all killed. They had with them supplies of goosedown bedding, which the Indians had never seen before. Not knowing the purpose of the bedding, the Indians slit open the casings and released the feathers, which for many months drifted with the wind over the scene of death, their whiteness creating a macabre contrast with the bodies.

Other travelers, too, encountered the horrors of an Indian attack as they drove their horses and mules over the mountain ridge, and Apache Pass soon won a name for itself as one of the most dangerous points along the Southwestern route. But whether these attacks were led by Cochise himself or whether he merely permitted other Indians to conduct them was not known to the whites. They understood merely that, dependent on the whim of the great chief, Apache Pass offered uncertain safety but not sure death.

Toward the Mexicans, however, Cochise took a different attitude. Although he had entered into a partial but not formal peace with the Americans, he still regarded the Mexicans as the traditional enemies of his people, and he had no objections to the Chiricahuas raiding them. More than one party of his warriors slipped south across the border and returned with supplies taken from the towns and ranches of Sonora.

These raids, combined with those of other Apache tribes, were a source of great embarrassment to the United States. When it had signed the Treaty of Guadalupe Hidalgo, it had agreed to protect the Mexicans from the Indians. But it soon learned this was impossible, at least at any reasonable cost. It also discovered that the territory it had acquired from Mexico did not include what many persons considered the best route for a future east-west railroad. Therefore in 1853, James Gadsden, the minister to Mexico, was instructed to negotiate a new treaty. Because Santa Anna's government was in serious financial straits, it was willing to sell the southern sections of what are now Arizona and New Mexico for $10,000,000. Included in this price, to the relief of the Americans, was a provision rescinding their obligation to prevent raids over the border. Cochise had proved too much for the diplomats and soldiers of the United States.

Under him, Geronimo's hatred of the Mexicans found no curb. The memory of his dead family continued to burn in his heart, and he was determined on further revenge. Most of the warriors, however, were satisfied with the results they had achieved at Arizpe and were not willing to take to the warpath so soon again. In spite of the prowess he had shown during the battle, Geronimo was not yet a recognized war leader with a following of his own, but he finally persuaded two other warriors to accompany him on a raid, and he left the United States at the head of this small party. They traveled south on foot and, after some reconnoitering, selected a small town in Sonora as the object of their attack.

In the early dawn, when the light was first breaking and the outlines of the buildings became faintly visible, they left the shelter of the nearby foothills and slipped toward the town. It lay quiet and still before them, its adobe walls bathed in shadows and the dusty streets deserted. The Apaches approached quietly, their moccasined feet making no sound on the ground. Five horses were tied up just outside the settlement, and the three Apaches decided to steal them. Using every caution, they worked their way toward the tethered animals, certain that no one had observed or heard them. Their knives were in their hands ready to cut the horses loose, when suddenly the town sprang awake. Heavy gunfire burst from the windows of the houses, shattering the dawn's quiet. Bullets sang through the air. Geronimo's two friends fell mortally wounded, and he, having no other choice, turned to run in an effort to escape the rain of lead. As he did so, armed Mexicans poured out of the doorways with their guns loaded and cocked. Some ran in his direction, while others paused long enough to saddle and mount their horses before joining the chase.

Every trick Geronimo had learned during his boyhood training as a warrior was useful to him that day, particularly his skill

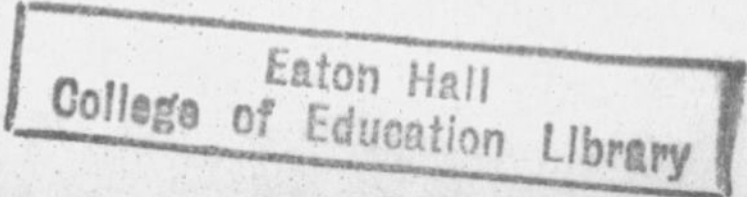

at running and his ability to hide in the most unlikely places. At least three times the Mexicans surrounded and almost captured him, but each time he eluded them and got farther toward the safety of the mountains. But he could not throw them off or tire them out, and they kept combing the countryside in search of him. On several occasions, he was able to kill one who came near him; but the hunt persisted with no respite, the angry townsmen seeking the lone Apache. With relief, he at last saw the sun disappear and darkness fall. The cool night crept over the desert, and in the blackness he turned north toward the Arizona border.

But the next day, he learned that he had not yet thrown off the pursuit. Mexicans on horseback were still riding in the direction he had taken, trying to cut him off from the border. He had not eaten or rested since that first fatal moment when the Mexicans had opened fire on him and his friends. His supply of arrows was exhausted. Except for his knife, he no longer had any means of defending himself and had to rely entirely on his ability to avoid detection. All day long the hunt continued, for the Mexicans, flushed with their earlier success, were determined to kill the remaining member of the tiny band. But Geronimo managed to remain hidden throughout the daylight hours, taking advantage of every bush, rock, and gulley and moving unseen from cover to cover. That night, he was able to throw the Mexicans off his trail, and the next day he was alone in the desert country and did not pause in his hurry to return home.

On his arrival, there was no rejoicing among the Apaches.

"Some of the Apaches blamed me for the evil result of the expedition," he said later, "but I said nothing. Having failed, it was only proper that I should remain silent. But my feelings toward the Mexicans did not change—I still hated them and longed for revenge. I never ceased to plan for their punishment, but it was hard to get the other warriors to listen to my proposed raids."

In spite of his defeat, he was able to persuade two other warriors to join him on another raid back into Mexico. After crossing the border, they picked out a town that was near the mountains and planned to attack it at daybreak. From what they could determine at a distance, it looked undefended, and so they lay down under the clear desert sky to sleep before the raid. During the night, Geronimo was awakened by the sound of gunfire and found that he and his two friends were under attack. A group of Mexican scouts, traveling through the country during the nighttime, had uncovered the Apaches' camp. The fusilade that struck them killed one of the three, but Geronimo and the remaining warrior managed to escape.

At sunrise, the two Indians were still hiding and trying to decide what to do next. They certainly could not carry out their planned attack against the town, and yet they did not want to return to the ranchería empty-handed. While they were making up their minds what to do next, they noticed a column of Mexican troops advancing from the south. The soldiers were mounted and well armed and had with them a packtrain loaded with enough supplies for a long journey. An attack on so many troops was out of the question, but Geronimo and the other warrior were curious to find out where the soldiers were going. Lurking behind cover, they kept up with the troops, who continued north toward the border.

The watching Apaches finally concluded that the column's commander planned to disregard the international boundary, march into the United States, and undertake to attack the Apaches in their own country. So the two warriors went ahead to give the alarm. Because they were deep in Mexico, it took them three days to reach the ranchería, arriving there around noon. Although Geronimo was discredited by his second failure in a row, the Indians listened to his news; and those warriors who were at the settlement—many of them happened to be away—made their defense ready. Later on the same day, the Mexican column appeared and killed three Apache boys with the first volley. The fighting raged until nightfall. Two Indian warriors died in the struggle, but as darkness came, the Mexicans, who had lost eight soldiers, decided to retreat from the mountains and return to their own country.

In spite of the failure of his two recent raids into Mexico, Geronimo's lust for Mexican blood was not yet sated, and he soon joined a war party of twenty-five Apaches. They followed the trail of the retreating soldiers on a retaliatory mission to avenge the deaths of the three boys and the two warriors. Shortly after they reached Mexico, their scouts discovered a group of Mexican soldiers accompanied by a company of cavalry. Although they outnumbered the Apaches, Geronimo was certain the Indians could overcome them by taking them by surprise. In the mountains toward which the soldiers were moving was a pass through which they would have to march. In such a spot, the advantage lay with the Apaches.

Outflanking the soldiers and getting ahead of them, the Apaches stationed themselves on either side of the mountain pass, their guns cocked and their arrows ready. Soon the first of the soldiers entered. The Indians kept still, so none of the Mexicans noticed the danger that surrounded them, and the men behind followed their leaders into the trap. When the entire band was in the confines of the pass, the Apaches attacked.

To their surprise, the Mexicans were not thrown into a panic. Instead, in an orderly fashion, they dismounted and formed a barricade with their horses, shooting from behind the animals' bodies and returning the Indians' fire with deadly effectiveness. The Indians fired from behind rocks and bushes, taking positions where they could see the enemy but could hardly be seen in return. Only the puffs of smoke rising from their rifle barrels showed where they were. But the Apaches were not winning, and they were being plagued by their perpetual handicap: They were running short of ammunition and arrows.

In an attempt to save what remained, the Apaches charged. Down the mountain slopes they came, brandishing their weapons and determined to pass the barrier of the horses' bodies. Anxious to demonstrate his courage, Geronimo was in the forefront, holding his Apache lance ready for hand-to-hand combat. As he came to the trail where the soldiers were gathered, he singled out an individual Mexican and raced toward him, intending to thrust the lance into his chest. The Mexican started to aim his gun at him, but Geronimo kept on coming, certain he could make the final thrust before the Mexican could pull the trigger. Just as he raised his lance to strike, he stepped with one foot into a pool of blood; and instead of spearing the soldier, he slipped and fell to the ground. The Mexican quickly shifted his grip on his gun and, taking it by the barrel, swung it in an arc. The butt crashed down on the Apache's head and knocked him senseless. As Geronimo lay unconscious, another Indian, who was directly behind him, saved his life by killing the Mexican with a lance.

The battle raged around Geronimo's inert body. Both sides fought desperately, because they each knew they could expect only total victory or total defeat. There was no possibility of surrender. The Indians kept attacking with their knives and lances, and the Mexicans defended themselves as best they could with their guns and swords. The ground was covered with the blood of the dead and wounded, and the air was hideous with cries of pain. In the end, the Apaches won; but as they looked at the dead Mexicans around them, they found no cause to celebrate. Their own losses had been too heavy to justify the attack.

Before leaving, they searched among the bodies for wounded Mexicans who should be killed and wounded Apaches who might be saved. During their search, they discovered Geronimo still alive, and one of them nursed him back to consciousness. Then they wrapped a bandage around his head and, along with their other wounded, started the journey back to Arizona. Geronimo had lost blood, and his head ached from the blow he had received, but he was able to keep up with the Apaches' fast pace and returned home safely.

Although most of Geronimo's thought during this period was absorbed in his struggle with the Mexicans, he still found time to marry another wife. (The only limit on the number of wives an Apache warrior could take was his ability to support them.) He also left the Dragoon and Chiricahua mountains and returned farther north, where relations between the Apaches and the Americans were increasingly tense and where the chief, Mangas Coloradas, was becoming more and more hostile to the new invaders.

His attitude was based on a set of circumstances quite different from those faced by Cochise. The Americans moving westward through Cochise's territory wanted access to the water at Apache Pass, but they had no desire to remain. The high, rugged mountains and the broad, arid valley that Cochise controlled offered nothing the Americans could not obtain more easily elsewhere. The territory of Mangas Coloradas, however, contained rich mineral deposits, and the miners who came to work them planned to stay.

Mangas Coloradas quickly learned two facts about the miners: Nothing could dissuade them from their search for wealth, and they preferred gold to all else. In an attempt to lure them away from his land, he approached them individually and, with the promise of secrecy, told each one that he knew the location of much larger gold deposits in other parts of the country. As he explained, he had no use for it. He could not eat it and it would not keep him warm. So why not tell his friend where it was? This tactic might have worked, but the miners did not keep their oaths of secrecy. In time, one spoke to another about his conversation with Mangas Coloradas, the two miners talked to a third, and soon the whole of Mangas Coloradas's plot became apparent to them.

When Mangas Coloradas next came to town, the angry miners seized him, strung him up, flogged him, and released him with the blood oozing from the welts on his back. They thought they had taught him a lesson, but they had no understanding of Apaches. The wounds meant nothing to Mangas Coloradas compared to the hurt to his pride. From that time on, he was the Americans' enemy; and although he was too wise—and too much an Apache—to wage open warfare against them, thereafter many a miner woke up in the morning to discover his horses and mules had disappeared or while riding the lonely trails of New Mexico found himself under attack from a hidden foe. As the bullets and arrows either narrowly missed him or brought him to the ground, he mistakenly cursed the treachery of Indians and not the impetuous anger of the miners.

Although Geronimo moved back to the Warm Springs Apaches during this period, he continued to concentrate his hatred on the Mexicans rather than engage in the harassment of the Americans. A year after the defeat of the Mexican soldiers in the mountain pass, he was able to gather together another band of twelve warriors who were willing to follow him. They crossed the international border and for four days traveled along the eastern edge of the Sierra Madres in Chihuahua. When they were close to the town of Casas Grandes, they made camp, rested for a day, and then successfully attacked a passing packtrain.

Driving the mules back toward Arizona, they took a route that led them through Sonora. Their success, however, made them careless, and one night they made camp without adequately looking over the surrounding country. In the darkness, some cavalry, whom the Mexicans had sent after them, crept up to the camp. And at daybreak, before the Indians realized they were cornered, the soldiers opened fire. During the first volley of shots, a bullet struck Geronimo a glancing blow on the side of his face near his left eye. The wound was not serious, but Geronimo was again knocked unconscious. "All the other Indians fled to cover," Geronimo said later. "The Mexicans, thinking me dead, started in pursuit of the fleeing Indians. In a few moments I regained consciousness and had started at full speed for the woods when another company coming up opened fire on me. Then the soldiers who had been chasing the other Indians turned, and I stood between two hostile companies, but I did not stand long. Bullets whistled in every direction and at close range to me. One inflicted a slight flesh wound on my side, but I kept running, dodging, and fighting, until I got clear of my pursuers. I climbed up a steep canyon, where the cavalry could not follow. The troopers saw me, but did not dismount and try to follow." And he added, "I think they were wise not to come on."

The warriors were now scattered in every direction, each

seeking a way to escape. As usual, they had previously selected a place where they would meet in the event of disaster, and so instead of trying to reassemble while still near the Mexican soldiers, they went back separately to the meeting place in Arizona, from which they returned to their home.

Shortly after the band returned from Mexico, some of the Apaches went north to trade for blankets with the Navajos, while others went on a hunting expedition. Geronimo, however, had not yet recovered from his wounds—his left eye was swollen shut—and he remained at home with some twenty other warriors. With most of the men away on peaceful missions, life at the ranchería was quiet. The women had less work to do when their husbands and fathers were away, and the few warriors merely loafed in the sun, played games, and enjoyed themselves.

But one morning, when the women rose as usual to light their fires in preparation for cooking breakfast, bullets whistled through the camp, killing many women and children and several of the warriors. The others raced to safety in every direction, but the attack had been so sudden that they had to leave most of their possessions behind them. What they could not carry back with them to Mexico, the soldiers burned, leaving the ranchería a smoldering ruin and Geronimo's band almost destitute. "A few warriors followed the trail of the troops as they went back to Mexico with their booty," Geronimo later said, "but were unable to offer battle. It was a long, long time before we were able to go on . . . [a raid] against the Mexicans." These were not like the old days when they had been able to mass the war party and attack Arizpe. For the struggle with two invaders at once, the Mexicans and the Americans, was beginning to take its toll among the Apaches.

VIII
A Lieutenant's Mistakes

WHILE Geronimo was fighting the Mexicans and Mangas Coloradas was trying to stop the Americans from infiltrating his land, Cochise was still having little difficulty with either. The Mexicans were cowed by the Chiricahuas, and the Americans were not attempting to set up permanent settlements in his territory. In 1858, however, a small group arrived to ask permission to build a stagecoach station and corral near the springs at Apache Pass.

After years of debate, during which the South and the North had been pitted against each other over the choice of a route, the federal government had finally offered a contract for the delivery of overland mail on a regular basis. John Butterfield, a New York stagecoach operator, had won it. Although he had used his political influence to secure the contract, much of the business world and many newspapers thought he was a fool, for the postmaster general was empowered to lay down many conditions. One of these was the route itself, which he decreed must swing south and then back north in what angry journalists described as an oxbow. Furthermore, the operator was required to start full service within one year after the signing of the contract. This meant Butterfield had to make the necessary road improvements, purchase livestock and coaches, employ his staff, set up his stations, and complete this monumental task by September, 1858.

On his 2,800-mile route, few points were more important to him than the spring at Apache Pass. Without that pool of water deep in the canyons of the Chiricahua Mountains, his stagecoaches could not cross southern Arizona and roll on to California. Butterfield was extremely wise in his choice of men, and those charged with the construction at Apache Pass fully understood the need for Cochise's friendship and set about gaining it.

By using presents instead of threats, they won permission to build the station and corral without interference, but Cochise did not allow them to take possession of the water. The station and corral were to be placed some distance away toward the west, close enough so the stock could be driven back and forth in a few minutes, but not so close that armed men, protected by the stone walls of the station, could control access to the spring. It was to remain available to anyone who wanted it, white or red, and neither group was to enjoy an advantage over the other.

The construction was finished in time for Butterfield to meet the terms of his contract. Although his men had made peace with Cochise, Butterfield was not overly trusting. The stone walls of the corral contained portholes through which his employees could shoot in the event of an attack, the kitchen and sleeping rooms were heavily built, and the station was well stocked with ammunition. It was really a small fortress in the middle of the Chiricahuas' territory. Its only weakness was its distance from the water. It could not hold out against a long siege, but the Indians rarely used that technique in their fighting.

Cochise certainly continued his forays into Mexico, and his warriors may have conducted some raids against Americans. At least some soldiers and settlers thought so. But he did not molest the coaches of the Butterfield Overland Mail. Four times a week, twice from the west and twice from the east, they braked to a stop at the stone station in Apache Pass. The passengers, weary from their long, jouncing ride, got out, stretched their legs, had a meal, and rested. Then they were off again behind a fresh team, the wheels grinding over the sand and rocks of the road. The passengers often saw the Indians. Sometimes a few of them were around the station itself, and there were usually large numbers camped nearby. But not an arrow or a shot was fired at either a stage or a team. In fact, relations between the Chiricahuas and the company were so friendly that Cochise entered into a contract to provide the station with wood.

Many of the other tribes, however, were more aggressive; and although the Americans were no longer obliged to protect the Mexicans, the civil and military authorities in the Southwest found themselves fully occupied defending their own citizens. The military responded by sending out punitive expeditions—sometimes successful and sometimes not—and by building forts. The civilian in charge of Indian affairs, Dr. Michael Steck, took a more realistic view. He recognized that if the Americans hoped to take over the Indians' land, the only real choice was to exterminate the Apaches altogether or to place them on reservations. In the latter case, he argued, the government would have to provide them with the means of subsistence, because they could not support themselves unless they were permitted to wander freely in search of game and other food. Of the two choices, he favored the second.

Dr. Steck's policies were at least partly successful. He even persuaded some of the Indians near the Gila River to expand their farming activities, and as a result many of them cultivated as much as 150 acres. In 1859, he went south to meet with Cochise near Apache Pass. The chief and the American talked together, and Cochise repeated his promise to allow the Butterfield stages to pass through his territory without molesting them. Dr. Steck doubted how long such an agreement could last and suggested to the government that the Chiricahuas should eventually be moved farther north. But for the time being, the safety of the east-west route had been reconfirmed, and all was well at Apache Pass.

In February, 1861, Cochise and some of his people were camped in Goodwin Canyon (now Cochise Canyon), which is only a short distance from the spring. A party of almost sixty soldiers, some of them dragoons and some of them infantry mounted on mules, entered the pass and stopped at the station to talk with Charles W. Culver, the keeper. They then made camp in Syphon Canyon, which lies between the spring and Goodwin Canyon.

For all his friendship with the Butterfield employees, Cochise was still wary of Americans; and he was concerned about having so many soldiers in Apache Pass. So he circled around them and visited the station, where he had two other friends in addition to Culver: the assistant keeper, Walsh, and a driver named James F. Wallace. He asked them what the soldiers were doing, and they assured him that the commander, Second Lieutenant George N. Bascom, had said he was taking them from Fort Buchanan, farther west, to the Río Grande. This was, therefore, a routine movement of men, and Cochise had nothing to be disturbed about.

As a consequence, Cochise decided to visit the lieutenant. Accompanied by his brother, two nephews, a woman, and a child, he went to the soldiers' camp. Bascom had already pitched his tent, and he invited the Indians to step inside, an invitation they willingly accepted. Besides the Apaches and Bascom, there were two other men present—a rancher, John Ward, who lived near Sonoita, not far from Fort Buchanan, and an interpreter, Antonio.

With Antonio's help, Bascom began to talk to Cochise. After a brief exchange of pleasant formalities, he abruptly and flatly accused Cochise of having stolen livestock from Ward's ranch and, at the same time, of having kidnapped the son of a Mexican woman who lived with him. Cochise was amazed at this sudden onslaught. Firmly and correctly, he denied the charge; and his denial was later substantiated when the boy grew up and became a member of the Apache scouts. An entirely different tribe had kidnapped him. Cochise, however, was willing to help the white men and said he would dispatch some of his warriors to find out what actually had happened.

Bascom refused this offer of assistance. When Ward had first reported the theft, he had been convinced the thieves were Chiricahuas. He still was, and so was Bascom. After a long delay, probably occasioned by a shortage of men at the fort, Bascom had been given command of the sixty soldiers with the assignment of recovering the boy and the livestock. That was the sole purpose of his visit to Apache Pass; he had lied to Culver when he had said he was taking his command to the Río Grande. He was there to serve Ward's interests, and he had no intention of returning to Fort Buchanan empty-handed. Furthermore, he was determined to hold Cochise and the other Apaches who had accompanied him into the tent as hostages until his mission was completed. When Bascom said this, Ward—as they had apparently agreed beforehand—slipped from the tent to alert the soldiers that Cochise was now a prisoner.

Cochise was furious at the false accusation and fearful for his own safety. Before Bascom could stop him, he drew his knife, slit a gash in the wall of the tent, and leaped through it. Outside, the soldiers were unprepared for this fast response. Almost before they knew what was happening, Cochise ran between them and escaped from the camp. They fired some fifty shots in the direction of the fleeing Apache, but all the shots missed, and he disappeared into his native mountains.

One of Cochise's nephews tried to follow him. He, too, leaped through the gap in the tent right after Cochise, but the soldiers were now ready. They clubbed him to the ground and bayoneted him. The others had no chance at all. They were immediately made prisoners by the soldiers.

If Bascom was planning to barter with hostages, Cochise needed some of his own to bargain with him. So as soon as he had gathered some of his warriors, he dashed to the stagecoach station. In addition to the other errors he had committed that day, Bascom had failed to warn the stagecoach employees about his plans. So while Bascom and his soldiers were attempting to take Cochise prisoner, bayoneting his nephew and holding the other Apaches as hostages, Culver, Walsh, and Wallace were going about their day's work as usual, unaware that Bascom had shattered their peaceful relations with the Indians. When

Cochise and his warriors appeared at the station, they had no hesitation about going out to talk to them.

The Indians immediately rushed forward to grab them. They captured the driver, Wallace, but Culver and Walsh broke free and ran back toward the station. Culver headed for the front door of the building, while Walsh ran toward the corral and the safety of its walls. Meanwhile Bascom had decided to break camp and return to the station himself. He and his soldiers arrived just about the time that Culver reached the front door. The Apaches had started firing at the two fleeing white men, and one of their bullets struck Culver, who fell wounded to the ground. The soldiers took hold of him and dragged him to safety inside the station.

At the approach of the soldiers, the Apaches began to withdraw, but the soldiers were taking no chances. Some of them guarded the station, while others filed into the corral to protect it against attack.

Walsh reached the outside of the corral in safety just at this moment. Digging his fingers into what handholds he could find, he began to climb. Finally he was able to get his head above the top and see the soldiers inside. One of them noticed him and, in a panic, thought he was an Apache. Quickly raising his gun, the soldier shot and killed Walsh, whose body tumbled backward onto the dirt outside the corral.

At the end of the day, Bascom still held as hostages the warriors and the woman and child who had first accompanied Cochise into his tent. But he had also killed one American—Walsh; Culver was wounded; Wallace was in the hands of the Apaches; and Cochise had turned from a friend into an enemy. For all this, Bascom was no closer to locating the stolen livestock and kidnapped child than he had been in the morning.

That evening, while Bascom rested safely in the station, the Chiricahuas were on the search for more hostages to trade with the white men for their own people. Some of their scouts noticed a wagon train entering the pass from the Sulphur Springs Valley. Not knowing that conditions had suddenly changed, the men driving the train took no special precautions. It was getting late and dark, so they casually made camp about two miles west of the station and were preparing for a quiet night, when the Apaches swooped down on them. The Indians did not want spoils, but men they could use as hostages. There were eight Mexicans and two Americans with the wagon train. The Apaches killed the eight Mexicans, who they thought would be of little use to them in bargaining with the American soldiers, tying them to the wheels of the wagons and burning their bodies. The two Americans, L. C. Jordan and Walter Lyons, they kept as additional hostages.

That same evening, Cochise returned to the hillside just east of the station, taking Wallace along with him. After attracting the attention of the soldiers, he drove a stake into the ground, attached a piece of paper to it, and left. Although the soldiers feared some sort of trap, they retrieved the paper and found it carried a message in English, probably written by Wallace at Cochise's request. It said simply, "Treat my people well and I will do the same by yours, of whom I have three." This was the first that Bascom knew of the attack on the wagon train.

The night passed without further fighting. On the following day, Cochise again appeared in sight of the station. He had a large number of warriors with him and also Wallace, whose hands were tied. Leaving the warriors in a ravine where they could protect him, he walked forward and indicated that he wanted to talk to Bascom. The lieutenant left the station with some of his men, including his sergeant, Reuben Bernard. With Wallace acting as interpreter, Cochise said he was willing to surrender Wallace in return for the release of all the hostages held by Bascom. But when the lieutenant learned from Wallace that the other two Americans were still alive, he insisted that they be included in the deal. Cochise flatly refused. Bascom could have Wallace, but not the others. Having gained what seemed to be the upper hand, Cochise did not want to surrender it. For even if he recovered the Indians taken prisoner, he still had to dislodge Bascom from the pass.

Wallace pleaded with Bascom to make the exchange, and so did Sergeant Bernard. In fact, Bernard pleaded so hard that he was later court-martialed for his extreme language. But Bascom would not consider the offer. The soldiers returned to the station, and the Apaches went back to their camp.

The rest of the day passed quietly, as neither side took any further action, each waiting for the other to give in. That night silence reigned in the canyons of Apache Pass, but the breaking of the new day brought fresh problems for Lieutenant Bascom and new opportunities for Cochise. For that was the day on which two stagecoaches were due to arrive after dark, one from the east and one from the west.

Bascom seems to have been unconcerned about anyone's safety except his own. He had failed to warn the men at the station that he was planning to seize Cochise as a hostage, and he let the wagon train enter the pass without getting word to the drivers of the dangers they faced. With careful use of his men, he might have been able to protect the routes into the pass or at least warn the approaching stages. But apparently he did nothing. Without any interference from the soldiers, Cochise's warriors placed bales of hay across the road, planning to ignite them when the westbound stage approached. The fires would create walls of flame through which the stage would have to pass and provide light for the Apaches to shoot at their target. Having finished their work, the warriors returned to camp but foolishly failed to post a lookout.

That day the stage was several hours ahead of time and began the ascent to Apache Pass well before dark. Skillfully guiding his team along the rough road, the driver saw the bales ahead and braked the stage in time to avoid running into them. The passengers jumped out, removed them quickly, and, realizing why they had been placed there, drove rapidly on, reaching the station at four in the afternoon without exchanging a shot with the Indians. The conductor of the stage was A. B. Culver, brother of the wounded stationkeeper, and he wisely decided not to go any farther but to remain under the protection of the soldiers.

Cochise had lost one stage, and he did not want to lose the other. On the western side of the pass, he made better preparations. He chose a point about two miles west of the station for an ambush and placed his warriors on the slopes of the surrounding mountains, so they could fire down on the stage as it went by. Between there and the station, he had his men put rocks in the road to stop the stage. At one point, where a bridge crossed a narrow but deep gulley, he ripped the rails from the bridge and destroyed part of its surface, hoping to cause an accident.

After midnight and long after the Chiricahua Mountains had been cloaked in darkness, the waiting warriors could hear the sound of the stage, its wheels grinding over the stones and the mules' hooves striking the dirt. They waited tensely as it drew nearer and nearer. When it appeared on the road below, the Indians opened fire. A dozen or more shots burst from their guns. One lead mule fell and tangled its traces, bringing the whole team to a halt; and the driver, King Lyon, slumped in the box, seriously wounded. At least for the moment, the stage was helpless.

In addition to the driver, there were six passengers on board, including William Buckley, superintendent of Butterfield's Fourth Division, which ran between Tucson and El Paso. All the passengers leaped out. Some fired their guns in the direction of the Apaches to hold them off. Others cut the lead mule from the traces and freed the rest of the team from the dead animal, while still others helped carry Lyon inside. Then either the conductor or Buckley mounted the box, took up the reins, and the stage was off again. Whoever drove the remainder of the night did well. The team, one mule short, started east, for the closest safety lay behind the walls of the station. Flight back to the west was now impossible.

When the stage approached the rocks the Apaches had placed in the road, the driver braked the team and brought it to a stop. Some of the passengers climbed out and quickly removed the rocks, while the others, using their guns freely, kept the Indians at a distance. Then the stage, to the Apaches' dismay, started up again. Suddenly the damaged bridge appeared ahead. The driver had no time to use his brake. The mules leaped in the air and landed on the opposite bank. The wheels of the stage slipped off the sides of the narrowed platform, but instead of toppling over, the stage slid across on its axles. When it reached the opposite bank, the wheels caught in the dirt again, and it continued safely down the road. In spite of Cochise's efforts, it reached the station about two in the morning.

By the next day, even Bascom himself had to realize he was in desperate straits and needed help. After talking to Buckley, the division superintendent, he decided to send to Fort Buchanan for assistance. At the same time, Buckley dispatched the driver of the westbound stage, A. B. Culver, to Tucson to notify the authorities of their predicament. For a man who had been taken completely by surprise, Cochise had done well in recovering his position. But for some reason, probably the independence of the individual Apaches, he was unable to maintain a continuous watch over the entrances to the pass. As a result, the messengers escaped unobserved and headed for their destinations.

The guards Cochise had placed at the springs were, however, more faithful in their duty. Sooner or later, as Cochise knew, Bascom would have to leave the station and go for water. The short distance from the corral to the spring had now grown to one of interminable length, fraught with danger. Dividing the company's and the military's livestock, Bascom sent a herd composed of half of each to the spring under a guard of about twenty soldiers and some of the Butterfield men. The waiting Apaches permitted them to reach the water, perhaps thinking that well-watered animals would be easier to handle and more valuable to them. But when the escort was driving the horses and mules back to the station, the Apaches attacked, firing at the men from the surrounding slopes. They killed one and wounded several others and in the confusion captured more than fifty mules.

But, unknown to Cochise, relief was on its way to Bascom. When the lieutenant's messenger reached Fort Buchanan and described what had happened, Assistant Surgeon Bernard Irwin volunteered to lead a small force of fourteen infantrymen to the rescue. The messenger to Tucson found two sources of help: a group of civilians from that city under the leadership of the Butterfield agent, W. S. Oury, and two companies of dragoons from Fort Breckinridge under First Lieutenant Isaiah N. Moore.

Irwin's soldiers moved quickly, covering sixty-five miles during the first day. On the second, they crossed Sulphur Springs Valley and saw a group of Coyotero Apaches with some stolen stock. Although his mission was to rescue Bascom from the Chiricahuas, Irwin engaged the Coyoteros in a short fight. He succeeded in taking three warriors as prisoners and recovered thirty ponies and forty cattle. Certain that there was little likelihood of his being able to enter Apache Pass unseen, he decided to drive the livestock ahead of him. In the event of an attack, he hoped the Indians' attention would be concentrated on stealing the animals rather than on killing his men.

But Cochise had a stroke of bad luck that prevented him from ambushing the relief party. While his men were driving away the livestock they had seized at the spring, they saw a column of soldiers to the north. These soldiers were completely unaware of Bascom's predicament and were on a routine transfer to a more eastern fort, but the Apaches thought they had been sent to circle around Cochise's position and attack him from the east. Consequently, they followed the soldiers and, in doing so, left the western entrance unguarded just at the time that Irwin reached it.

The safe arrival of Irwin's command meant Cochise was losing in his attempt to recover the Indians held as hostages, and the appearance the next day of the two companies of dragoons and the group of civilians confirmed his fears. Instead of bargaining with him over an exchange of prisoners, the Americans were committing more and more men to the struggle and obviously preparing to fight it out. As an Apache, Cochise was not willing to battle with such a large force, especially since it might grow bigger and bigger as the Americans sent in more reinforcements. From the first, he had tried to be reasonable, even though Bascom's original accusation had been false. He had offered to help the lieutenant, but the officer had refused his assistance. He had taken prisoners only in an attempt to trade them for those Bascom had captured by treachery. This offer, too, had been turned down. Now, abandoning all hope of regaining his people, he allowed his warriors to kill the three American prisoners and mutilate their bodies with their lances. Then he and the Chiricahuas left Apache Pass.

With the Indians gone, the force now assembled at the station scouted the country. It came across Cochise's deserted ranchería and set fire to what was left. It also discovered the bodies of the three Americans, so badly mutilated that Wallace could be identified only by his gold teeth. The sight infuriated the soldiers and civilians, who immediately proposed hanging the six warriors they now held—six, that is, if they included the three Coyotero Apaches, whom Irwin had captured and who had had nothing to do with the battle.

Bascom tried to act as a restraining influence. The captives, he said, were prisoners of war and therefore should not be killed. Irwin, however, argued that the three Coyoteros were his and he had a right to do with them as he wished. Lieutenant Moore, who commanded the dragoons, was as bloodthirsty as Irwin and supported his position. He pointed out to Bascom that he was the ranking officer at Apache Pass and would take full responsibility. In the face of these arguments, Bascom reluctantly consented to the execution. The six Indians were later marched to the site where the Americans' bodies had been discovered, and there they were hanged from an oak tree to serve as a warning to all Indians. Irwin later commented, "The punishment was an extreme mode of reprisal but was demanded and justified by the persistent acts of treachery and the atrocious cruelties perpetrated by the most cowardly and intractable tribe of savages infesting the country." So much for Cochise's efforts at peace or his attempts to be helpful.

After the execution, the troops left Apache Pass. Bascom received public commendation from the commanding general for his part in the action and, a few months later, was promoted to captain. The stage continued to roll through Apache Pass, but Cochise was no longer there to cut wood for the station. He had gone on the warpath, and his hatred of Americans was now as great as that of Mangas Coloradas.

IX

The Battle of Apache Pass

MANGAS COLORADAS and Cochise, both of them now completely disillusioned by the Americans, began intensifying their raids against the invaders and noticed with satisfaction that they were having a telling effect. In July, 1861, for example, Fort Buchanan, from which Bascom had been dispatched, and Fort Breckinridge, which had sent the dragoons to his rescue, were evacuated and their stores burned. The soldiers garrisoned at them retreated east toward the Río Grande, and the Apaches watched them leave with a sense of relief and victory. With the withdrawal of many soldiers, the few settlers that remained in the country gathered together for mutual protection in such centers as Tubac and Tucson, because it was no longer safe to live in the open countryside. It looked as though a few more years of fighting would eliminate the Americans altogether.

But the optimism of the chiefs was unwarranted. The collapse of the Americans' defenses resulted not from the attacks of the Apaches but from their own internal differences. Having preached to the Indians against raiding and killing, they were now raiding and killing each other on a scale that would have appalled the Indians. On April 1, 1861, General Pierre Beauregard had demanded the surrender of Fort Sumter and, at four thirty on the following morning, had fired the first shots of the Civil War. The greatest enemies of the Americans were no longer the Apaches but their own fellow citizens, and the garrisons at Breckinridge and Buchanan were needed to defend the Southwest from a Southern invasion.

The threat came from Texas. The Texans knew they were safe from a direct attack by the North and were therefore free to take the offensive. The Territory of New Mexico, which included present-day Arizona and New Mexico, presented a prime target. Although it was a wild and dangerous land, its capture by the Confederacy could be an important asset once peace was restored, and it would also provide direct access to California.

To effect the conquest, Confederate Colonel John B. Baylor moved westward in the summer of 1861 at the head of a detachment of soldiers. Installing himself and his men in the small town of Mesilla, he proclaimed himself governor of what he called the Territory of Arizona. A Union force of some 400 men attacked him there, but he defeated them quickly and easily. Then, with reinforcements under Brigadier General H. H. Sibley, the Confederates moved across the Río Grande at Valverde and soon held Albuquerque and Sante Fe.

They quickly discovered, however, that conquering the territory's principal cities was one thing, protecting its citizens from the Indians another. With the Northern and Southern troops preoccupied with maneuvering against one another, the Apaches were running wild. By the fall of the year, Baylor was complaining to the Confederate War Department that he did not have nearly enough men under his command to defend the smaller settlements from the Indians.

Colonel E. R. S. Canby, the Union commander, was having equal problems in the areas still under his control. He reported to the Union War Department that Indian attacks were on the increase, particularly in the South, and recommended that the government follow the policy of putting them on reservations. But the resources of the nation were devoted to the struggle between North and South, and little was left over for handling the Indians.

Colonel Baylor, by March, 1862, had become so desperate that he ordered the extermination of all Apaches. His men were to entice them with promises of peace and presents and then slaughter them. Only the children were to be spared, and these were to be sold as slaves to help defray the cost of the program. (To the credit of Jefferson Davis and his Secretary of War, this order brought an end to Baylor's future career in the Confederate Army.) General Henry Sibley, the Confederacy's commanding officer, was not as vicious as his subordinate, but he recommended making the Indians slaves.

Meanwhile the balance between the Confederacy and the Union in the Southwest was beginning to shift. Although the South won its early victories over the North with ease, the North was rallying its forces. In February, 1862, a group of Colorado miners, untrained and undisciplined but eager for a fight, formed the Pikes Peakers and marched south to counterattack the Confederates in New Mexico. They caught General Sibley on his way to capture Fort Union, a post about ninety miles northeast of Santa Fe. Both sides claimed a victory in the subsequent battle, but the ragtail army of miners prevented Sibley from taking Fort Union and gaining control of its supplies. This was a significant loss for the Confederates.

Farther south, about a hundred Confederate soldiers marched westward, reached Apache Pass, went through it safely, and arrived at Tucson. Part of this command went even farther west to Yuma, Arizona. This represented the extent of the Confederacy's advance into the Southwest. For in California, General James H. Carleton was assembling a force of approximately 1,800 volunteers to march east against the Confederates. Unable to oppose such a large body of men, the small detachment in Yuma and Tucson began its retreat to the Río Grande. The Apaches were waiting for it. At Dragoon Springs, to the west of Apache Pass but still within Cochise's territory, they came down on the soldiers while they were in camp. In the fighting that followed, the Confederates lost at least three men and much of their supplies and livestock. But the Apaches did not follow up the attack and permitted the soldiers to retreat safely through Apache Pass.

Mangas Coloradas, his wounds well healed but his pride still smarting from the miners' whiplashes, was now determined to make an all-out attempt to drive the Americans out forever. To do so, however, he needed help, and so he sent word to Cochise in the early summer of 1862 asking him to join him.

But Cochise refused. He was concerned about the large influx of Union soldiers at Tucson, for the California Column had arrived, and from what Cochise knew, it might be planning to proceed farther east into his territory. If that were to be the case, he would need every warrior for his own defense. So instead he asked Mangas Coloradas to help him.

Mangas Coloradas, curious to know more about the new danger that seemed to be threatening the Apaches and anxious to assist his fellow chief, discussed the situation with his warriors. After obtaining their agreement, he left New Mexico at the head of some 200 men, crossed the steep mountains and broad valleys that separated him from Cochise, and arrived among the Chiricahuas during the early summer of 1862. This well may have been the largest assemblage of Apache warriors in history. Even then, they probably only totaled somewhere between 400 to 700, far fewer than the thousands later estimated by some of the military and, at best, less than half the number of the enemy they were preparing to fight.

As they waited in their mountain stronghold, the Apaches saw three white men approaching from the west—two civilians and an Army sergeant, who were carrying dispatches to Canby, the Union commander in New Mexico. The three men reached the pass on the evening of June 18 and hoped to slip through it under the cover of darkness. But that night, as they rode along the narrow road with the mountains rising on either side, the Apaches attacked. Two of the white men were killed. The third, by a miracle, was able to escape in the confusion and continue eastward in safety. (For all his heroism, he never reached Canby; the Confederates captured him before he had completed his mission.)

Two days later, more white men appeared. Apache Pass had become crucial to the waging of the Civil War in the Southwest. If the Union strategy was to prevail, Carleton had to maintain communications with Canby and move his own column eastward. Both of these actions depended on travel through the pass. The new group of soldiers was under the command of Lieutenant Colonel E. E. Eyre, a man who was inexperienced in dealing with the Indians. He left Tucson on June 17 and safely followed the trail of the Butterfield stages to the Chiricahua Mountains. The Indians, of course, knew of his approach, but they permitted him to enter the pass unmolested and to water his horses and men at the spring.

Instead of attacking him immediately, the Apaches decided to talk to him. A short distance from the spring, some of the soldiers were guarding the livestock that had already been watered; and because they were detached from the main body of troops, the Indians thought it might be safe to signal to them. Waving a white flag—they had early learned this custom of the white men—they came in sight of the soldiers, who fired four shots to warn the others that the Apaches were near. Then one of them went to report personally to Eyre.

Taking an interpreter with him, Eyre went to the spot where the soldiers had first seen the Indians. There were now about seventy-five to a hundred of them gathered there, many of them mounted and all of them carrying firearms. Eyre tried to get close enough to talk with them, but the Apaches were cautious. They had been the victims of the white men's treachery so often that they did not trust the white flag Eyre was carrying with him. Finally they decided Eyre's intentions were entirely friendly and that he was not luring them into an ambush. One of them came forward and indicated he would like to hear what Eyre might have to say.

Eyre explained that the troops were Americans and that they only desired to be friends with the Apaches. In the opinion of the Apaches, this statement was ridiculous. After Bascom's attempt to take Cochise prisoner for a crime he had not committed, the Apaches had little respect for Americans' professions of friendship. But they were not prepared to attack the relatively large number of men under Eyre's command. So they pretended to accept his offer of friendship and asked him for presents. Drawing on his supplies, Eyre gave them what food and tobacco he could spare and then rejoined the soldiers at the spring.

While Eyre was talking to one group of Apaches, another was keeping careful watch over the water hole in the arroyo bed. Three soldiers, unaware of the danger surrounding them, wandered off by themselves. Some of the Indians followed them, hiding behind bushes and rocks, until the three men were too far from the spring for help to reach them. Quickly the Indians fired, and the three soldiers rolled over dead. The sound of the shots was heard at the spring; and as soon as Eyre returned, he was notified of the shooting and told that three men were missing. He immediately ordered thirty soldiers to go in search of them. They finally found the bodies. Keeping his head, Eyre realized his assignment was not to fight Indians but Confederates. As long as the Apaches made no further attempt to halt his progress through the pass, he was not going to engage them in battle. To do so would probably cost him much time and many casualties, neither of which the Union cause could afford.

Later that day, he moved his men into the San Simon Valley, where, in the open, they would be less susceptible to attack. The Apaches let him go. But later a few of them crept up on the camp and fired some shots into it. They killed one horse on the picket line and wounded an assistant surgeon, but that was the extent of the damage they inflicted.

The next few weeks passed peacefully at Apache Pass. The Indians were in complete control of their mountains, and no white men appeared. But Mangas Coloradas stayed on, because the Indians still did not know what the concentration of troops at Tucson would do. If, as they suspected, more Americans tried to travel through the pass, the Chiricahuas would need all the warriors they could assemble.

The next white men came from the east. Looking down from their mountains, the Indians noticed a column of dust rising from the floor of the San Simon Valley advancing toward the Chiricahuas. The Apaches knew no Indians would be approaching from that direction and in that fashion and correctly surmised it must be a small group of white men. Once the travelers reached the pass, they would probably be on the alert, so the Apaches decided not to wait but to ambush them before they entered the mountains.

They could do this, because the rains had carved a gully two miles east of the entrance to the pass. This gully extended about a quarter of a mile into the plain and was approximately six to eight feet deep and three or four yards wide, large enough to hold a considerable number of men. Because it was cut into the flat surface of the plain, it was invisible to a rider at a distance any greater than fifty yards, which was close enough to permit an ambush.

Some of the Apaches quietly left the mountains and assembled in the gully, hidden from the view of the approaching white men. Peering from behind the bushes at the top of the gully, the Indians watched the men come nearer. They were thirteen miners from Pinos Altos, the town where Mangas Coloradas had been beaten. Unaware of any danger, they were riding along carelessly, their guns in their slings and their pistols in their holsters. Hardy and experienced, they would take every precaution as soon as they came to the mountains, but the Apaches could see they did not expect to be ambushed on the flat plain where there was no apparent place for a group of Indians to hide.

Still and motionless, the Apaches waited, their guns and bows ready, as the unsuspecting white men drew nearer and nearer. When they had come within fifty yards of the gully, the Indians rose from their hiding place and began firing. Bullets and arrows showered from the gulley. Almost half of the white men were killed during the first volley, falling to the ground with blood streaming from their wounds. The others, taken completely by surprise, fell into a panic at the violent, unsuspected assault. Futilely they tugged at their guns, trying to get them free and, at the same time, turned in desperate flight. But they were too slow. The Apaches leaped from their gully and followed them. One by one, the white men fell under the hail of bullets and arrows. At the end of the fight, not a single white man was left alive. The jubilant Apaches walked among the dead to make certain no one was shamming. Then with their usual disdain for corpses, they left the bodies lying along the road and returned to report their victory to Cochise.

The Apaches, waiting in their mountains and looking across the plains on either side, next learned that a large detachment of soldiers was coming from the west, larger than any that had passed through Apache Pass before. General Carleton had ordered Captain Thomas L. Roberts to lead the advance and set up a camp on the San Simon River on the east of the Chiricahua Mountains. To accomplish this, he assigned him 126 soldiers and 242 horses and mules, along with a wagon train of twenty-six wagons. The wagon train was under the command of Captain John C. Cremony, who had been with Bartlett at Santa Rita del Cobre and to whose tent the two Mexican boys had run.

The soldiers safely reached the crossing of the San Pedro River in the San Pedro Valley, just north of the present city of Benson, Arizona. The terrain here was defensible, and the walls of the Butterfield station offered protection. At this point, Roberts divided his command in two. Knowing the danger of being caught with insufficient water in this dry desert country, he planned to lead one group of his men on to Dragoon Springs. If he found enough water for the entire command, he would send back for the others. Those that remained behind consisted of the wagon train and its guard of cavalry, both under Cremony.

That night, a violent thunderstorm broke over the desert. Black clouds rolled across the sky and were split by long flashes of lightning, which lit the peaks of the surrounding mountain ranges. The rain came down in sheets, striking the floor of the desert and running off it almost as though it were made of adobe bricks. The water poured into the arroyos, which in a few moments turned from dry, sandy riverbeds into roaring streams and emptied themselves into the San Pedro.

Although the Apaches did not usually attack at night, Cremony thought they might take advantage of the confusion created by the storm, so he doubled his sentries, built a warm fire in the fireplace, and lay down on the dirt floor of the station without taking off either his clothes or his firearms.

About two o'clock in the morning, the guards woke him, for Indians were approaching from the west, south, and north. But instead of attacking the station, they were carrying firebands, for Mangas Coloradas and Cochise had sent out messengers to assemble even more warriors. Because of the contour of the land in that area, fire signals could be seen at only a short distance, so the messengers bore brands in the darkness. The gleams of light in the black night were the signal for the Apaches to gather together. All available help was needed.

To the white men at the station the sight was eerie. Cremony was prepared to fire at the lights but decided against it. If these Indians were planning to attack, he thought to himself, they would not have revealed their presence, and there was no point in provoking them into a fight.

At least one of the Indians came within 200 yards of the station. But their instructions were to alert other Indians, not to battle the white men, so they did not come closer to pit themselves against Cremony's soldiers. They even permitted the messengers that Roberts sent back from Dragoon Springs to reach the station without hindrance. These men, who had struggled against the storm, brought word that Cremony was to move forward, because there was enough water at Dragoon Springs for the men and livestock.

He reached the springs without interference from the Apaches, since Cochise and Mangas Coloradas had decided to base their strategy on Cochise's experience with Bascom. During those hectic few days, the Americans had revealed their utter dependence on the spring at Apache Pass. The Indians knew of other sources of water in the mountains, but the Americans did not; and sooner or later, just like Bascom, they would have to enter the small canyon, where they would be especially vulnerable to attack. In an effort that was unusual for Apaches, they attempted to make access even more difficult by erecting crude breastworks of stone on two of the nearby hills. Instead of placing all the stones closely one on the other, they left a number of holes where they met. These served as gun ports through which the Indians could safely fire on any men below. This time, the two chiefs were determined to slaughter the invaders.

Neither Cremony nor Roberts knew what lay ahead of them. Cremony understood the Apaches—he was one of the few white men who studied their language and tried to learn their customs—but even he did not anticipate the large number of warriors that were waiting for them nor the extensive preparations they had made.

At five o'clock on the afternoon of July 14, Roberts left Dragoon Springs ahead of Cremony and began the march to Ewell Station, fifteen miles from Apache Pass, and then on to the pass itself, a distance of about forty miles. He had with him sixty infantrymen, seven cavalrymen to serve as scouts, a tank of water, and two howitzers. Under the cover of darkness, he crossed the broad Sulphur Springs Valley. The brilliant starlight of the desert outlined the peaks of the Dos Cabezas Mountains and the high ridges of the Chiricahuas. In between them, the soldiers could see the lower gap that represented their goal, Apache Pass. All was silent except for the sound of marching feet, the occasional clatter of hooves as a cavalryman returned from a scout to report, and the creaking of the howitzers as they rumbled across the floor of the desert.

At dawn, the world changed. The light crept up behind the mountains, silhouetting them against the clear blue sky. As the sun rose, the nighttime coolness quickly gave way to the desert's heat. Only a few hours before, the men had been comfortable; now the sweat was pouring from their faces and the glare of the sun seemed almost intolerable. Yet they still had many miles to go.

Along the way, Roberts ordered a halt. While the men stood

at their ease or slumped exhausted on the ground in whatever shade they could find, a few of them gathered brush, made a fire, and, using their small supply of water, brewed coffee for the others. There was just enough water for one cup for each man, and they drank it greedily, swishing the moisture in their mouths before swallowing it. Then they picked up their arms and began marching again, the dust rising from their tired, plodding feet.

Just before noon, the Apaches watched them enter the pass and start their ascent to the summit; but they held their fire, for in addition to the ambush at the spring, they had laid another in the narrow canyon that led to the station house. At the summit, Roberts ordered his men to turn off the main road and follow the road to the south that went to the station house. Not a sound was heard, until suddenly shots rang out from both sides. Curls of smoke rose from the rocks where the Apaches were hiding. The soldiers returned the fire, but with little effect because they could not see the hidden enemy. Wisely, Roberts ordered a retreat back to the summit, where the land was more open. The Apaches watched him withdraw with little or no concern, knowing he had to have water and that he could not return as far as Dragoon Springs to obtain it. Sooner or later, he would have to push forward through the ambush to the springs beyond the station house.

Roberts knew this, too, so he ordered the howitzers loaded and skirmishers placed on his flanks. Then, under heavy fire, he advanced toward the station and finally reached it. Its walls offered the soldiers safety from the Apaches' bullets, but they still had the few hundred yards to go from the station to the spring itself. Every time they moved toward it, the Apaches shot from behind their stone breastworks, turning the small canyon into a place of death. It was late in the afternoon, and the Apaches believed they had the American force trapped, unable either to advance or retreat.

They then saw the soldiers bring forth what they thought were merely two wagons, but which were actually the howitzers Roberts had brought from California. The Indians kept up a steady fire on the men surrounding them and had the satisfaction of seeing one of the two overturned through the mismanagement of the men handling it. It lay on its side on the sandy riverbed until cavalrymen ran forward, righted it, and aimed it toward the slopes where the Apaches were hidden behind their breastworks of stones.

Roberts gave the command to fire. The roar of the howitzers filled the air, and the smoke bellowed from their muzzles. The Apaches were taken completely by surprise. They had felt secure and safe behind their crude fortifications and certain the white men were doomed. Now all this was changed. The howitzers turned the balance against the Apaches, who could not withstand the repeated shots hurled in their direction. In spite of the well-laid plans of Cochise and Mangas Coloradas, they had no choice except to retreat.

In the lull, the soldiers were able to get to the spring, fill their canteens, and return to the protection of the station. The Apaches, however, did not give up hope. They had been stunned by the howitzers and had suffered heavy losses. Under such circumstances, they would normally have withdrawn and left the Americans in possession of the pass. But they knew they would probably never again assemble so many warriors or have such an opportunity to destroy so many white soldiers. So although they moved back from the springs, they remained in the nearby mountains.

In addition to the safety of the men under his immediate command, Roberts was gravely concerned for the wagon train, which was lumbering across the desert somewhere to his rear. Should it reach the pass and start the ascent to the summit, the Apaches could easily destroy its escort and capture the large amount of supplies it carried. So after supper he dispatched six of the cavalrymen to warn it to make camp until he could send further orders or arrive himself with help.

The Apaches, not having recovered from their shock, did not notice the messengers until they had left the mountains and entered the Sulphur Springs Valley. Some fifty warriors then saw them and rode in pursuit under the personal leadership of

Mangas Coloradas. The dust rose from the hooves of their horses as they closed in on the fleeing soldiers. The Americans could not afford to turn and fight, for they were greatly outnumbered and could expect no help from either Roberts or Cremony. Spurring their horses, they attempted to stay ahead of the Apaches, who now began shooting at them. The Indians' fire was effective. Two American horses were killed outright; their riders each climbed up behind one of the other soldiers and continued their flight. Another horse, although still able to run, was mortally wounded, and the sergeant's elbow was fractured.

During the frantic dash across the plain, one of the cavalrymen, John Teal, lagged 200 yards behind the others, his weary horse unable to keep up with them. Mangas Coloradas, with approximately fifteen other Apaches, was able to get between him and the other five Americans, who obviously could not return to his assistance. To have done so would have been sure death for them all. So Teal turned southward in an effort to throw off the pursuit, but his horse was too tired to keep ahead of the Indians.

The soldiers were certain Teal was going to die, but Teal himself had no intention of giving up his life easily. Dismounting, he made himself into as inconspicuous a target as possible and started shooting with his carbine. The Apaches were surprised at the rapidity and accuracy with which he could fire with this new weapon, which was better than theirs, and hesitated to come closer. So instead of charging, they began to circle around him at what they thought was a safe distance.

The uneven fight continued for an hour. Mangas Coloradas realized that the advantage of time lay with the Indians, so there was little point in rushing the lone soldier with his deadly gun. Sooner or later, he would exhaust his ammunition, and then he would be helpless. Unknown to Mangas Coloradas, however, Teal had noticed the chief's great stature and his obvious superiority to the other Apaches and was determined to kill him. As the warriors circled, he saw his chance and fired. Mangas Coloradas felt the pain of the bullet entering his chest and fell from his horse. The other Apaches were startled to see their chief slide to the ground. They let out a cry of despair and, concerned over his safety, forgot all about Teal, who rose to his feet and started in the direction his companions had taken toward the wagon train.

Mangas Coloradas's wound was serious. The Apaches had great confidence in their medicine men, but they knew the removal of the white man's bullet would require the services of a white man's doctor. The Americans certainly would not help them, so they decided to take their chief to Mexico. Putting him on a horse and assisting him as best they could, they headed down the chain of mountains toward Chihuahua. After days of travel, they stopped outside of Janos and visited a doctor who resided there. Whatever his personal feelings may have been, the doctor had to treat the wounded Apache. For the Indians made it clear that if he failed and Mangas Coloradas died, they would punish him and his family. Under this threat, which the Apaches were capable of carrying out, he did the best he could, and Mangas Coloradas eventually recovered. But he was no longer a factor in Cochise's defense of Apache Pass.

Teal, pushing on by himself in the darkness, late that night reached Ewell Station, where he found that the other cavalrymen had arrived. Cremony had moved the wagons into defensive positions and had issued extra ammunition to all his men. If the Apaches attacked, he was ready for them. But the Indians, discouraged by the wounding of Mangas Coloradas, had broken off the fighting and returned to the Chiricahua Mountains.

For all his careful planning, Cochise had suffered three serious setbacks during the day's battle. The firing of the howitzers had demoralized his warriors and driven them from their ambush; Roberts's messengers had been able to escape and warn the wagon train; and the wounding of Mangas Coloradas had been a severe blow to the Apaches' morale, as well as depriving Cochise of an able leader.

But at least Cochise had Roberts in a difficult position. The

American commander could not remain indefinitely at Apache Pass, nor could he permit the wagon train to approach the mountains unguarded. After allowing his tired, hungry soldiers to eat their suppers and take a short rest, he divided them into two groups. One, under a lieutenant, was to remain at the station and defend it. The other, under Roberts, was to march westward until it met up with Cremony's wagon train and provide it with an escort.

Darkness had covered the Chiricahua Mountains when Roberts's men picked up their guns and quietly left the station. They moved silently through the night, following the road to the west and holding their guns ready to fend off an attack. But the attack did not come. The Apaches, never expecting that the white men would leave their hard-won position at the station, had relaxed their guard over the western approach, and the soldiers reached the valley safely.

At about two o'clock in the morning, they arrived at Ewell Station. Roberts's men had marched some forty miles from Dragoon Springs to Apache Pass, engaged in a long fight with the Indians, and then marched fifteen miles back to the wagon train. They were exhausted, and Roberts allowed them three hours of rest before setting out again at five o'clock in the morning.

For the first part of the trip, Roberts placed half his small force of cavalry 300 yards in advance of the wagon train and ordered the remainder to bring up the rear at an equal distance. He then placed his infantry on either side and began to march. If Cochise had attacked him then, the Apaches might have won a startling victory. Pinned down on the plain without water and without his howitzers, Roberts and his men might have died. But Cochise did not attempt to fight him, because he was still concentrating his effort and attention on the spring at Apache Pass.

After the barrage fired by the howitzers, the soldiers had stormed the heights above the springs; but they had not attempted to hold them during the night. Tired as they were, they could not have resisted the Apaches in the darkness, so they had withdrawn to the station. During the night, the Apaches had retaken the slopes surrounding the springs. Cochise realized the white men would have to get to the water again; and although they had defeated his warriors with their howitzers the day before, he hoped that somehow the next time he could hold out. On this hope he based his entire strategy.

When Roberts reached the entrance to the pass, he ordered his command to a halt and regrouped them. He sent out his infantry on either side of the road as skirmishers, holding only a small number in reserve. The cavalry concentrated on guarding the wagon train and making occasional forays up the adjoining canyons. By these tactics, Roberts hoped to keep the Apaches from reaching the wagon train itself, and he was successful. Cochise, relying wholly on keeping the Americans from the water and knowing that the wagon train was well protected, did not attack. And Roberts was able to reach the safety of the station.

The next morning found his force in serious straits, for some of the animals were already dying of thirst. If he were to get through the pass—or even to survive—he had to clear the way to the spring again. His first step was to give his men a good breakfast of fried bacon and flapjacks, although there was no water with which to make the coffee the men most wanted. He then ordered the wagon train and the mules into the stone corral of the station, arranging the wagons in a square with the mules chained inside. This gave the defenders two lines of protection—the walls of the corral and the wagons themselves. All the teamsters, who numbered almost thirty, were given rifles and ammunition and told to guard the train. Roberts understood that those wagons with their supplies could be a prime target of an Apache attack, and he did not want his soldiers to be distracted from the next phase of his operation.

Next he lined up the two howitzers, which had served him so well the day before, heading them in the direction of the spring. Twenty infantrymen were assigned to operate and guard them, and the soldiers filled their boxes with twelve-pound shells and spherical case shot. Others of the infantry were designated to serve as skirmishers on the flanks, and the fast-moving cavalry were held in reserve. Cremony, having missed the fighting the day before, wanted to lead his men in a charge up the slope. Saluting Roberts, he said, "Captain, you have done your share of this fight; I now respectfully ask for my chance. If you will throw your shells on the heights above the springs, I will charge the latter with my men and clean out the Apaches in a very few moments. I certainly think," he added, "this concession due me."

Roberts wisely refused him permission. As he explained, the men under Cremony were the only cavalry he had, and they were essential to the success of his move to the San Simon River. Furthermore, Cremony was later to take the empty wagons back to Tucson, and Roberts simply could not afford to risk losing either him or any of his troops.

At the sound of a bugle, the men began moving the howitzers up the canyon, pausing at intervals to fire. The air was split by the sound of the discharges, the shells rose above the Apaches' positions, and the outcome was a repetition of the day before. The breastworks that the Apaches had built for themselves could not protect them from this sort of attack. Some were wounded or killed, and the others, realizing their position was hopeless, began running in twos and threes for better cover out of the range of those mysterious, death-dealing "wagons." As they ran, they came within aim of the American skirmishers, who shot at the disappearing Indians with terrible effectiveness. Seeing that the Indians were routed, Roberts ordered Cremony's cavalry to charge. The horsemen pursued the Apaches until the terrain became too rough and steep for their mounts. To make certain no Indians were lurking near the spring itself, Roberts, as a final step, fired several more shots with the howitzer in its direction.

Then all became quiet in the small canyon. The soldiers, without any further interference, marched to the spring and drank their fill. The mules and horses, some of which had not tasted water for many hours, were driven to the small grove of trees where the water gushed from the ground, and they, too, drank until they were satisfied.

In all this fighting, the American casualties had been only a few dead or wounded. By depending too much on his ambush at the spring, Cochise had lost the opportunity of killing them when they would not have been able to use the howitzers; and Roberts's reliance on those two guns, rather than on making charges against the Apaches' position, had saved many American lives. As one of the Indians remarked years later to an American, "We would have done well enough if you had not fired the wagons at us."

As it was, the Apaches were so stunned by their inability to hold the pass and by the horror created by the howitzers that they made no further attempt to interfere with Roberts and his men. No more shots were fired as the captain led his men back up the narrow canyon to the summit. Ahead of him lay the broad San Simon Valley, stretching for miles north, east, and south. On the far rim of the plain stood the Peloncillo Mountains, the blue haze of summer cloaking their foothills. Roberts advanced carefully, taking every precaution against a surprise attack, but the canyons were silent and still. The rumbling of the wagon train and the howitzers, the clatter of the hooves of the horses and mules, the echoing of the drums and bugles, and the tramping of the men were the only sounds. Otherwise, Apache Pass was as deserted and quiet as it had been busy and active only a few hours before.

At four o'clock in the afternoon, the Americans reached the San Simon River and made their camp. Although he had defeated the Apaches, Roberts did not dare risk sending his men back through the Chiricahua Mountains. So when Cremony was ready to return with the empty wagon train, he ordered the captain to take the more northern route. Cremony waited until after sundown before setting out. In the twilight and then the night, the dust rising from the wheels of the wagons would be less visible to any Indians watching from the mountains. In addition to his small detachment of cavalry, Roberts assigned him seven infantrymen. These tried to sleep in the jolting wagons during the nighttime journey so they would be refreshed and ready to guard the train during the day. While they dozed, the cavalrymen rode at the front and rear of the wagon, occasionally sweeping its flanks.

Heading in a northeasterly direction, Cremony took his men up the San Simon Valley. In the starlight, he could see the outlines of the Chiricahua and Dos Cabezas mountains in the distance and the hollow between them, where the battle had taken place. By the next morning, he had entered the pass between the Dos Cabezas Mountains and the Pinalenos. Although it offered less water than Apache Pass, the rainy season had started, and Cremony had relatively few men to provide for.

When the sun rose and his movements were exposed to the Apaches, he brought the train to a halt. The teamsters drove the wagons into a U-shaped formation and unharnessed the mules, placing them inside the rough corral, while the cavalrymen tied their horses to a picket line that was strung across the open end. For all the secrecy of traveling by night, the Americans had not passed unnoticed. The Apaches had already found them and were moving across the surrounding slopes in the hope of making a successful attack. But Cremony had chosen his ground well. No matter what the Apaches did, they could not get inside the superior range of the Americans' guns. Finally, they gave up. The teamsters and cavalrymen lay down in the wagons to sleep, and the infantrymen took on the duty of guarding the train.

At sundown, the men again harnessed the teams, the cavalrymen saddled their horses, the wagon train started off, and Cremony met Carleton at the San Pedro River without any further fighting.

Deeply discouraged by their failure to defeat Roberts, the Apaches made no effort to impede Carleton's passage through the pass. If they had not been able to stop Roberts's smaller force, they could see no hope of doing so with Carleton's larger one. The strategic importance of the pass was immediately apparent to Carleton, and before marching on, he detailed a hundred men under Major T. A. Coult to stay behind to guard it and build a fort, which he named Fort Bowie after a colonel in the California Volunteers.

The Apaches were dismayed to see this large force remain, but they felt powerless to drive the Americans out. Under the watchful eyes of the Indians, the soldiers began building a stone wall around the tents they had pitched on a slope above the old stage station. Within a few weeks, they had erected stone breastworks four and a half feet high and three feet wide at the bottom, tapering off to two feet at the top—the type of fixed fortification the Apaches were unable to attack successfully. In addition, Coult carried out his orders to maintain a permanent guard at the spring itself so the Apaches could not regain possession of it and to provide escorts for all Americans traveling through the pass.

The Apaches, although unwilling to make a direct attack against the breastworks, kept watching for some weakness in the Americans' defense. A few times during the remainder of the year, Cochise attacked an isolated soldier or a small detachment, but the casualties he inflicted were slight. And Fort Bowie remained a permanent threat to the Apaches—a white man's stronghold in the Chiricahuas' lands and a guardian of the Americans' east-west route.

X

Red-hot Bayonets

CARLETON, as he moved east, had little difficulty winning New Mexico back from the Confederates. The Southerners' failure to capture the supplies at Fort Union had been a serious setback. Furthermore, although they had taken the towns easily, they had not gained the support of the people. New Mexicans disliked Texans, who composed the majority of the Confederate troops, and were glad to assist the Union forces whenever they could. But Carleton, like other military commanders in the Southwest, soon learned that the Indians were a worse enemy than any white army. White armies stood up and fought; they could be attacked or outmaneuvered and their supply lines cut. Apaches simply melted away in the face of superior strength, and their only source of supplies was the land itself. But when an opportunity appeared, they returned to strike again, usually at the white men's weakest point. In spite of the presence of the California Column, the Southwest was still unsafe.

One of those who continued fighting and raiding was Geronimo. That summer, while Cochise was attempting to defend Apache Pass, Geronimo led another expedition into Mexico. He took his band down the western slopes of the Sierra Madres and camped in the foothills of the mountains, waiting for a packtrain to appear on the trail. About ten o'clock one morning, four unsuspecting riders passed near the Apaches' camp, driving their mules. There was no fight. At the sight of Geronimo and the eight warriors who had followed him on the raid, the Mexicans fled and left the Indians in possession of the packtrain. The animals were laden with blankets, saddles, calico, tinware, and loaf sugar. Only the addition of firearms and ammunition could have made the capture more nearly perfect.

But in spite of the supplies Geronimo had captured during his raid, times were hard for the Apaches. Carleton, having driven the Confederates back into Texas, turned his full attention on the Indian problem. The civilian authorities advanced their own reason for the Apaches' outbreaks. The Indians, they said, were forced to raid because of the scarcity of game. (This argument was largely true; the white men's slaughter of the buffalo herds in particular had deprived the Indians of one of their basic means of subsistence.) The solution, according to the civilian authorities, was to put the Indians on reservations and provide them with the means of staying alive. This policy would be more humane and less expensive than conducting large-scale troop operations.

Carleton, however, did not agree. In October, 1862, he was issuing orders that the Indians should be pursued and killed whenever possible, thus adopting the same policy of extermination that had failed so many military commanders before. But he did not utterly discard the idea of using reservations and made attempts, sometimes successfully, to establish them.

His first target was the Mescalero Apaches, who lived in New Mexico well to the east of the Chiricahuas and south of the Warm Springs Apaches. In the winter of 1862–63, he reported to Washington that he had completely subdued this tribe. Three hundred and fifty Indians were either at Fort Sumner in New Mexico or on their way there. With this objective accomplished, he was ready to turn to his second target: the Apaches under Mangas Coloradas.

The heat of summer had given way to the cold of winter, and the winds were blowing across the plains of southern New Mexico. In the Black Mountains the snows were falling, and the upland areas were covered with white. The trees in the deep canyon bottoms had shed their leaves, and the nuts were falling from the piñons. But this winter was different from any other for the Apaches. For years, they had fought under Mangas Coloradas, driving the Mexicans from Santa Rita del Cobre and harassing the Americans. But the great chief was growing old and weary. None of his efforts to regain supremacy over the Indians' lands had truly succeeded. At Apache Pass, both he and Cochise had been defeated; he himself had been wounded; and the hated miners were still living at Pinos Altos. From time to time, he had led his warriors in raids against them, but he had never succeeded in dislodging them. Ever since the arrival of Bartlett and the boundary commission, Americans had remained in New Mexico.

Unaware that a campaign was being launched against him, Mangas Coloradas decided to explore the possibility of making peace. With three of his warriors, he visited some of the settlers near Pinos Altos. They told him that if he surrendered, the white men would provide him and his tribe with blankets and food. He returned with this news, and the Apaches held a council to discuss it. Many of the warriors were for accepting the white men's offer. Like Mangas Coloradas, they, too, were weary of the continual fighting. Others, of whom Geronimo was one, were suspicious, because the white men had broken their word so often. After much talking, approximately half the tribe decided to surrender with Mangas Coloradas. The others would remain in the wilderness and see what happened. Out of fear of treachery, the surrendering Apaches took more than half the arms of the tribe. Thus, if they were attacked, they would have the means of defending themselves.

They were not a happy group as they began the journey to Pinos Altos. Always before, they had been a strong, independent people, prepared to fight their enemies, visit their friends, or hunt for game. Now they were unsure of themselves and the future and ready to submit to the invaders. In return for peace, they hoped to receive blankets and food. But they knew that even the most favorable terms would not permit them to roam their deserts and mountains freely.

Shortly after they reached the vicinity of Pinos Altos, the

white population was reinforced by a group of prospectors who were headed for California. They made camp at the site of old Fort McLane, about fifteen miles south of Santa Rita del Cobre. The fort had been abandoned at the outbreak of the Civil War, when the garrison had been moved eastward to help defend New Mexico from the Confederate invasion, but the location provided a good resting place for the weary travelers. They were about thirty in number, not enough to hold off a determined Apache attack, but they were well armed and kept a constant guard. And Mangas Coloradas was tired of fighting. His purpose was to make peace, not kill more Americans.

As they rested, the prospectors considered what to do next. For many weeks, they had been journeying under the leadership of an experienced Westerner, Joseph Reddeford Walker, but they had been unable to find a safe route to California. Everywhere the Apaches had followed them. By day, they had seen the columns of smoke rising from the Indians' signals; in camp, the guards learned to fire at any bush they had not noticed the night before, for often it was held by an Apache using it as cover to creep closer to them.

Failing to find a northern route through the mountains, they had turned south to pick up the trail of the old Butterfield stage and had reached the pass at Steins Peak in the Peloncillo Mountains. This was northeast of the Chiricahua Mountains and the last stop before reaching Apache Pass.

After drinking the water that made Steins Peak a stage station, they set out to discover the cause of a column of smoke they had noticed earlier. They thought it might be a smoke signal, but instead of finding Indians, they discovered the bodies of three white men strung by their ankles from a piñon tree. The smoke came from small fires that had been lighted under each man's head. The flames had been only a foot away and had burned the hair and flesh from the skulls. Walker's men were both horrified and afraid. This, they were certain, was the fate destined for them if they persisted in following the southern route to California, so they hastily cut down the bodies, buried them, and turned back.

Later they found eight more bodies. All but one of them, a

man with thick, dark hair, had been scalped. Another had been bound by thongs to a cactus and then burned with firebrands. Some of the charred brands were still lying on the ground nearby.

Such a sight did not inspire confidence in Walker's party. Yet the Apaches, although they often tracked them, did not attack. Thirty armed men, particularly under the leadership of an experienced frontiersman who never relaxed his guard, were a formidable enemy. And the Apaches were certain that time was on their side. All they had to do was follow the travelers, and sooner or later they would blunder. Then the Indians could kill them and take their supply of arms. The relentless tracking, the almost constant presence of Apaches, sometimes hidden and sometimes in view at a distance, had worn down the morale of the prospectors, and they had retreated eastward to escape the menace. While resting at the site of Fort McLane, they decided they must capture an important Apache hostage or they would never get farther west.

Purely by chance, the prospectors were joined at Fort McLane by a company of California Volunteers under the command of Captain E. D. Shirland. Mangas Coloradas, of course, had no way of knowing that this was the advance party of a four-company force under General J. R. West, who had been assigned by Carleton to subdue Mangas Coloradas's tribe. The soldiers listened with interest to the prospectors' plan to capture a hostage, and some of them agreed to go to Pinos Altos and help in the attempt.

Under the watchful eyes of the Apaches—it was almost impossible for anyone to travel in that country without the Apaches seeing them—a group of the prospectors, accompanied by some of the soldiers, went to Pinos Altos, reaching the settlement by nightfall and making camp.

The next morning, the Apaches were watching to see what these white men would do. After the Americans had eaten their breakfast and the daylight made their actions visible, they hoisted a white flag where the Apaches would notice it. This was the signal for which Mangas Coloradas had been waiting. He moved with his warriors onto a hill near the town and let himself be seen. The prospectors and soldiers called to him. Although their Spanish was poor, their intentions were clear. They wanted to make a treaty with him. Mangas Coloradas moved closer so as to be able to talk better. The white men repeated their generous terms for peace. The chief questioned them suspiciously, but their answers were always the same. They proposed to be friends with the Apaches.

Leaving the majority of his warriors on the hillside among the rocks that served them as natural fortifications, Mangas Coloradas, with two or three other Apaches, walked down to talk to the Americans. One of the white men later wrote that "his dress consisted of a broad-brimmed, small-crowned chip or straw hat of Mexican manufacture—a check cotton shirt, breechcloth or clout, and a high pair of moccasins or moccasins with legs to them like boots, only that they fit the legs closely. Mangas was apparently fifty years of age and a large athletic man considerably over six feet in height, with a large broad head covered with a tremendously heavy growth of long hair that reached to his waist. His shoulders were broad and his chest full and muscular. He stood erect and his step was proud and altogether he presented quite a model of physical manhood. If Mangas ever had any or many peers amongst his people in personal appearance, I never saw them during the five years experience in that country."

Even in surrender, he was an imposing figure. He came up to the white men with their flag of truce and began speaking with them. They greeted him with smiles. Then suddenly, before he could resist, they turned their guns on him. He was a prisoner, they said, and they would kill him if his warriors attempted to rescue him.

Mangas Coloradas was bewildered by this hostility in place of the friendship he had expected, but he listened as the prospectors told him they were holding him as a hostage to ensure their safe travel through the land of the Apaches. If they reached central Arizona, they would release him and let him go back to his family and friends. But if any Apaches attacked them, they would kill him immediately. The warriors who had come down the hillside with him were to return to the tribe with this message. Unable to do anything else, Mangas Coloradas told his friends to depart. But he warned them not to rely on the white men's promise to let him go. These were not Mexicans but Americans, and the tribe might never see him again.

Much pleased with their accomplishment, the prospectors and soldiers went back to Fort McLane with their prisoner and arrived there just as General West came up with the other three companies under his command. Curious to see what the chief looked like, West walked out to where the prospectors had him in custody. The two men made a strange contrast—the enormous Indian, his black hair falling over his shoulders, towering above the general in his white man's uniform.

The next day, General West, who had had nothing to do with the chief's capture, decided to take charge. Bluntly he accused him of having plundered two Union wagon trains at the Río Grande del Norte some months earlier. The capture of the wagon trains, one loaded with clothing and the other with artillery ammunition, had been a serious loss to the government. Mangas Coloradas denied the charges leveled at him by the general, but the general refused to believe him, never stopping to consider that the raid had been conducted well outside Mangas Coloradas's usual territory. Infuriated by what he considered the chief's stubbornness, West demanded physical custody of him for the Army. The prospectors, who had been sincere in their promise to release him if they reached central Arizona safely, had no choice but to give him up.

All the remainder of that day, two soldiers were assigned to guard the chief. The weather was cold, and they built a fire from the logs of the old fort and kept the chief near it, as much for their own comfort as for his. That night, because of the bitter weather, everyone except the sentinels retired early. Before crawling between his own blankets, General West gave a final order to his men: If Mangas Coloradas attempted to escape, he was to be shot.

The civilians' camp was separate from that of the soldiers and slightly to the west. One of their sentry lines was about 150 yards long and ended at the fire, where Mangas Coloradas was lying, watched by his guards. One of the soldiers' sentry lines also ended at this point, coming in at right angles to the line paced by the civilian.

Silence, cold, and blackness fell over the camp. Except for the sentries, the men lay huddled in their blankets. The only light in either camp came from the fire where the guards were watching Mangas Coloradas. All was quiet in the winter night except for the pacing of the sentries as they marched back and forth, listening in the darkness for the sound of an enemy.

A little before midnight, a civilian sentry, Daniel Connor, noticed that Mangas Coloradas was moving restlessly in his blankets. When he reached the far end of his line and turned around to come back, he saw the soldiers were doing something to annoy and disturb the chief. But each time he reached the fire, the soldiers were still. Connor's curiosity was aroused. Something odd was going on, and he was determined to find out what. Coming up to the fire, he turned as usual, but as soon as he passed outside the range of the firelight, he turned again and stood there. The two guards were heating their bayonets in the fire and then laying them against Mangas Coloradas's feet and legs.

Connor did not approve of the soldiers' conduct, but he did not try to interfere with them. Every time he returned to the fire, the two guards looked innocent and sleepy. Every time he left it, Mangas Coloradas stirred, trying to avoid the searing impact of the hot metal against his flesh.

Just before midnight, Connor was in the middle of his beat and returning toward the fire, when he saw Mangas Coloradas, weary of the persistent torture, rise on his elbow and remonstrate with the two soldiers, telling them in Spanish that he was no child for them to play with. In response, each soldier immediately aimed his gun and fired a shot into the chief's body. Then they drew their six-shooters, and each of them fired two more shots into his head. The chief fell dead, his body motionless on the cold ground and the flames from the fire dimly lighting the scene of murder.

XI

War Without Victory

THE sound of the guards' shots roused the whole camp. Soldiers and civilians leaped from their blankets and grabbed their guns, thinking they must be under attack. But the only sign of violence was the bleeding body of Mangas Coloradas, lying beside the fire. In response to West's questions, the sentinels reported that the chief had attempted to escape and they had shot him in accordance with their orders. As nothing further could be done in the darkness and as the camp was not in danger, the soldiers and civilians left the corpse where it was and went back to sleep.

The following day, West held a brief investigation. The position of the body, still encumbered with blankets, and the marks of the bullets where they had struck the frozen ground told what had happened. West, however, was not interested in the truth but sought in his dispatches the glory he was incapable of earning for himself in the field. His official report made heroes of himself and his men. Mangas Coloradas, he told his superiors, had been captured only after a battle between the Apaches and the soldiers and had been shot while attempting to escape.

Within a few hours after the chief's murder, West ordered a detachment of soldiers to Pinos Altos to kill more of the Apaches. They arrived there just before daylight and took up a position in an old log cabin. When daylight came, they decoyed the Indians within gunshot and fired, killing two. Then they stripped the corpses of their clothing and rode back to camp, wearing the dead Apaches' moccasins and buckskins.

The same morning, one soldier proposed scalping Mangas Coloradas. He tried to borrow Connor's knife for the purpose, but Connor refused to lend it to him. So the soldier went to the camp cook, obtained a bowie knife, removed the chief's scalp, wrapped his long hair around it, and placed it in his pocket. No officer interfered.

The body lay all morning near the fire. At noon, a few men were detailed to wrap the corpse in a blanket and carry it outside the camp. They dumped it in a gulley and covered it with earth. A few days later, they dug it up again, cut off the head, and preserved the skull as a trophy, saying they intended to send it East to a museum.

After the behavior of the Americans, the Apaches of New Mexico no longer had any doubts about the white men's intentions. The capture of Mangas Coloradas under a flag of truce and his subsequent murder, as well as the unprovoked attack on the remaining Indians, convinced them that peace with the Americans was impossible.

"They had gone," Geronimo said later, "happy that now they had found white men who would be kind to them, and with whom they could live in peace and plenty. But," he added, "no word ever came to us from them. From other sources, however, we heard that they had been treacherously captured and slain. In this dilemma we did not know just exactly what to do, but fearing that the troops who had captured them would attack us, we retreated into the mountains near Apache Pass.

"During the weeks that followed the departure of our people we had been in suspense, and failing to provide more supplies, had exhausted all our share of provisions. This was another reason for moving camp."

On their way to the Chiricahua Mountains, they came across four white men driving a herd of cattle. They killed the men and took the cattle with them into the mountains, where they prepared to butcher the animals. While they were engaged in this work, some troops found and attacked them. Because they had given most of their weapons to the Indians who had gone with Mangas Coloradas, the Apaches were at a serious disadvantage. In the uneven fight that followed, they used spears and arrows against the guns of the soldiers but could not do so successfully. In a short time, Geronimo had lost his spear and used up all his arrows. The soldiers surrounded him, but he was able to escape by dodging from one side of his running horse to the other. The Apaches, who had lost one warrior and six women and children, scattered in every direction and later regathered at a point fifty miles distant that they had designated as their meeting spot in the event of a disaster.

Here they were later attacked again by the same soldiers. By ten o'clock in the morning, the last of the Apaches' spears and arrows were gone, and they fought with clubs and stones, unable to inflict much injury on the troops but at least holding them off until nightfall. The darkness gave them a chance to retreat farther into the mountains, where the soldiers could not use their horses to follow them. The next day, the scouts who had remained behind to watch the Americans reported they had left. But in a few days, another detachment of troops located them and again attacked. The battle that followed was so costly to the Apaches that they decided to break up into smaller groups, each finding its own place to live.

Although Carleton's policy of offering the Indians a choice between extermination or going on a reservation was creating havoc among the Indians, it was not accomplishing the results the white men desired. Some Indians made peace; some were killed; and certain tribes were subdued, principally the Navajos and the Mescalero Apaches, who lived east of the Río Grande and were one of the tribes of Plains Apaches. But those Indians who were neither conquered nor killed became more hostile than ever. The Army could not locate and destroy them, and they roamed the country, raiding and killing whenever the opportunity offered.

In the land of the Chiricahuas, the Apaches' main effort was devoted to dislodging the soldiers at Fort Bowie. Little had been done to improve the fort since it was first established, and it remained a crude fortification. Its site had been chosen solely because it commanded the springs and without regard to any other consideration. The living quarters for the men were mostly pits dug into the ground, whose crude roofs leaked badly whenever the rains swept the pass. The garrison was sufficiently large to hold out against a direct attack and to provide escorts for those who wished to travel through the pass, but it could not go out on patrols against the Chiricahuas. The initiative, therefore, lay with Cochise. He harassed the troops and travelers, and in September, 1863, he captured all the horses at the fort, leaving the soldiers without any mounts.

For Geronimo, the months passed peacefully. The rainy season came and went; the arroyos flooded with turbulent water, then subsided and became once more tracks of sand across the desert. The snows drifted over Apache Pass and covered the peaks of the Chiricahuas only to melt again when the desert burst into bloom on the arrival of spring. The Apaches with Geronimo's group remained aloof from the white men. They heard that some of the Apaches were able to secure provisions from the Americans if they agreed to live in certain places and to stay at peace. But there was no need for the small band to accept such terms, for they had enough supplies to lead their simple lives comfortably.

During this period, Geronimo's influence among the other Apaches had continued to grow. Although he was not a chief, the older men listened more and more to his advice and sought out his counsel. In part this was because of his demonstrated courage and ability in fighting, in part because he could express himself well and was persuasive in his talking, and in part because his ideas were in themselves good. He was an ambitious man, and his position among the other warriors pleased him. He enjoyed the life he led in the Chiricahua Mountains. He had prestige, he had plenty of food and other supplies, he had the freedom he loved so much, and he was remote from the American settlements and troops. The white men, it appeared, were penned up at Apache Pass.

But the following fall all that changed in a single day. A detachment of soldiers—Geronimo thought they came from San Carlos on the Gila River—found the ranchería and launched a surprise attack. In the fighting, four warriors, five women, and seven children were killed, and the remaining Apaches were forced to desert their camp without taking their supplies with them. As soon as the Indians had gone, the soldiers systematically destroyed everything they could not carry away with them, moving from dwelling to dwelling with their torches. When the Apaches returned, nothing was left. They were without horses, blankets, clothing, or food; and winter was close at hand.

They needed help and thought of Victorio. Following the death of Mangas Coloradas, he had become chief of the Warm Springs Apaches. It was a sorry group that traveled to New Mexico. They had little food or ammunition, and the only livestock they owned were two horses they had captured from an American and a Mexican. Even for Apaches, who never accumulated many goods, they were a destitute lot. But Victorio welcomed them and gave them enough provisions for the winter. In addition, game was plentiful, as it had not been that year in the Chiricahua Mountains. Soon the band was eating well again, and Geronimo was ready to lead another expedition against the Mexicans.

Twenty warriors were willing to follow him. They traveled south through the land of the Chiricahuas and entered Sonora near the present-day city of Bisbee. Continuing south, they first went into hiding in the mountains and then emerged to attack several communities, securing enough supplies to make the raid well worthwhile. By then they were about forty-five miles west of Arizpe, the town where Geronimo had been given his name. A mule train, protected by only three drivers, came along the trail. The Apaches attacked. Two of the drivers escaped and one was killed. When the Indians examined their booty, they found that the mules were loaded with bottles of mescal, the native liquor made from agave. As soon as they could, they chose their campground and started drinking as fast and as hard as possible. In the usual Apache fashion, they were soon drunk and began fighting among themselves, using their weapons against their own companions. The camp became a shambles of drunken Indians engaged in battling each other. Geronimo, too, had drunk some of the liquor, but he was still sober enough to be aware of the danger they were in. If the Mexicans found them now, they would be slaughtered.

He tried to stop their arguments, but without success, for they had long since passed the point where they would listen to reason. As the liquor took over, however, they fell, one by one, into a stupor, lying wherever they had dropped or crawled. Soon the ground was covered with the bodies of senseless warriors, and Geronimo alone was conscious. He extinguished their campfires, emptied all the bottles onto the ground, and drove the mules some distance from the camp to help prevent the drunken warriors from being discovered. Then he returned to take care of the wounded. Two of the Apaches had been seriously hurt during the fighting. An arrowhead was buried in the leg of one of them, and a spear point in the shoulder of another. Drawing his knife, Geronimo operated on both men, a task made easier by their drunken state. After he was finished, he stood guard by himself and spent the night hoping the Mexicans would not find them. Fortunately, they did not, and the next day, when the Apaches were sober enough to move, they loaded their wounded on the mules and started home.

Much of Geronimo's life during this period was spent on just such raids into Mexico. He would gather a band of warriors, lead them into Mexico, steal whatever he could, and return to the ranchería to divide the spoils. All this while, he was learning more and more about fighting, for although his bands sometimes escaped without firing a single shot, at other times they were engaged either by civilians or soldiers. Once the Mexicans climbed unseen to a cliff above their campground and opened fire on them. By scattering in every direction, the Apaches avoided serious casualties, but they had to leave their camp unprotected. The soldiers entered it and recovered all the loot. But in spite of occasional failures like this, Geronimo's reputation as a warrior continued to grow, and with it his prestige.

Although he was not asked to lead large bands, increasingly he was the leader chosen by smaller ones.

He was also learning more and more about the geography of the country. His travels took him through the lonely mountains of the American Southwest and northern Mexico. He learned the locations of the canyons and the passes and where to find water. On one journey, he followed the Yaqui River in Sonora as far south as its outlet into the Gulf of California, the largest body of water he had ever seen. It shone in the sunlight, and not knowing about the oceans, he thought it a large lake. His knowledge of the land was an enormous advantage, enabling him to travel swiftly and unseen along routes that were unfamiliar to either Mexicans or Americans. Thousands of square miles of some of the most rigorous territory in the Western Hemisphere were familiar to him. No American officer had a command of the terrain that approached Geronimo's, for none had traveled so far or so frequently through it.

Although Geronimo and many of the Apaches were concentrating their efforts against the Mexicans, the Americans were experiencing extreme difficulties in controlling the others. Carleton's policy of extermination succeeded in killing a few and creating worse enemies than ever out of those remaining. In 1864, he launched a massive drive in an effort to repeat the Americans' earlier successes in subduing the Mescalero Apaches and the Navajos. He gave the governors of Sonora and Chihuahua permission to cross the international border in pursuit of Apaches and requested Governor John N. Goodwin of Arizona to muster a civilian force to assist him. But in spite of the fanfare with which he started, the only results were a few more Indian deaths and even greater anger on the part of those left living.

The following year was marked by great changes, not only in the Southwest, but throughout the entire United States. Lee sent word to Grant that he was ready to meet him at Appomattox and surrender. And so the fighting between the Americans, which had cost many more lives than the wars with the Apaches, came to an end. An assassin's bullet, aimed as surely as an Apache's but fired in what people considered civilized surroundings, brought death to the President of the United States and ushered in the weak administration of President Johnson. In the Southwest, the California Volunteers were disbanded, leaving New Mexico and Arizona practically defenseless. And to compound the confusion, military control over Arizona was transferred to the Department of the Pacific, so that it and New Mexico now came under separate commands. This step, taken for economy reasons, made it difficult to coordinate action between the two areas.

The Apaches took full advantage of the situation. Although some of the individuals of some of the tribes remained at peace on reservations, many of them took to the warpath. The Indians practically overran southeastern Arizona, spreading death and destruction wherever they went, and they actually captured Fort Buchanan and its supplies—a surprising achievement. Because the Americans responded by attacking friendly Indians as well as those on the warpath, they gained more enemies. By June, 1865, many people thought parts of Arizona would have to be abandoned.

The governor of the territory went to San Francisco in an attempt to get a loan to aid the defense of the citizens, but no banker was interested in such risky business. The commander of the Department of the Pacific, however, responded immediately by sending reinforcements amounting to 1,000 men under General J. S. Mason and, for the purpose of efficiency, set up Arizona as a separate command. The Indian Office promised its cooperation and instructed its superintendent to remain subservient to the military's wishes. Mason continued the previous policy of offering protection to any Indians who promised to stay peacefully on a reservation. For this purpose, he went to Fort Bowie to hold a council with the Chiricahuas, but they had been betrayed so many times, they did not want to meet with him. His military offensive was also ineffective. At Prescott, for example, Indian attacks were so frequent that the judge had difficulty keeping court in session because the jurors had to leave the box so often to help defend the town.

In New Mexico, Carleton tried to keep peace with Victorio's Warm Springs Apaches. One of his officers met with Victorio at Pinos Altos and found the Warm Springs Apaches willing to appoint a delegation to inspect a proposed reservation. But when the delegation failed to appear, the officer ordered his soldiers to shoot down all Apaches. This aggressive attitude destroyed any remaining chance of peace.

President Andrew Johnson, busy in a futile attempt to develop a humane policy for the reconstruction of the South and to put down a political rebellion within his own party, was unable to formulate a forceful and coordinated Indian policy. Nor could the men in the field agree among themselves what to do. Some argued for intensive warfare. Others believed the Apaches could be quieted more easily and less expensively by giving them some means of subsistence. In actuality, neither view could have led to success, given the circumstances that then prevailed in the Southwest.

Annihilation was a goal beyond the reach of the Army. It had neither enough men nor enough experience. The area it had to patrol was vast and difficult to traverse. More than one commander realized that better results could be obtained during the sporadic campaigns by concentrating their men, but that left many scattered settlements open to attack. On the other hand, when they spread their troops out, manning each of the posts, they had insufficient soldiers to launch an intensive offensive. Also, they still did not know how to fight the Apaches. Many of the officers performed well in individual combats and on individual patrols, but no one could formulate an overall strategy that would compensate for the Americans' weaknesses and the Apaches' strengths. The best mounted cavalry could not keep up with the Indians even when the Indians were on foot. The cleverest officers could not figure out how to block the Apaches' mountain trails. The most alert soldiers had difficulty locating an Apache ambush. And the Apaches' tactics of scattering in every direction, moving only in small bands, and refusing to fight a superior force were more than the Army could cope with. Added to all this was the

Apaches' ability to travel without any dependence on traditional supply lines, thus making themselves less vulnerable to attack. Unless they changed their strategy, the Americans needed thousands of additional soldiers to overcome their enemy.

The prospect of keeping the Apaches on reservations was also dim. The Department of the Interior was not well enough organized to operate a system of reservations successfully. Appropriations for rations were insufficient to meet the Apaches' needs and make it worthwhile for them to give up their independence. There was little real coordination between the civilian and military authorities, and because responsibility was divided, no one knew who held the final authority. A further complication was the attitude of the settlers. Most of them hated the Apaches, and every so often they would go on the offensive themselves. When they did, they often killed the Americans' friends and missed their enemies, thus breeding further distrust in the Indians' minds.

Capping all this was widespread corruption. Army quartermasters would brand mules with a "C" meaning condemned and sell them for personal profit. Other supplies would be disposed of in a similar manner. Purchases were often made on the basis of politics or friendship. Beef contracts for the military and for the reservations were big business, and more than one fortune was made by delivering less meat than the government paid for. As usual, corruption not only cost the public money, it also led to inefficiency.

From time to time, the territorial government of Arizona, despairing of help from Washington, made efforts toward assuming a major role in handling the Indian question. These usually followed a familiar pattern. In 1866, for example, a bill was introduced into the territorial legislature that would have provided for a hundred rangers at a cost of $12,000 a month. That was a year in which all the taxes raised by the territory totaled only $1,200 to $1,300. With so little income, the territorial government obviously could not afford to buy the rangers' supplies, so the bill provided for a single contractor who would be paid in interest-bearing bonds. As calculated by the bill's sponsors, the contractor (and the legislators knew who he was to be) would have eventually received $150,000 worth of these bonds. The purpose of the proposed legislation was clearly the profit of the selected contractor rather than protection from the Indians, and the debt would have hung over the territory for many years. Other efforts, if they were not designed to build up personal fortunes, simply resulted in undisciplined, untrained civilian actions. It was these that so often resulted in the deaths of friendly Indians.

By 1868, little had been accomplished, and many lives had been lost. General E. O. C. Ord, the new commander who was responsible for Arizona's safety, received urgent pleas that he send more troops, but he had no more troops to send, and the financing necessary for additional ones was not forthcoming from Congress. But he did order the men in the field to be more aggressive, and they made almost thirty patrols deep into Indian country. The results illustrate the ineffectiveness of the Americans' fighting methods: An average of less than one Indian was killed on each patrol. So Ord vacillated between two extremes. At times he thought the maintenance of the troops was too expensive to be worthwhile and the number of men should be reduced in the interest of the country as a whole. At other times, he ordered more aggressive tactics.

By 1869, when Ulysses S. Grant was inaugurated President and replaced the unhappy, ineffective Johnson, the situation had not improved. Some of the Americans' campaigns had worked effectively, and some of the Indians were on reservations. Constant warfare had worn down the Warm Springs Apaches, and Loco, the chief of one band, was ready to make peace, provided his people could live near their former lands at Cañada Alamosa, just to the west of the Río Grande in New Mexico, and be allowed to hunt over a wide area. The Indian agent who negotiated with the chief received little help, however, from Santa Fe or Washington, and as the winter approached, he realized that either the whites must take constructive steps or face the possibility of an even more intensive war.

On October 10, he met with Loco, who had been joined by Victorio and several Mescalero leaders. The presence of the latter made the agent fearful that the various Apache tribes were working in greater collaboration than ever before and therefore presented a more serious threat than in the past. Although he had not heard from those in authority, he persuaded the Apaches to gather their people at Cañada Alamosa and promised to do what he could for them. But the weeks went by with no response from the authorities. The Apaches grew restless, particularly as those whites who did not want peace threatened to attack them. The Indian agent did everything possible to hold their confidence and even stayed with them overnight to demonstrate his trust in them. Finally, in January, 1870, just when he had decided he probably could restrain them no longer, word arrived that Washington had allotted $2,800 for their care. The plan then worked so successfully that more Indians agreed to come in, and by October, 1870, almost 800 Warm Springs Apaches had gathered at Cañada Alamosa.

But the peaceful relations that developed with Loco and Victorio were not duplicated elsewhere. In an eleven-day period during August, 1870, the Chiricahuas killed twelve Americans, wounded one, and destroyed $10,000 worth of property. The troops could do nothing about it even though the cavalry sent several bodies of men in pursuit of Cochise. But later in the year, Cochise suffered a serious defeat and appeared to be ready to talk about peace, but little came of the opportunity his willingness presented.

General William T. Sherman had succeeded Grant as commanding general of the United States Army, and was so discouraged by the conditions in Arizona that he thought the area had been settled prematurely. Perhaps the best course to follow, he speculated, was to advise the settlers to leave, then withdraw the military and turn the land back to the Indians. General Grant, however, saw cause for hope. He realized the Indians, not only in the Southwest, but elsewhere, too, had often been treated unjustly. Perhaps a change in policy might remedy the errors of the past and bring peace where war now existed. As a consequence, he formed the Board of Indian Commissioners, composed mostly of men with religious feelings and humanitarian temperaments. Congress appropriated enough money for them to start work and see what they could accomplish. But there was still no clear change in the Americans' policy. The commissioners were working for peace; many Army commanders were still pursuing the Indians vigorously; the white settlers were complaining about the lack of protection they were receiving; many citizens in the East were disturbed by the inhuman treatment of the Indians; and the Indians themselves, caught between these conflicting attitudes, hardly knew what to do. They had little faith in the white men, but they could not fight on forever. So some made peace, and some made war, and few of them benefited from whichever course they followed.

Geronimo remained aloof from all this. He had struck up a friendship with Mangas, son of Mangas Coloradas, and went on at least one raid with him into Mexico. They captured a herd of cattle after killing two of the cowboys guarding them, but near Arizpe, they met a troop of Mexican soldiers. The Mexicans chased them, forcing them to desert their herd. In the mountains, the Apaches dismounted, because they could fight better in that rough wilderness on foot, so the Mexicans rounded up their horses and rode away. Mangas and Geronimo returned to the ranchería without any loot and without even the horses they had ridden into Mexico. Tired of the taunts of the other Apaches, most of the warriors wanted to go back to Mexico, and Geronimo agreed to lead them. This time they successfully attacked several settlements, secured many supplies, and regained their standing among their fellows.

Thus Geronimo spent his days. The snows fell on the Black Mountains and on the Chiricahuas. The spring winds blew for days on end across the plains of southern New Mexico. The summer sun turned the desert into an inferno. But even with the passing of time, vast regions of the Southwest remained unknown to the Americans. Many canyons had never felt the imprint of a foot other than an Apache's. Many water holes and mountain passes remained undiscovered. And there was still some space for a free soul like Geronimo.

He wandered between the Warm Springs Apaches and the Chiricahuas, never attaching himself permanently to one or the other. He was restless and increasingly resentful of the Americans, for he realized their continued presence posed a threat to the life he loved so well.

XII

Massacre at Camp Grant

BY 1871, conditions in the Southwest had not noticeably improved, and with the exception of some of the government contractors who were growing rich, no one was satisfied. A government report noted that relations with the Apaches had been relatively peaceable until the Americans had adopted the Mexicans' policy of extermination. "This policy," it continued, "has resulted in a war which, in the last ten years, has cost a thousand lives and over forty millions of dollars, and the country is no quieter nor the Indians any nearer extermination than they were at the time of the Gadsden Purchase." It estimated that continuance of the war would cost $3,000,000 or $4,000,000 a year.

Yet in much of the territory, white men still could not live or work in safety. Stagecoaches were stopped by the Indians, wagon trains attacked, ranches and mines raided. Many settlers fled their homes and took refuge in the larger communities, where they could not find work because of the overcrowded conditions. Jobless and frustrated, these men wandered through the streets, voicing their complaints to anyone who paused to listen. And there were many listeners, because the entire territory suffered from the spreading chaos.

The soldiers were dissatisfied and hampered by Washington's conflicting policies. Nor were the Indians happy. They could neither dislodge the Americans nor come to terms with them. Some, like Victorio, had agreed to go on a reservation; others, like Cochise, were still openly at war; while yet others, like Geronimo, fluctuated between the two extremes, sometimes appearing on a reservation and sometimes taking to the warpath. None of these ways of life suited them. They were unhappy with the restrictions of the reservations. Yet the actions of the military, although ineffective in bringing about peace, took a toll of these Indians that remained free. Greatly outnumbered by the white men and fighting with inferior arms, many of the chiefs were becoming discouraged. Cochise, for example, although he boasted that his warriors killed ten Americans for every Chiricahua killed, saw his tribe dwindle and wondered whether it could continue to survive.

Eskiminzin, chief of the Aravaipa Apaches, was another who had doubts about the future of his people. The Aravaipa Apaches, who normally lived near Aravaipa Creek to the north of Tucson and just south of the Gila River, had been harassed by the soldiers. And a military post, Camp Grant, had been established at the juncture of the Aravaipa Creek and the San Pedro River. Like many of the posts in the Southwest, it was not much of an installation—an adobe kitchen, some sheds, deteriorating tents, and some ramadas made of upright saplings covered with cottonwood boughs to provide shade. Several corrals, a blacksmith's shop, a sutler's store, and a few other buildings completed the camp. It was garrisoned by a relative handful of men under Lieutenant Royal Whitman. Yet, located where it was, Camp Grant prevented the Aravaipa Apaches from reclaiming their homeland.

Among the residents at the post was an Aravaipa boy who had been taken captive in 1869. He was perfectly happy, for the soldiers clothed him, fed him, and took good care of him, but his family wanted his return. The Aravaipas did not dare attack Camp Grant, so Eskiminzin permitted some of the family to go to Camp Apache near the White River and talk to the commanding officer. (Camp Apache, located in the midst of the northern Apaches and just south of the Navajos, was an important post and later became a fort.) Because the Aravaipas were now at peace with the Americans, the commanding officer wrote a note to Whitman ordering the boy's release and told the Aravaipas to take it to Camp Grant.

Five women, including the boy's mother, were chosen to carry the message. In February, 1871, they arrived at Camp Grant under a flag of truce. The guards, having little to fear from women, permitted them to approach, read the note, and sent for Whitman. With the help of his interpreter, Whitman talked to them. The boy was then brought to them, but although he was glad to see them, he did not want to go back with them. Life at the camp, with the Americans' food and clothing, was far better than the rugged existence at the ranchería. Unable to prevail on him, the women remained with the Americans for two days. During that time, Whitman saw to it that they were well cared for, and when they left, they said they would like to come back. Whitman told them they could.

On their arrival at the ranchería, they repeated to the other Aravaipas what the boy had said and how he preferred life among the Americans. They also told how well Whitman had treated them. Eskiminzin was interested. This sounded as though it might be a better life than the one his people were leading, and Whitman appeared to be a man whom the Indians could trust. So he allowed the women and some of their friends to return to Camp Grant to trade for manta, a cloth used by the Indian women. He also asked them to tell Whitman that he would like to talk to him personally. Curious to hear what Eskiminzin had to say, Whitman sent back word that he would be glad to see the chief.

Within a few days, Eskiminzin arrived at the camp with about twenty-five of his band. Short even for an Apache and somewhat given to weight, Eskiminzin was a Pinal Apache who had married an Aravaipa and joined her tribe. Now he was the leader of a band of approximately 150 Indians, mostly Aravaipas but including a few Pinals. He and his people had no home, he explained, and they were tired of fighting and fearful each time the cavalry came near them. He wanted a permanent peace with the Americans. Whitman advised him to go to the White Mountains of Arizona. That was the home of the White Mountain Apaches and included the site of Camp Apache. The government was attempting to set up a reservation there, and provisions had been made to issue rations to the Apaches who agreed to live there.

But Eskiminzin did not want to go to the White Mountains. "That is not our country," he said to Whitman. "Neither are they our people. We are at peace with them, but have never mixed with them. Our fathers and their fathers before them have lived in these mountains and have raised corn in this valley. We are taught to make mescal our principal article of food, and in summer and winter here we have a never-failing supply. At the White Mountains there is none, and without it now we get sick. Some of our people have been at Goodwin [an important post farther east on the Gila River] and for a short time at the White Mountains, but they were not contented, and they all say, 'Let us go to the Aravaipa and make a final peace and never break it.' "

Whitman recognized the justice and logic of Eskiminzin's request. Although he had been in Arizona only a few months, he realized, as many in authority did not, that all Indians were not the same, even though they might be Apaches. They had different ways of living, and their existences depended on one of the many specialized environments in Arizona. Few areas within the United States offer such diversity—snowy mountains, sun-baked plains, vast forests, and expanses of desert where mesquite trees and cholla cactus predominate. Life in one region was not like life in another, especially for the Apaches, who depended so entirely on what nature gave them. On the other hand, Whitman had no authority to make peace with the Apaches, provide them with food, or set up a reservation. Yet he could see no point in fighting the Indians if they wanted to settle down peacefully. So he told Eskiminzin he could make camp about half a mile from the post. Then he wrote a report to the commanding general, who made his headquarters near Prescott, Arizona, and asked him for instructions.

Although Eskiminzin was happy with the lieutenant's decision, Whitman himself was worried because he was greatly exceeding his authority. But he issued rations to the Apaches and then set them to work bringing hay to the post. "I arranged a system of tickets with which to pay them and to encourage them," Whitman wrote later, "and to be sure they were properly treated, I personally attended to all the weighing. I also made inquiries as to the kind of goods sold them and prices. This proved a perfect success; not only the women and children engaged in the work, but many of the men. The amount furnished by them in about two months was nearly 300,000 pounds." The plan worked so well that several other small bands asked to come in. Whitman gave them permission, too, and the number of Apaches around Camp Grant kept increasing until it reached about 500. Yet the weeks passed, and no reply came to the report Whitman had sent to the department commander asking for instructions. Everything he had done seemed to him to have made sense, but he still had no authorization for his actions.

Some of the Apaches wanted to go farther off to search for mescal. This posed a real problem for Whitman. The mescal was necessary for their survival—it had been one of the reasons they wanted to come back to Aravaipa Creek—but he could not control them at a distance with the few men under his command. So he spent hours among the Indians explaining their situation and that in return for the soldiers' protection they must never fight other Americans. He also personally issued the passes for these trips away from the camp and carefully noted how many Indians went out each time. Most of the groups were composed largely of women, a point that reassured him. As soon as they returned, he checked on the amount of mescal they had brought back to make certain they had actually been gathering the plant and not raiding against the Americans. As a result, he was confident their journeys had all been peaceful.

After six weeks in this delicate position, with hundreds of Apaches camped near his post and no reply to his report to the commanding general, he finally received an answer from the department headquarters. It consisted solely of the return of his original report along with a comment that he had not included the proper briefing. Whitman had accomplished what no other officer had done: He had subjugated hundreds of Apaches without the loss of a single life. But the Army cared more about formalities than it did about results. So Whitman was left without any instructions.

In April, he finally received verbal confirmation that his course of action had been all right. Captain Frank Stanwood arrived to supersede him as commander of Camp Grant, although Whitman was to remain at the post. Stanwood had talked to the commanding general and had been instructed to treat any Indians at the post as prisoners of war. He conducted a personal investigation of the Indian camp and the way it was controlled. Then, perfectly satisfied with what Whitman was doing, he left on a protracted scouting expedition in the southern part of Arizona Territory.

Gathering hay for the one Army post was not enough employment for the Apaches, so Whitman persuaded the nearby ranchers to hire the Indians when they were harvesting their grain. This, too, worked out well. No one complained about the manner in which the Indians performed their tasks; and one rancher, Charles McKinney, who lived on the San Pedro River, became a close personal friend of Eskiminzin. The chief often visited him, and the two men enjoyed each other's company.

But Whitman was still concerned. As he wrote later, the Apaches "had so won on me, that from my first idea of treating them justly and honestly as an officer of the Army, I had come to feel a strong personal interest in helping to show them the way to a higher civilization. I had come to feel respect for men who, ignorant and naked, were still ashamed to lie or steal, and for women who would work like slaves to clothe themselves and [their] children, but, untaught, held their virtue above price. . . .

"I had ceased to have any fears of their leaving here, and only dreaded for them that they might at any time be ordered to do so. They frequently expressed anxiety to hear from the general, that they might have confidence to build for themselves better houses, but would always say, 'You know what we want, and if you can't see him you can write and do for us what you can.' "

Although the Indians had great confidence in Whitman, the white men at Tucson did not. For months, the leading citizens, in the mood of the times, had been complaining about the Army. It was inefficient and ineffective, they said, and Washington did not understand the problems of an area in which white men could not live and work safely. On several occasions, they held public meetings to discuss the Indians and the threat they posed. Tucson's newspaper faithfully reported every Indian attack in the hope the news would spread nationally and force the government into greater action. Emotions ran higher and higher, and Whitman emerged as a principal target. Here was an Army officer, paid out of the public treasury, who was not pursuing Indians; he was befriending them. Soon the citizens began blaming Whitman's Aravaipa Apaches for almost every Indian outbreak in the southern part of Arizona; and in April, 1871, they decided to do something about it.

Under the leadership of six of Tucson's most prominent citizens, they recruited a force of almost fifty Mexicans and nearly a hundred Papago Indians. Longtime enemies of the Apaches, the Papagos lived near Tucson and were at peace with the white men, but they still hated all Apaches and were ready to go to war with them. A recent Apache raid, during which they had lost some livestock, had further inflamed their tempers.

Leaving the city inconspicuously, the Americans and Mexicans met the Papagos a few miles northeast of Tucson. There they were joined by a wagon containing guns and ammunition sent to them by the adjutant general of Arizona Territory, who had taken them from the state arsenal. Avoiding the main road to Camp Grant, the group marched toward the Rincon Mountains, following the wash of the Tanque Verde River. Darkness fell as they wound their way along the tortuous and difficult trail. Because it was rarely used by anyone except occasional Indians, the chances of their being seen on it were slight.

At two o'clock in the morning, they had crossed the summit and were descending the other side of the mountains. The men were tired from their long climb, so they made camp for the night in an open area where a stream had formed a pool of water. The next day at dawn, they rose and began marching down the valley of the San Pedro River along a trail that followed the riverbed. After marching awhile, they came to a spot where they would be hidden from view. Here they made camp for the rest of the day because they did not want to be near Camp Grant during daylight. A military patrol or an Apache hunting party might see them and spread the alarm.

About five o'clock in the afternoon, they started out again. They thought they were approximately sixteen miles from the Aravaipas' ranchería. An easy march would bring them to it by midnight, the hour they planned to attack. But as the evening hours passed, the country did not look as they had expected it would, and they were afraid they might have underestimated the distance. Two Mexicans and a Papago went ahead, while the rest of the men increased their pace. One of the Mexican scouts returned and said that, judging from the appearance of the terrain, they must have camped that day thirty miles, not sixteen, from the ranchería. The group was now in serious trouble. If they could not reach the ranchería before daybreak, their plan would fail. But they decided to go ahead as fast as they could and hope they would make it.

Behind them in Tucson, the commanding officer at Fort Lowell had become suspicious. It seemed to him that too many men had left town, and he had heard talk about a possible raid against Whitman's Aravaipas. At four o'clock in the afternoon, he wrote a message to the lieutenant warning him that the Apaches might be attacked and sent two mounted infantrymen to carry it to Camp Grant. They took the military road on the other side of the mountains, which, although longer, was easier and faster.

The Aravaipas slept quietly that night. Because of a shortage of water, they had moved farther up the canyon and were about five miles from the soldiers' protection. But they were not concerned, because their arrangement with Whitman was working well and they had implicit faith in him. Many of the warriors had even gone off hunting or gathering mescal with no fears for the safety of their women and children. The only guards that night were a man and woman sitting by a fire on top of a bluff.

Dawn was approaching when the tired men from Tucson reached the sleeping ranchería. Quickly the leaders made their plan of attack. Several Papagos were detailed to kill the two guards first. Moving quietly, they reached the unsuspecting couple and murdered them. Then the slaughter began.

The remainder of the Papagos swept through the ranchería from three sides, while the Mexicans and Americans occupied the bluff where the two sentries had been killed. The Papagos used their bows, their knives, and their war clubs. Again and again, they would swing their clubs at the heads of sleeping or defenseless Aravaipas, crushing their skulls and spattering their brains on the ground. According to later reports, there were instances in which young girls were raped by the Papagos, then mutilated and killed. Many of the Aravaipas who woke and tried to escape were cut down by the fire of the Mexicans and the Americans who had stationed themselves on the bluff. The shouts of the dying and the sounds of bullets filled the early morning air, but they did not carry the five miles to Camp Grant. The soldiers remained completely unaware of what was taking place.

Eskiminzin was one of the few who escaped. He woke during the attack, grabbed his youngest daughter in his arms, and ran from the ranchería. Somehow he slipped through the line of Papagos and escaped the bullets of the Mexicans and Americans. But the other members of his family were not so fortunate. His two wives and five other children were all killed.

The fight—if it could be called a fight—was over in about half an hour. The Mexicans and Americans then walked through the ranchería, shooting the wounded and even sending bullets into the bodies of those already dead just to make certain. Then they set fire to the wickiups, gathered together the twenty-eight children whom they had taken prisoner, and started back to Tucson, pleased that they had killed so many but had suffered no casualties themselves.

Whitman was sitting at breakfast that morning when the messengers from the commanding officer of Fort Lowell arrived with the warning. He immediately sent two of his interpreters to the ranchería to tell the Aravaipas to gather their belongings and come to Camp Grant at once. But when the interpreters arrived, they found only corpses and smoldering ruins left by the men from Tucson. On hearing their report, Whitman assembled a party of twenty men and sent them out under the post surgeon to care for any wounded they might find, and he offered a hundred dollars to any of his interpreters who would go into the mountains and tell the survivors that none of the soldiers was to blame for the disaster. Even for so high a reward, no interpreter was willing to take the risk.

The following day, Whitman himself led a burial party, knowing the Indians would see what was happening and realize the soldiers were showing respect for their dead. This might persuade them to return. His hopes came true, and he later wrote, "They began to come in from all directions, singly and in small parties, so changed in forty-eight hours as to be hardly recognizable, during which time they had neither eaten nor slept. Many of the men, whose families had all been killed, when I spoke to them and expressed sympathy for them, were obliged to turn away, unable to speak, and too proud to show their grief. The women whose children had been killed or stolen were convulsed with grief, and looked to me appealingly, as though I were their last hope on earth. Children who two days before had been full of fun and frolic, kept a distance, expressing wondering horror. I did what I could; I fed them, and talked to them, and listened patiently to their accounts. I sent horses into the mountains to bring in two badly wounded women, one shot through the left lung, and one with an arm shattered."

The Aravaipas were completely stunned. One question that they asked repeatedly Whitman could not answer: Why had government guns been used against them? Those weapons, taken from the state arsenal by the adjutant general and marked "AT" for Arizona Territory, were impossible to explain, and they convinced the Indians that this was not an unofficial attack by individual enemies.

Even though he could not give them reasons for the tragedy, Whitman was somehow able to keep the Indians' confidence. One of them said to him: "I no longer want to live; my women and children have been killed before my face, and I have been unable to defend them. Most Indians in my place would take a knife and cut his throat, but I *will live* to show these people that all they have done, and all they can do, shall not make me break faith with you as long as you will stand by us and defend us, in a language we know nothing of, to the great governor we never have nor never will see."

In this spirit, the Aravaipas began the sad work of rebuilding their ranchería. And Eskiminzin and Whitman picked up the threads of their former existence and, trying to forget the horrors of that sunrise attack, looked to the future.

But the future was not bright. A cavalry patrol from Camp Apache came upon the Aravaipas by surprise. Scared of all Indians, they became frightened and fired on Eskiminzin and his friends. Fortunately their aim was poor and they killed no one before Eskiminzin was able to explain that his band was friendly and was under the protection of Camp Grant.

But the incident sickened Eskiminzin. Twice he had made peace with the white men. Twice they had attacked him. Whitman, he was sure, had good intentions, but the Army seemed unable to defend the Aravaipas. The only course was to drive all white men from the country, for there could never be peace between those people and his.

Before leaving the reservation, he went to see Charles McKinney, the rancher with whom he had become so friendly. As he usually did, McKinney greeted the chief warmly and invited him for supper. They had their meal together, talking and laughing and enjoying each other. But when it came time for Eskiminzin to depart, he drew a pistol from his belt and shot McKinney in the head. As the sound of the shot died in the night, he went away, leaving the dead man where he had fallen.

Eskiminzin had not wanted to do this. But as he later explained, he had to teach his people that there could never be friendship between them and the white men. He had chosen to kill McKinney to set an example for the others to follow. "Anyone can kill an enemy," he said, "but it takes a strong man to kill a friend." Then he led his warriors on the warpath.

XIII

Efforts at Peace

NEWS of the horrors that had taken place at Camp Grant quickly swept the country. Although many Western newspapers praised the massacre as an act of self-defense, most others denounced it as an act of barbarism. In Washington, many officials, including President Grant, voiced their indignation at the irresponsible and inhuman slaughter. And among the Apaches, the incident was regarded as additional evidence that the Americans could never be trusted.

At about the time of the massacre, but before the news of it had reached Washington, the Army relieved the commanding general in Arizona and replaced him with Lieutenant Colonel George Crook. The assignment had been offered Crook before, but he had turned it down. He was weary of fighting Indians, he did not like the Arizona climate, and he thought holding such a post with his relatively low rank would cause jealousy among his senior officers. But the pressures were too great for him to resist. He was a noted fighter, and the people of Arizona wanted someone who would battle Apaches, not feed them.

Crook's philosophy toward Indians was simple and, assuming that the Americans had a right to their land, completely honorable. Unlike many civilians and soldiers, he believed they should not be cheated on their rations and that promises to them should be kept, not broken. He ordered his officers never to make an agreement with the Indians that they did not have the authority to enforce. But after many years of experience with them, especially in the Northwest, he believed they would not remain at peace until they had first been conquered. They had to be made fully aware that the Americans were stronger than they.

Of all the officers in the Army, Crook was probably the one most able to put such a policy into practice. He was a determined and intelligent fighter, one who never took unnecessary risks but never gave up. He was also imaginative and flexible, able to adapt his methods of fighting to those of his enemy. One of his most appealing personal traits was his complete modesty. Describing his arrival at Tucson, an officer who served under him wrote: "He came . . . without the slightest pomp or parade, and without anyone in San Francisco, except his immediate superiors, knowing of his departure, and without a soul in Tucson, not even the driver of the stage which had carried him and his baggage, knowing of his arrival. There were no railroads, there were no telegraphs in Arizona, and Crook was the last man in the world to seek notoriety had they existed. His whole idea of life was to do each duty well, and to let his work speak for itself."

Although he was a man of action who liked to be in the center of the fighting, Crook was not at all impetuous. In Tucson he spent his first days gathering all the information he could about the Apaches by talking with both civilians and soldiers. From them, he learned that the Mexicans knew more about the Apaches than did the Americans and that they could travel almost as fast and with almost as little equipment. He therefore employed some fifty of them as scouts and, with five companies of cavalry, marched through the land of Cochise to Fort Bowie. He hoped to encounter some of the Chiricahuas and engage them in battle, but Cochise was too clever to fight so strong a force, and his warriors remained hidden.

From Fort Bowie, Crook made a sweep along the Dos Cabezas Mountains, where he saw a small party of Indians. He planned to trap them at a spring, but the failure of one of his officers to advance at the right moment permitted the Apaches to escape.

Abandoning his attempt to lure the Chiricahuas into battle, he left the lands of Cochise and marched to the Aravaipa Mountains and from there to Camp Apache, where he dismissed his Mexican scouts. Although he had learned their value during his short time in Apache country, he realized Indians themselves would be even better. At Camp Apache, he talked to some of the White Mountain and other Apaches who were living there under the Army's protection. Because they were tired of the restrictions of reservation life and glad to return to the adventurous existence they had once led, they were willing to serve in the Army against Apaches. This was entirely consistent with the Apaches' tradition of individualism. Just because some Apaches remained at war with the Americans did not mean that the others were required to fight them also. Each warrior had the right to make his own choice, and some of them chose to serve under Crook.

Although relatively unnoticed at the time, Crook's decision marked the first dramatic change in the Americans' strategy since they had commenced their invasion of the Apaches' territory. Instead of continuing to use the principles of European warfare, Crook intended to fight the Apaches on their own terms and in their own way. Regular troops would still play an important role, according to his plans, but in the future, when the Apaches fled to their mountain refuges, they would be pursued by their own people.

After assembling his scouts, Crook left Camp Apache and started on a patrol along the Mogollon Rim. One day, reading some newspapers he had received, he learned that President Grant was sending Vincent Colyer, Secretary of the Board of Indian Commissioners, to investigate the Camp Grant massacre and also to try to find a peaceful solution to other Apache problems. Crook was contemptuous of this plan. "I had no faith in the success of his enterprise," Crook later wrote about Colyer. "But," he added, "I was afraid if I continued my operations and he was to fail, I would be charged with interference. So I at once countermanded all my orders looking to active operations against the hostiles, and directed all persons under my control to furnish Mr. Colyer all the assistance within their power in the carrying out of his peace policy."

Colyer, a Quaker by faith and an artist by profession, went to Santa Fe, where he learned that the settlers living near Cañada Alamosa had decided to follow the example set by the people of Tucson and perhaps exterminate all the Apaches they could. Their attitude was expressed in a resolution passed at a public meeting held that year:

"Resolved, That the people of Grant County, New Mexico, organize themselves into a posse and follow their stock to wherever it may be, and take it by force wherever found, even if it be at the sacrifice of every Indian man, woman, and child, in the tribe.

"Resolved, That if opposed by the Indians, or their accomplices, be they Indian agents, Indian traders, Army officers, let them be looked upon as our worst enemies and the common enemies of New Mexico, and be dealt with accordingly."

The probate judge who forwarded the resolution to the authorities added a note in which he said that if the citizens "carry out their program, the Camp Grant massacre will be thrown entirely in the shade. . . ."

Hurrying to the agency, Colyer found the Apaches had heard of the impending violence and had fled. Nothing could induce the chiefs to leave their hiding places and join Colyer in a council. Alarmed at the possibility of another massacre, he went to the valley of the Tularosa River to examine its potential as a reservation. Because it was a considerable distance from any white settlement, it was less likely to be attacked. The land was arable, and there was plenty of wood, water, and game. But he did not know the country well enough to realize that the winter climate in the valley would be far too severe for the Warm Springs Apaches. So he ordered the agent at Cañada Alamosa to make the move as soon as the Indians returned from their flight. When the Apaches learned their new fate, they protested strenuously and predicted a cold winter. But the agent had to obey Colyer's orders, although he promised to make every possible effort to have Colyer's decision rescinded later.

Believing he had solved one problem, Colyer himself left New Mexico and went to Camp Apache. The commanding officer received him enthusiastically, and so did the Indians, for he had ordered $2,000 worth of food and clothing for them. In a few days, nearly 400 Apaches assembled for a peace council. Colyer and the commanding officer argued that it would be better to remain at peace with the Americans than fight them, and the Apaches agreed. Colyer then set up a generous allotment of land as a reservation for them, and the commanding officer warned them that if they strayed away from it, they would be hunted down and killed.

Satisfied that he had made progress with those Apaches, Colyer next wanted to talk with Eskiminzin. Since leaving Camp Grant, the Arvaipas had run into further ill fortune. In July, they had attacked a supply train going from Tucson to Fort Bowie. The train with quantities of food and ammunition looked like an easy target. At times when some of the wagons lagged behind, it stretched out for nearly two miles, and it appeared that the military escort was concentrated in front and that the rear had been left unguarded. Eskiminzin took this into consideration when he set up his ambush. He arranged to have a small band of warriors attack the undefended rear, while he and the remainder of the warriors took up a position at the front, where they could divert the soldiers if they attempted to go back to the train's defense.

Unfortunately, the rear was not unguarded. A number of soldiers had been assigned to march behind the wagon train but, growing weary of the walk across the hot desert, had climbed into the wagons and so were invisible to the watching Apaches. When the smaller of the two groups of Aravaipas attacked, the soldiers emerged and began firing. This unexpected resistance upset Eskiminzin's plans by delaying the Indians who were trying to capture the wagons at the rear. Although he tried to hold the advance guards' attention and prevent them from turning back, he was unable to do so, and they joined their companions in the defense.

Eskiminzin had only two choices: to desert his fellow Apaches or engage in an open battle. He chose the latter. In the subsequent fighting, the Aravaipas suffered heavy losses—some thirteen killed—and Eskiminzin himself was wounded in the arm. Yet the Apaches had killed only one American, slightly wounded a few others, and failed to take any supplies. It was a disastrous defeat, and when word reached the Aravaipas that Colyer wanted to talk to them, Eskiminzin was willing to make another effort for peace.

The two men met at Camp Grant near the scene of the massacre. Eskiminzin's old friend, Whitman, was present, and the three tried to repair the damage of the past. Colyer may not have always been practical, but he was motivated by the highest idealism, and his attitude appealed to the Indians. After listening to him talk, Eskiminzin said he was such a good man that he could not have been born of mortal parents. Crook, when he heard this, thought the chief was simply playing on Colyer's vanity—and succeeding. But Eskiminzin agreed to stay at Camp Grant as long as Whitman remained in charge. This angered Crook, who had as little use for Whitman as he did for Colyer, believing the lieutenant was an ineffective officer and gullible in dealing with the Indians.

At Prescott, Arizona, Crook met Colyer personally. Colyer was affable and told him he was delighted Crook agreed with his peace policy. Crook firmly informed him that his position was quite the opposite. Nothing he had seen in Arizona had made him reverse his previous opinion: The Apaches had to be conquered before they would make a lasting peace. Being under orders to do so, however, he would cooperate with Colyer in every way he could, but he was certain Colyer's efforts were doomed to fail.

And to a large extent, they did. No man in the few months given Colyer could have satisfied the conflicting demands of the military, the civilians, and the Indians, have established and organized the necessary reservations, and thus have brought peace to the Southwest. The problem was far too complicated, particularly in view of the government's self-contradictory policies. Here at one time was the chief civilian authority working toward peace through conciliation while the chief military authority was laying his plans for an offensive, plans he could put into operation just as soon as Colyer was gone. Nevertheless, Colyer did succeed in adding to the system of reservations, and he persuaded some Indians, like Eskiminzin, to return to peaceful ways in spite of the wrongs they had suffered.

When Colyer left, Crook was greatly relieved and began making ready to recommence his offensive. His hand was strengthened by another change of attitude in Washington. An Indian attack on a stagecoach near Wickenburg, Arizona, resulting in the death of six Americans, attracted nationwide publicity. The Western press picked up the cause of the settlers, and the federal government decided to adopt a much firmer policy toward the Indians. All the roving tribes were to go on reservations immediately, and those that failed to do so were to be hunted down. All warriors were to be listed and required to carry identification papers, and their presence on the reservations was to be verified daily. Furthermore, Crook was given practically complete charge of all Indian affairs in Arizona.

Crook did not take to the field right away, for he had no intention of squandering his troops on minor skirmishes. Instead, he gathered all possible information about the Indians and their movements and prepared to launch a major campaign that would settle the problem once and for all. In December, 1871, he sent out word that all Indians must be on the reservations by February 15, 1872, or risk severe punishment. As a result, many Indians flocked in during the winter. On February 7, 1872, he reiterated his warning and prepared to start his offensive the same month. But he had barely begun to send out his troops when the government reversed itself again, and he received orders to avoid warfare if at all possible.

President Grant, dissatisfied with Colyer's achievements, selected a new peace commissioner, General Oliver Otis Howard, a one-armed veteran of the Civil War. Howard, a deeply religious man, had worked among the blacks after the conclusion of the Civil War, because, as he told Crook, he believed he had been placed on earth to be "the Moses to the Negro." His next most important mission, he thought, was to help the Indians.

Conflict between the two officers was inevitable. Crook was a down-to-earth person, one of the ablest fighters in the Army, and a man with no pretensions. Except on the most formal occasions, he wore battered civilian clothes, and he liked to be with his troops at the heart of the fighting. On the other hand, Howard, for all his good intentions, was somewhat self-centered. According to Crook, he was fond of speech-making, his two favorite subjects being "How I Was Converted" and "The Battle of Gettysburg." No sooner had he arrived at Prescott than he announced that he had been asked to address the soldiers. The commanding officer, who had little respect for him, questioned him closely and finally determined that the request had come from Howard's own aide. Such conduct earned Crook's scorn, but he was too well disciplined to show it openly.

Whitman had been arrested and was facing a court-martial. In his absence, the Aravaipas were reported to be growing restless, so Howard ordered Whitman back to Camp Grant and went there with Crook to hold a conference with the Indians. As Crook wrote later, "At this post was a Lt. Royal E. Whitman, who had deserted his colors and gone over to the 'Indian Ring' bag and baggage, and had behaved himself in such a manner that I had preferred charges against him. He was then under arrest, awaiting trial. There was more or less feeling against me at this post. One of the first things General Howard did after his arrival was to parade up and down the garrison, arm in arm with Whitman." Crook apparently did not know that Whitman was a relative of Howard's first wife, so it was only natural that the two men should spend time together. To him, Howard was publicly endorsing Whitman's cause against his own. This led to more ill feeling on Crook's part.

When the Aravaipas had assembled, Whitman took Howard out to the meeting place. The warriors were already sitting on the ground, waiting to hear what the general would say. But Howard, instead of talking to them, dropped to his knees and began to pray in a loud voice. The startled Aravaipas leaped to their feet and quickly fled, leaving the Americans completely alone.

At last Whitman saw Eskiminzin peering around the corner of a building and beckoning to him. He went over to talk to his old friend, and Eskiminzin flatly accused him of being a traitor. Why, he asked, had he brought a man among them to make such bad medicine against them? Whitman laughed in reply and said this was Howard's normal manner for starting any important business, just as normal as an Indian's spitting on his hands before drawing a bow. Eskiminzin was satisfied with the explanation, the other Aravaipas came back, and the conference began.

One of the principal issues was the return of the children who had been taken captive by the raiding party from Tucson. Howard had persuaded some of the people who were now caring for them to bring them back to Camp Grant on the promise that they could keep any children whose parents were no longer living. This was completely unsatisfactory to Eskiminzin, who argued that the children were Aravaipas and should grow up with their own people whether their parents were alive or not. Nothing Howard could say would make him change his mind, so Howard promised to take the question up with higher authority. This reply greatly angered the foster parents; and the United States Attorney for Tucson, who was present, denounced Howard as a brute and a liar, while Howard retorted that he would have the official dismissed from his position.

But the council was generally successful. Howard agreed the Aravaipas should be moved farther away from the large white settlements and selected an area on the Gila River south of the agency at Fort Apache. Before the year was out, the San Carlos reservation was officially established. At the conclusion of the meeting, Eskiminzin picked up a stone and said that not until it melted would he break his word. Crook regarded this promise with cynicism, saying Eskiminzin had made it so many times that "he had it pat." Howard, however, was impressed and asked Eskiminzin if he could come to their ranchería even if the Aravaipas were on the warpath. The chief liked Howard, but not that much. He told the general he could only do it if he wanted to get killed.

After the conference at Camp Grant, Howard returned to Fort Apache and was successful in arranging treaties between some of the other Apaches and their traditional enemies. Then he left for Washington, taking with him several important chiefs. It had been agreed beforehand that such a delegation might be impressed by the Americans' power and that their appearance in various cities would help to increase constructive interest in the Indian question.

In spite of Howard's successes, two major problems remained. The Warm Springs Apaches, who had been moved to Tularosa under protest, were growing more and more restless. Just as they had predicted, the winter of 1871-72 had been severe, and they had suffered seriously from the cold and inclement weather. In the spring, the agency had fenced in a few acres of land and attempted to persuade the Apaches to take up farming. But this was so foreign to their usual way of life that they refused to do it. All they wanted was to return to Cañada Alamosa.

Many of Victorio's warriors, including Geronimo, had left him to join Cochise and the Chiricahuas, who were still on the warpath. Although Fort Bowie continued to guard Apache Pass and the troops there offered a check to the Indians, southwestern Arizona and northern Sonora were still unsafe areas for either Mexicans or Americans, and no one knew when the Chiricahuas might attack. So in August, 1872, Howard was instructed to return to Arizona to try to settle these two difficulties.

The situation at Tularosa was approaching a crisis. The Warm Springs Apaches had been told again and again they could return to Cañada Alamosa but that they would have to wait for Howard's arrival. As they did not want to spend another winter at Tularosa, they finally delivered an ultimatum to the Indian agent: If Howard did not appear within a week, they would all leave.

Frederick Hughes, who was on the agency staff, went in search of the general and met him on the trail not far from Tularosa. "To my surprise," he wrote later, "I found Howard traveling with no other escort than his aide-de-camp, his clerk and . . . [his] guide, quite a contrast to Colyer's mode of traveling . . . while on the same mission when he was accompanied by two troops of cavalry." Although Howard had his share of faults, personal cowardice was not one of them.

The general quickly saw that Colyer had made a grave error in moving the Warm Springs Apaches to Tularosa and that the land was utterly unsuited to them, so he immediately gave orders to have them returned to Cañada Alamosa. This at once settled that problem, but the larger one remained: How to even find Cochise, much less make a peace with him?

Both Victorio and Hughes, with whom he discussed the question, agreed he would never locate Cochise if he went with an escort of soldiers, and they also said that the one white man who could help him was a scout named Thomas Jeffords. A curious friendship had sprung up between Jeffords and Cochise, and Jeffords had even visited the chief in the Dragoon Mountains, something no other American would have dared do. Victorio also said there was one Apache who might assist him. That was Chie, a son of Mangas Coloradas, who in spite of his hatred for Americans as a result of his father's murder might be persuaded to work for peace. After Howard talked to them, both Chie and Jeffords said they would accompany him on his mission, but both repeated the warning that they could take no soldiers with them, for Cochise was suspicious of the military.

Before they turned westward toward the Chiricahuas, they first had to visit Cañada Alamosa. Victorio wanted Howard personally to see the land he loved so well, and Howard did not dare offend the chief. Also, Jeffords thought they might find Ponce, another Apache chief, near there. Ponce was a good friend of Cochise's and an excellent interpreter from Spanish to Apache. If he could be persuaded to go with them, too, his friendship and linguistic ability would be assets. After inspecting Cañada Alamosa, they found Ponce and his band gathering corn at the edge of a river. Ponce said he would go with Howard, too.

The small party of nine, Apache and American, moved south and west to Silver City, near Santa Rita del Cobre. The mines were prospering, and the town had a small hotel, where the travelers could spend the night in comparative comfort. But relations between the miners and the Apaches had never been good, and in the evening Howard learned that the citizens of Silver City planned to kill Ponce and Chie in the morning. He kept this fresh problem to himself, but he roused his men early on the following day, and the people of Silver City woke to find their intended victims gone.

One settler, however, raced after them. His brother had been killed by Apaches, and he was determined to take an Apache's life in return. Somehow he got ahead of the travelers without being seen and suddenly appeared on the trail in front of them with his gun drawn. The peace of the Southwest hung on that moment. If he killed Chie and Ponce while they were under the protection of Howard, no Apache would ever again trust an American. There was no time for the travelers to draw their own guns in defense, but Howard acted quickly and bravely. He spurred his horse and came between the settler and the Apaches, so that his own body protected them. Then he told the settler that if he wanted to kill the two Apaches, he would have to shoot President Grant's emissary first. This caused the man to stop; and seeing he could not get between Howard and the Apaches, he turned his horse and rode away. Howard's quick action not only saved the prospects of peace, it also earned him the respect and confidence of the two Apaches.

When the party reached the mountains of the Mogollon Rim, Chie went ahead and lit nine smoke signal fires. This was a sign to any Apaches that might be nearby that nine men had come in peace. In a little while, he began to bark like a coyote, and soon the listeners heard a bark in answer. Chie ran off in the direction of the sound and later came back with a small band of Chiricahuas. Water was short in the southern mountains, so they had come north for a while, and they were willing to talk to Howard. Their principal advice was that even nine men were several too many if they hoped to see Cochise. So Howard, who was willing to do anything to accomplish his mission, sent four men back to Tularosa, leaving only himself, his aide, Jeffords, Ponce, and Chie.

Turning southward, they reached the west side of the Dragoon Mountains, where they made camp, and Chie went on ahead to talk to the Chiricahuas. Cochise consented to let the three white men enter his mountains and sent two young Apaches to Howard as guides. But no one knew what his final intentions were—whether he would kill them or not. Although the Dragoon Mountains are a smaller range than the Chiricahuas, they are equally wild. Their foothills, too, are marked by eerie rock formations and boulders providing ideal cover for an Apache ambush. The guides led Howard into this strange land and took him five or six miles up a narrow canyon that suddenly opened into a grassy, forty-acre valley. It was surrounded on all sides by rock cliffs approximately a hundred feet high. The place was easily guarded, because the only way in or out was along the narrow bed of the stream that had cut the canyon.

The campground was filled with women, children, and a few old men, but there was only one warrior, an inauspicious sign. The warrior greeted them cordially but would not tell them where Cochise had gone or when he might return to talk to them, and he gave no indication whether the Chiricahuas planned peace or war.

Howard believed he had at least one afternoon and night to make a friendly impression on the Apaches, so he gathered some of the children around him, took out his notebook, and picked up an arrow. "What is that?" he asked, and they replied by repeating his own words, "What is that?" Then he said, "Apache," and they realized he wanted to know the Indian word, which he wrote down in his book when they told him. His interest in learning their language appealed to them, and soon they were bringing him all sorts of objects and telling him their Apache names. He played this game with them until dark, while the women watched and laughed. That night, when he lay down on the ground with his saddle for a pillow, some of the Apache children came and slept next to him. In the darkness that now covered the canyon, Howard whispered to his aide, "This does not mean war."

The next morning, Cochise appeared, accompanied by some of his family. When he saw Jeffords, he jumped from his horse and embraced the American twice. Jeffords told him who Howard was, and Cochise walked up to the general, shook his hand, and said good morning to him in Spanish. Then he led him to the council ground some distance off, where the warriors had gathered.

First Ponce and Chie told the men what they knew about Howard and what he had done for the other Indians, and Cochise seemed pleased at what the two Apaches said. Then they told Jeffords to ask Howard the purpose of his mission. To this, Howard replied that he had been sent by President Grant to make peace with the Chiricahuas.

Cochise replied by relating in detail his earlier encounter with Lieutenant Bascom and explained why this had led to years of war. But although he had killed ten Americans for every Apache lost, his tribe was growing smaller and smaller and would soon disappear. He was willing, therefore, to talk about peace, but it would take him at least ten days to get the scattered Chiricahua bands together and hold a council. Howard said he would remain as long as necessary to achieve peace. He also promised Cochise he would ride to Fort Bowie and personally tell the commander there to send out orders to all the troops that they were not to attack any of the Chiricahuas while they were assembling.

Howard set off across the Sulphur Springs Valley with Chie as a guide. They were mounted on mules and ahead of them they could see the notch in the line of mountains that marked Apache Pass. Chie was somewhat afraid, knowing the attitude of many soldiers toward Apaches, but the incident outside Silver

City gave him faith in Howard. They reached the fort safely, Howard gave his instructions to the commander, and the following day, he returned to the Dragoon Mountains, bringing with him a quantity of supplies.

Cochise had moved his camp to a new location, looking toward the west. On a high rock, about half a mile away, he had erected a tall pole on the top of which was a white rag that could be seen at a distance. To gain favor with the chief, Howard laid a piece of canvas on the ground and, using it as a table, served a meal for Cochise and several other important Chiricahuas. This act proved so popular that they ate this way three times a day while they waited for the warriors to assemble.

They came in small groups, for in true Apache fashion they had not left their mountains in large numbers. Day after day, one or more bands returned to the Dragoons. Among them was Geronimo, who was weary of life on the Warm Springs Reservation and had joined the Chiricahuas.

When all the warriors had arrived, Cochise called a council. The women sat side by side in a large circle with the men in the center. After some singing and discussion, Cochise told Howard they were willing to make peace.

The reservation that Howard and Cochise agreed upon was about seventy miles square and included the Dragoon and Chiricahua mountains. Except for one small adobe house at Sulphur Springs and, of course, Fort Bowie, which was to remain, there were no buildings on it. This land was to belong to the Chiricahuas for all time. Cochise laid down one other condition. He would accept no one as agent except Jeffords. This was a heavy responsibility to place on the scout, but Jeffords, in the cause of peace, accepted. On only one point did Howard and Cochise differ. Cochise wanted to know if making the treaty with the Americans prevented his warriors from raiding in Sonora. Howard replied that he had no authority to negotiate on behalf of the Mexicans, but the United States had peaceful relations with them and could not permit the Apaches to cross the border for warlike purposes. Cochise accepted this statement.

Meanwhile, at Howard's request, some of the officers had

come from Fort Bowie and camped ten or twelve miles away at Dragoon Springs, where they waited news about the treaty. The next day, Howard took Cochise and some of his warriors to visit them. Geronimo seemed as pleased as the others with the agreement they had reached and asked Howard if he could ride with him on his horse. When Howard said yes, Geronimo leaped up over the tail of the horse onto its back and then took another leap forward, so he could put his arms around Howard. In this fashion, they rode toward the men he had long considered his enemies.

When Geronimo saw the soldiers, however, Howard could feel him start to tremble; and Cochise was so nervous he had his warriors spread out in what Howard later described as "a sort of skirmish order." In this formation, they could go forward to attack, seek cover, or retreat. But no incidents occurred. The terms of the treaty were confirmed in the presence of the officers, and Howard was able to return to the East, leaving behind him greater peace than the Southwest had known for years.

XIV

More Broken Promises

MANY of the Apaches were dubious about the new arrangement, including Cochise himself. Fred Hughes, who was transferred to the new agency from Cañada Alamosa a few weeks after the treaty, later wrote: "I found the Indians upon my arrival still very timid, for it must be remembered these Indians had been constantly on the warpath for fourteen years when they made peace with General Howard. Some of the young warriors had been born and raised during the time the tribe had been at war with all mankind, and quite a number of them had no remembrance of when their tribe had been at peace. A few days after my arrival, Cochise made his first visit to the agency.

"To show how suspicious the old fellow still was, he came accompanied by about fifty warriors. They made their camp about half a mile from the agency but within sight. They then commenced sauntering up to the agency in squads of two's and three's until some fifteen or twenty had reached there. Then seeing everything was all right, they took Jeffords down to where Cochise was and brought him up."

But the chief's confidence in Jeffords proved justified. And although the Army, as permitted by the treaty, maintained the fort at Apache Pass and marched through the reservation, no soldiers attacked the Chiricahuas. The Nednis heard about the peace, and 200 of them came north to talk with Jeffords. After several days of conversation, they agreed to accept the same terms as Cochise.

But Jeffords was in a difficult position. The Apaches were too widely scattered to permit him to hold regular roll calls. He could not patrol the vast area covered by the reservation except with troops, and their presence would have set Cochise on the warpath again. And he was also dealing with many warriors who were not Chiricahuas. The reservation was in the corridor that had been used for years by other Apaches in their travels north and south, and they continued to pass through it. Many bands came from other reservations, and so did many bands that had not surrendered. To maintain control of this delicate situation, Jeffords had only diplomacy and his friendship with Cochise.

Nevertheless, the arrangement worked reasonably well—certainly better than the open warfare that had prevailed before. Early in 1873, Crook, who questioned the wisdom of the treaty, moved up troops and sent several of his most experienced officers to talk with Jeffords and Cochise. Apparently they were satisfied, for he took no further action.

About this time, the governor of Arizona Territory visited the chief and later wrote: "His height is about six feet, head large and well proportioned; countenance rather sad, hair long and black, with some gray ones intermixed. . . . He wore a shirt with pieces of cotton cloth about his loins and head, and moccasins covered his feet, which constituted his costume."

They talked about Lieutenant Bascom and the injustice of what he had done. Cochise also told of his liking for General Howard and explained that "for a long time previous the only friends he had were the rocks, that behind them he had concealed himself and they had often protected him from death by warding off the bullets of his enemies." He assured the governor that he was determined to remain at peace.

Geronimo had originally told Howard that he, too, was ready for peace, but after a few months on the reservation, he found he did not like the life. It was pleasant to be issued beef rations and to have food without working for it. It was not pleasant, however, to be under the scrutiny of the Americans or to be unable to travel away from the reservation without carrying a white man's pass. In a short time, he gathered his family and his belongings and moved back to New Mexico to be near the Warm Springs Apaches and Victorio.

Although Victorio was a great warrior, he was not a warlike man; and whenever he could, he tended to remain at peace. At this time, he was not fighting the Americans but was living again, by Howard's orders, at Cañada Alamosa. This was the land he loved so well, and as long as he could remain there, he was content. This unadventurous life did not please Geronimo either, and he soon returned to Mexico and joined Juh and those Nednis who had not come north to the Chiricahua reservation or who, like Geronimo, had also left it.

They made their camp in the mountains and spent a year conducting minor raids against the Mexican settlements. Although the potential danger was great, they hid their ranchería so carefully and moved through the desert and mountains so cautiously that the Mexican soldiers never found them. They then returned with some of their spoils to Arizona, where Jeffords, with the help of Cochise, was still maintaining the precarious peace.

In 1874, the delicate balance was upset when Cochise became seriously ill. The Apaches came in from the mountains and gathered in silent groups to wait word of their chief's health, but no medicine man had power enough to cure him. On June 8, Cochise died.

"I shall never forget their lamenting over Cochise's death," Hughes wrote later. "Quite a number of Indians were camped near the agency, mostly women and children, and they had evidently gathered there to await the news of their chief's death. When it came, the howl that went up from these people was fearful to listen to. They were scattered around in the nooks and ravines in parties, and as the howling from one ranchería would lag, it would be renewed with vigor in another. This was kept up through the night and until daylight next morning. Everything then became quiet, and throughout the next day almost the stillness of death reigned."

Some of the Apaches placed Cochise's body on a litter and carried it and his possessions into the Dragoon Mountains. Where they went no American knows, but they placed the body in a cave and screened the opening so no white man would ever find it. Then they returned to the other Apaches and joined in the difficult task of choosing a successor for Cochise.

Cochise had hoped his son Taza would become chief and that his other son, Nachez, would support his brother. A medicine man named Eskinya had different ideas, however, and although the wishes of Cochise were known, Eskinya attempted to become chief. Although he failed, his efforts split the tribe. The majority of the Chiricahuas followed Taza, but a group gathered around Eskinya. With this disruption in tribal politics, Jeffords began to lose his authority over the Indians, because he no longer had a single powerful friend to help him enforce the agency's regulations.

Problems were also developing at the San Carlos reservation. No agent seemed able to control the Indians there, and Crook had to intervene to maintain discipline. In 1874, the year Cochise died, Washington appointed a new agent at San Carlos, John Clum. An Easterner in his early twenties, Clum became agent largely through the accident of being a member of the Dutch Reformed Church, one of the religious denominations associated with President Grant's efforts to bring peace to the West. He had come to Santa Fe in search of adventure, and when the government was looking for a new agent, the church had suggested his name.

Although he knew nothing about Indians, he did know a great deal about people, and he realized Apaches were people, too, and might respond to sympathetic treatment. When he found Eskiminzin was again at peace with the Americans but had been placed in leg irons at the whim of an American officer, he had the leg irons removed, thus making a friend of the chief. He set up Apache courts to try cases against Apaches, and he established an Apache police force to maintain order.

The Apaches respected his efforts to let them govern themselves, and the policemen in particular were devoted and loyal to him.

He needed all the loyalty he could get, because in another switch in policy, Washington decided to concentrate more of the Apaches at San Carlos rather than leave them on the lands originally designated as reservations. This meant breaking the agreements made with several tribes, and it failed to take into consideration the Apaches' history or their way of life. Although they were related to each other, some of the tribes were not friendly. Concentrating them in one place often resulted in placing traditional enemies near each other. Furthermore, the land around San Carlos was not suited to the habits of many of them. They knew the desert well and traveled through it with ease, but they were not accustomed to spending entire summers in a climate as hot as the one at San Carlos. To many of them, San Carlos was little more than a deathtrap. Nevertheless, with the help of his native police, Clum succeeded in transferring the Indians who had lived near the Verde River and in assuming control of the agency at Camp Apache.

These changes had little appreciable effect on Geronimo's life. He visited New Mexico and Arizona regularly, but most of the time he was with Juh and the Nednis in Mexico. Without his knowing it, however, events were closing in on him. Jeffords never regained his control of the wilder elements among the Chiricahuas and other Apaches. To complicate the situation even further, his beef rations were cut, so he did not have enough meat for the Indians in his custody. This forced him to order them all off hunting, which further diminished his control. Geronimo and Juh had made one of their periodic trips north to visit their friends and were on the reservation at the time. They joined Eskinya's band, rather than Taza's, in moving into the Dragoon Mountains, where, far from Jefford's influence, the two factions of Chiricahuas began fighting among themselves.

Several Indians were killed, but Taza and Nachez, faithful to the wishes of their father, returned to the agency. Eskinya and his brother, Pionsenay, remained away, along with Juh and Geronimo. Although they disliked and distrusted white men, Eskinya and Pionsenay had made the acquaintance of the attendant at the Sulphur Springs stage station. He had a supply of whiskey and was willing to sell some of it to the Indians for ten dollars a bottle. This was dangerous business, and he certainly knew it, but the profit at that enormous price was attractive.

Filled with excitement after their recent fight, Eskinya and Pionsenay went to the station to buy liquor. After they had drunk it, they came back for more, but the attendant, realizing they were intoxicated, refused to sell them any. Thrown into a rage, Eskinya and Pionsenay killed both the attendant and his assistant and stole the arms and ammunition from the station as well as the remaining whiskey. Naturally, they started drinking it right away, and the next day they killed another American and stole some livestock. The peace Jeffords had built up was now broken. Since he no longer had Cochise to help him, he called on the Army. With its help, he cornered Eskinya and Pionsenay's band in the Dragoon Mountains, but he could not capture them.

Washington's reaction to the new crisis was to punish all the Chiricahuas for the acts of a few, and the government ordered John Clum to go to the Chiricahua reservation, remove Jeffords as agent, and take the Indians back with him to San Carlos.

Clum moved carefully. First, he obtained the cooperation of the Army. Crook had recently been transferred to the Department of the Platte, but his successor agreed to move the Sixth Cavalry into southern Arizona to reinforce the troops already stationed there. Clum planned, however, to avoid a direct confrontation between the soldiers and the Indians if possible. The soldiers were to come into action only if all else failed. He hoped he could accomplish his assignment with fifty-four Coyotero and Aravaipa Apaches, who were members of his police force.

At Tucson, he met with Frederick Hughes, who had worked with Jeffords and knew the Indians well. Hughes agreed to set out immediately for Fort Bowie. "I first met the two boys of

Cochise," he wrote, "informed them of the intentions of the government and advised them to go peacefully. They stated they were sorry, that neither they nor their band had been engaged in the recent outbreak, that the killing had been done by a band under the leadership of Eskinya. They would also consent to be removed to San Carlos but wanted me to try and get them a place above the reservation . . . so they could live apart from the other Indians. I promised to do all I could for them to that end."

Next Hughes talked to Eskinya, who freely admitted that he and his brother had murdered the two white men but pleaded they were drunk at the time and that the station attendant had abused them. He also said he and his brother would not go to San Carlos, but, if they were allowed to remain in the Chiricahua Mountains, would stay at peace with the Americans. Because Clum had not yet arrived at Apache Pass, Hughes returned to Tucson to give him a report of what the Apaches had said.

In the arguments among the Apaches, Juh and Geronimo naturally sided with Eskinya and Pionsenay. The San Carlos agency was too well controlled under Clum and too far from Mexico. To move there would be to destroy the life they were leading and liked so well.

The day Hughes returned to Fort Bowie from Tucson, they joined Eskinya in an attack on Taza's camp, which was twelve or fourteen miles from the pass. By doing so, they hoped to force Taza to join them on the warpath. The fighting was severe, with four or five dead on both sides. Eskinya was among those killed, and Pionsenay was wounded. Taza sent a messenger to Fort Bowie with news of this fresh outburst of violence, and as soon as it was dark enough not to be seen, Jeffords, Hughes, and thirty soldiers left the fort and went to Taza's assistance. They approached his camp in the darkness and found everything quiet, for Taza had successfully repulsed the attackers.

The next day, when Taza and the soldiers were on their way back to Fort Bowie, Juh, Geronimo, and the others returned to

Taza's campground but were greeted by a volley of shots fired by both Indians and soldiers. The joint opposition of Apaches and Americans made them realize any further fighting would be pointless, but they still did not want to go to San Carlos. On the other hand, they knew southern Arizona was filled with troops, so escape was all but impossible. The only hope was a resort to trickery.

They, therefore, made signs they wanted to talk to the white men and avowed they would go to San Carlos like the others. Taza and Nachez said they would meet with the Americans at Fort Bowie at nine o'clock in the morning, but Juh and Geronimo, trying to gain time, said they could not be there until four in the afternoon. Both factions kept their promises, but although Taza was ready to move immediately to San Carlos, Geronimo and Juh asked for twenty-day passes so they could gather their families. Twenty days of freedom was all they needed to get across the border and deep into the Sierra Madres. Clum talked to Hughes, and Hughes told him not to issue them. Geronimo and Juh then reduced their request to ten-day passes. Once again, on the advice of Hughes, Clum refused. Finally he did consent to give them passes for four days. Taking the precious papers, Juh and Geronimo raced back to their camp, killed their dogs, whose barking might reveal their whereabouts, and the old horses, which would slow them down, and headed for Mexico. Hughes surmised what they were up to. But Geronimo and Juh had wasted no time. When the troops arrived to intercept them, they were already gone. A few days later, Clum left for San Carlos with his scouts and the more than 300 Chiricahuas who had remained.

The events at Fort Bowie had little direct impact on Geronimo's way of living. Back in Mexico, he continued raiding the settlements and hiding in the mountains, just as he had done before. The only change occurred when he came north. Then, instead of visiting the Chiricahuas, he went to New Mexico and stayed in secret near the Warm Springs Apaches at the agency at Cañada Alamosa. Occasionally he revealed his presence by raiding some lonely ranch in Arizona or New Mexico, causing an uproar among the citizens. But no one knew where he hid, and the Army could not find him.

In February, 1877, he made his appearance among some of the settlements along the Rio Grande, where he was trying to sell some of the cattle he had stolen. There his band came across an Army lieutenant. Since the lieutenant did not have a sufficient force to attack Geronimo's warriors, he simply talked to them and was glad to get away alive. But during this brief encounter, he learned that Geronimo was then making his headquarters at Cañada Alamosa. Adhering strictly to military protocol, he gave the information to the general commanding the Department of Arizona, to which he was attached, instead of to the general in charge of New Mexico. When the general received the news, he sent it directly to the War Department in Washington, which in turn transmitted it to the Department of the Interior. Twenty-four days after the lieutenant had discovered Geronimo's hiding place, Clum received telegraphic instructions to take his Apache police to Cañada Alamosa and capture him.

The first that Geronimo knew of the Americans' plans was when Clum arrived at the agency, after having marched all the way from San Carlos on foot. As he had only twenty-two of his policemen with him, Geronimo did not regard him as a threat and readily accepted his invitation to come in and talk to him. Just at daybreak, Geronimo and the other warriors, all well armed, entered the parade ground at the agency to confront the white agent. Except for the chief of the Apache police, Clay Beauford, two agency employees, and Clum, there was not another white man within miles, for the soldiers Clum had previously requested had not arrived.

Clum lost no time in accusing Geronimo of having broken his word at Fort Bowie and told him he would now have to go to San Carlos. Just as flatly, Geronimo replied that he would not go and threatened the lives of Clum and his police if they attempted to make him. Almost imperceptibly, Clum raised his left hand and touched the brim of his hat. At this prearranged signal, the doors of the agency's commissary flew open and out came the first of more than eighty additional Apache police. Unknown to Geronimo, Clum had left this force behind when he first approached the agency, instructing them to come up after dark, when they could not be seen. Although taken by surprise, Geronimo was prepared to fight. Slowly he moved his thumb toward the hammer of the Springfield rifle he was holding in order to cock it. Clum noticed the gradual movement and dropped his right hand to the butt of his pistol. This was another prearranged signal. The original twenty-two police immediately raised their guns, aiming them directly at Geronimo and the other leaders among the warriors.

Geronimo realized he had been outmaneuvered. Just before his thumb reached the hammer, he hesitated. At that moment, a wild Apache cry broke out over the tense scene on the parade ground. An Apache woman, thinking Beauford was about to fire on the men, had thrown both her arms around his neck. Beauford, a powerful man, wrestled with her for a moment and threw her to the ground; but in the interval, the Apaches' attention had been distracted, and the remaining reserves had emerged from the commissary.

Clum now had Geronimo and his men caught in a potential crossfire, so Geronimo offered to talk further.

Clum insisted the Apaches must first give up their arms. Motioning to Beauford to keep Geronimo covered with his rifle, he moved forward and lifted Geronimo's gun from his arms. It was a bitter, humiliating moment for the Apache, one he would never forget. He glared at the white man who had so insulted him, but he was powerless. The police, following Clum's example, then removed the guns of several of the other leaders. And with that, the rest of the warriors laid down their arms.

Clum invited Geronimo and six other leaders to step up to the porch of the agency and sit down. Geronimo, he repeated, had broken his word once before. Now he and his leaders would be treated as prisoners until the time came to leave for San Carlos. Geronimo leaped to his feet, his eyes flaming defiance. His hand gradually reached for his knife, his only remaining weapon. With that knife he had fought many battles and killed many men in hand-to-hand fighting. Perhaps he could do so again. But before his fingers touched the handle, one of the Apache police jumped forward and snatched it away from him. At the same moment, twenty of the police cocked their rifles and aimed at him and the six other leaders. The police then took the knives away from the other men also.

Because the agency did not have a guardhouse, Clum ordered them placed in the corral with ten men on guard at all times. Before the order was effected, however, he had second thoughts. As they passed the blacksmith's shop, he remembered Geronimo's continued defiance right up to the last moment. So he asked the blacksmith to make leg irons for all seven men. The smith fashioned them out of wagon tires and linked them in pairs with eighteen-inch lengths of chain. Then he riveted one set on each of the leaders, and the police escorted them to their makeshift prison in the corral.

The next day, Victorio, who had heard something unusual was taking place at the agency, came to see for himself what was going on. Clum suddenly decided to take him to San Carlos, too. Above all things, Victorio loved the land around Cañada Alamosa, but he did not want war with the Americans. Reluctantly and sadly, he sent messengers to the Apaches' camps, telling them to assemble.

The seven shackled men were placed in wagons and went ahead. The rest followed within about a week. For Clum, it was a dangerous march. The soldiers he had sent for earlier had now arrived, but his Apache police resented them. News of an Indian raid farther south brought orders for him to send some of his police to that area. Finally, with only twelve soldiers and about twenty-five of his police, he proceeded to escort hundreds of resentful Indians a distance of more than 400 miles.

For the Apaches, the journey was a sad one. Most of them shared Victorio's love for Cañada Alamosa and dreaded the prospect of living at San Carlos. To make their situation worse, just before they set out, one of them came down with smallpox. The dread disease spread among them during the march, and on the way eight of them died of it. They faced other dangers, too. As they passed one mining town, the inhabitants, fearful of all Apaches, shot at them. But neither the police nor the soldiers took any retaliatory action. In fact, relations between the two groups of guards was tense. One night, open fighting broke out between them during a gambling game. The scouts overcame the soldiers and then, fearful they might be punished, took refuge among the other Apaches.

With each sad step of their moccasined feet, the Indians left their homeland farther behind. The tree-covered mountains and grassy uplands gave way to the desert. The land looked poor to them, and they saw no place in which to live. But they had to obey Clum's orders or go to war.

They reached the agency safely, and Clum found an unwelcome surprise waiting for him. During the years he had been agent he had used the military occasionally, but knowing how the Indians hated the soldiers, he had struggled hard against their intervention in reservation affairs. Indeed, at one time, he said he could handle the whole Apache problem with his police alone and at much less expense than the Army could. Some people in high office had supported him, but the government in Washington had again reversed its policy. Troops had returned to the agency with orders to conduct an inspection. Clum believed—and undoubtedly was correct—that the beef contractors were behind the move. In fact, one even told him as much. Without the Army, they would not grow rich, for if the soldiers were replaced by a handful of Apache police, they would lose a profitable market for their meat.

Clum's protests were of no avail. In spite of his record, which had been excellent, the Army remained in control, and in July, 1877, he submitted his resignation and moved to Tucson. Some people were sorry to see him go. The governor of Arizona, who had appreciated his effective efforts in bringing order to the territory, regretted his resignation openly; and numerous of the Apache chiefs foresaw trouble. One of these was Eskiminzin, who had become a devoted follower of Clum's. Beauford, the chief of the Apache police, resigned in disgust at the same time.

One man was happy, however, and that was Geronimo. Clum

had had little use for him, regarding him as a renegade and murderer who deserved to be hanged. While he remained as agent, he continued to treat Geronimo as a prisoner and kept him in irons. But within a few weeks after Clum's departure, the Army struck off the irons and set him free to live with his family.

Of all the Indians crowded into San Carlos—crowded, not by American standards, but by the Apaches'—the most unhappy were the Warm Springs Apaches. Neither Victorio nor his tribe could adjust to the change from their beloved Cañada Alamosa to the heat of San Carlos. Although they did not want war with the white men, they were restless and ready to break out.

The opportunity came on September 1, 1877, when Pionsenay slipped north without being seen and raided the reservation to rescue some of the Chiricahuas. During the confusion that followed, Victorio quickly made up his mind. With the troops occupied with Pionsenay's raid, the Warm Springs Apaches had the chance they had been waiting for.

Accompanied by Loco, one of the other leaders, Victorio fled from the reservation with more than 300 Warm Springs Apaches. They probably intended to head for Mexico, but the troops and the San Carlos police were less busy with Pionsenay than Victorio had expected. A group of scouts, police, and volunteers immediately chased and caught up with him. During the fight that followed, the Warm Springs Apaches were able to get away, but they lost all their horses. They moved northward, killing at least twelve ranchers and stealing stock, but the battle was a losing one. They had numerous skirmishes with the soldiers, and their casualty lists rose. Finally, they decided to surrender to the commander of Fort Wingate in New Mexico.

The Army did not know what to do with them. Fort Wingate was not equipped to hold them. To place them with the Navajos would only lead to trouble and bloodshed. And, above all, they could not go back to San Carlos, where the Indians were still in a state of uproar. With considerable wisdom, the Army decided to send them back to their old agency at Cañada Alamosa and keep them there until the Department of the Interior decided what to do. The general also promised Victorio he would take every step within his power to get permission for them to remain there.

At San Carlos, the agent who had succeeded Clum had his hands full, but he cooperated with the Army and received its help in return. He established subagencies, so the various tribes were not all clustered around one central point. And he made Geronimo captain of the remaining Chiricahuas, hoping to placate him and gain his support.

But Geronimo was restless and kept thinking of his friends who were again leading a free life. Liquor was forbidden at San Carlos, but it was available, and one day in 1878, Geronimo got hold of some, could not control himself, and drank too much. He began unjustly berating his nephew who was with him. Nothing the nephew said made any difference, and Geronimo continued his scolding in bitter terms. As a result of his uncle's words and probably also as a result of the depression that sometimes accompanies the overuse of alcohol, the nephew later killed himself. Geronimo was ashamed of himself, and his feeling of guilt added to his dislike of reservation life. The time had come, he believed, to leave San Carlos and return to Mexico. Gathering his family and some of the Chiricahuas, he left the reservation prepared to fight any white man who attempted to force him to return.

On the way south, the fleeing Chiricahuas encountered a wagon train, which was just what they needed to obtain supplies. The drivers were completely unaware of the danger they were in and were taken by surprise. The struggle was brief. In a short time, all the drivers were dead, and the Apaches were feasting on the food they had captured. Then they were on their way south again, racing against the troops they knew would be sent to intercept them.

Just north of the sanctuary offered by the Mexican border, the troops overtook them. The Apaches took cover behind rocks and fired at the troops from long range but with poor results. One old warrior told them they could never win in this fashion and urged them to charge. With him at their head, they ran toward the soldiers, but the fire they faced was so severe they were forced to retreat, rejoin their families, and continue the race to Mexico. After a few more skirmishes, they crossed the border and reached the safety of the Sierra Madres, where they resumed their raids against the Mexican settlements. This was the life, free of the heat of San Carlos, free of the impoverished land, and, most of all, free of the white men's restrictions.

Geronimo was wise to have left when he did, for the government in Washington had still learned nothing about Indians and particularly Apaches. At San Carlos, rations were short; the agent spent much of his time on his mining interests; nearby settlers were agitating to reduce the size of the reservation, particularly those areas that might contain minerals; and the agent was suspected of corruption. One investigation indicated he was collaborating with the beef contractors and taking other freedoms with the government's money, but the investigation suddenly halted.

At Cañada Alamosa, Victorio and the Warm Springs Apaches were living happily and at peace, but when the Department of the Interior finally got around to resuming charge of them, its officials insisted they return to San Carlos again. Some of them were compelled by the threat of force to do so, but Victorio slipped away with some of his warriors and hid in the high mountains of southern New Mexico. The weather was so severe, however, that he finally returned to the agency at Cañada Alamosa, willing to surrender if he would be permitted to live there. Once again, the officials were not clear what to do. They decided to send him to the Mescalero reservation, where some of the Warm Springs Apaches were already taking refuge. He agreed to go—it was better than San Carlos, in his opinion—but then changed his mind and took to the mountains once more. Life as a hunted fugitive was hard, so he again surrendered and said he would go to Mescalero.

The agent there agreed to have him, provided he remained at peace, and arrangements were made to bring back the Warm Springs Apaches who had earlier been taken to San Carlos. But the civilians were in no mood for peace. If the Department of the Interior and the Army would not punish the Apaches, they would. So they swore out a warrant for the arrest of Victorio on charges of murder. Victorio learned about it, and he knew what little chance he would have in front of an American jury. Hardly a rancher in the country would have acquitted him.

He was worried, and with the arrival of some soldiers and civilians on the reservation, he became convinced the agent had betrayed him. He accused the agent, but the agent paid no attention to him. Infuriated, one of the younger Apaches grabbed the agent by his beard and dragged him around the office. Then Victorio gathered his men—they numbered no more than seventy-five, if that—and their families and left the Americans' custody.

They moved down the lovely valley that leads up to the agency at the town of Mescalero, but they were not concerned with its beauty. After years of intermittent peace and fighting, Victorio had now declared war on all Americans, regardless of who they were. He led his people into the desert near Three Rivers, across the broad valley that contains the White Sands, those huge blowing dunes that glisten in the sunlight, to the San Andres Mountains and deep into the heart of the Black Range. These mountains were a natural fortress for the Apaches—wild, remote, not well known to the Americans, and containing forested uplands and enormous canyons. This was to be the refuge for the women and children during the coming days, while Victorio and his handful of warriors fought the Americans and raided for supplies.

Victorio had two unusual advisers. One was his sister Lozen, a beautiful woman who never married but fought with the warriors. She was courageous and skillful and, in the Apaches' opinion, she had magical power. She would stand with her arms outstretched, chant a prayer, and slowly turn around. By the sensations she felt in her arms, she could tell where the enemy was and how many they numbered. The other adviser was an old chief named Nana, a kindly grandfather known for his gentleness and wisdom and also for his skill on the battlefield. His grandchildren had difficulty in reconciling his reputation as a warrior with the gentle manner in which he treated them.

The weeks that followed were marked by some of the most intensive fighting in the Southwest. Victorio had repeatedly tried to make peace with the Americans. All he had asked was to be allowed to live in his homeland at Cañada Alamosa. The Americans had promised him he could and then had broken their promise several times. Now they had threatened him with a charge of murder. After all these years, his temper had at last exploded, and he saw his existence only in terms of preserving his people and killing Americans. With the help of Lozen and Nana, he proved a sagacious fighter. To save ammunition, for example, he laid an ambush in which American soldiers were killed by rocks rolling down on them. He dodged and twisted and turned. When the troops did encounter him, they could not pin him down; and after the fighting, they buried their dead and carried off their wounded. No one knew exactly how many white men were killed, but many estimates placed the number as high as 175. Then he left the field of carnage and fled to Mexico.

Although Geronimo and Juh disliked both Mexicans and Americans, they were having second thoughts about fighting them. The life of a fugitive, with every man's hand turned against them, was dangerous and unpleasant. At San Carlos, they at least did not have to post guards every night and fear their sleep would be broken at daylight by the sound of their enemies' bullets. Nor did they have to worry about starvation, for although rations might be short, the government supplied some food.

Winter came, and with it, more hardships. In January, 1880, while Victorio was still in Mexico, Juh and Geronimo, discouraged by all they had gone through, came north and crossed the border into the United States again. At the small outpost of Camp Rucker, they offered to surrender to the lieutenant in command and return voluntarily to San Carlos to make another attempt at reservation life.

That spring, while Geronimo and Juh remained on the reservation, Victorio went on the rampage again. In May, he even raided San Carlos itself, and, during a skirmish with the Chiricahuas, tried to persuade Geronimo and Juh to leave. Those two warriors refused, however. They had adjusted, at least temporarily, to reservation life.

But with or without the help of the Chiricahuas, the Warm Springs Apaches were determined to continue their warfare against the Americans and Mexicans. Victorio was like a man gone mad. He raided here and raided there. Wherever he went, he left bloodshed behind him. But the pressure of the combined Mexican and American offensives against him was beginning to tell. He was greatly outnumbered. No matter how many white men he killed, there were more to take their places, whereas whenever he lost a warrior, he was much weaker. When the Americans and Mexicans fired a volley, they could replace the bullets easily. Victorio had to count his, for he had no source of supply except what he could capture. Finally he decided to take refuge in the mountains of Mexico.

On his way, he stopped at Tres Castillos in northern Chihuahua. He knew about a lake in a grassy plain and, after consulting with Nana, decided the Mexicans would not find him there. But they soon learned where he was and planned to ambush him. In this offensive, they had been joined by representative American forces. Before attacking, they ordered the Americans to leave. Some of the Americans suspected it was because they planned to practice treachery.

Not counting two hunting and raiding parties that were out, only seventeen of the Warm Springs Apaches survived the subsequent massacre. Victorio was not among them. That night they gathered to care for their wounded in the darkness, for they did not dare to light a fire. One of the Apaches who was a small boy at the time later described the scene. When they had finished bandaging the wounded, he said, ". . . Nana talked to us. The chief had died as he would have wished—in defense of his people. . . . He had died as he had lived, free and unconquerable. We knew well the fate of Mangas Coloradas and of

Cochise. They, too, would have preferred death in battle; they would have envied Victorio. So—we were not to mourn for him. He had been spared the ignominy of imprisonment and slavery. . . . His courage was to be an inspiration of those left to carry on our race, and fortunately there were enough women and warriors that our people might increase.

"It was for us to rally and carry on the struggle."

XV
Revenge and Freedom

NANA was an old man with a lame leg, but on the death of Victorio, the warriors turned to him without hesitation as their new chief. In their present plight, they needed the best of leaders; and Nana was courageous, tireless, and, above all, wise.

Shortly after the massacre, some of the warriors who had been raiding for supplies came in. They had captured much ammunition, but one of them remarked bitterly that they had done so too late. Nana quietly replied that it was never too late as long as a single Apache remained alive to carry on.

During the fighting, the Mexicans had taken many prisoners, and Nana wanted to rescue them if he could. The soldiers had divided into two groups, one going south and the other north. The one going south was too large to be attacked by so few warriors, so he followed the smaller one. Because of his knowledge of the terrain, he was able to get ahead of the soldiers and lay a careful ambush, which the Mexicans unsuspectingly entered. There were too many men, however, for the Apaches to attack them, but the hidden Indians noticed the Mexicans had a single prisoner with them, a young Apache girl. As she passed, one of the Apaches whistled like a quail. The girl recognized the signal and looked in his direction. He whistled again. Quickly she dropped from her horse and ran toward him. A Mexican soldier came in pursuit, but the warrior shot him and saved the girl. Uncertain about the number of Apaches surrounding them, the soldiers fled.

Three days later, the Apaches returned to the site of the massacre. Many of the Indian bodies had been burned, and the rescued girl told them she had smelled much burning flesh, although she had not known the cause. Victorio's body was there, his ammunition belt empty and his own knife protruding from his heart. He had preferred suicide to the humiliation of capture.

Repeating Victorio's tactics, Nana led his band northward to the Black Range and from there conducted a series of raids against the Americans, both to obtain supplies and wreak revenge. The troops pursued him across the deserts and through the mountains. Ranchers formed posses to kill him. But the kindly old grandfather with the lame leg was too much for them. Approximately 1,000 soldiers were assigned the task of pursuing him, but they rarely even met up with him; and when they did, it was usually because they had ridden into an ambush.

The public was in an uproar. Newspapers and citizens denounced both the Apache leader and the Army officers who could not catch him. Outside the larger communities, no white man felt safe. When a rancher doused his lamp in the evening, he was not sure he would still be alive when the sun rose the next day. Passengers on stagecoaches kept their guns loaded and ready, while the drivers stayed alert for signs of the Indians. Prospectors were cautious about entering the remote regions and gave more care to their rifles than they did to their picks. The statistics were at best uncertain, with every death blamed on Nana; but during his brief campaign in 1881—a campaign that lasted only a few months—he killed approximately thirty to fifty Americans. Then, well equipped with ammunition and other supplies and with Victorio's death avenged, he melted away. Following trails known only to the Indians, he eluded both the American and Mexican troops and disappeared into the vastness of the Sierra Madres.

The outbreaks of Victorio and Nana should have taught the

Americans that, after years of warfare and bloodshed, the Apaches were still capable of meeting force with force, violence with violence. But they did not. Instead of improving conditions at San Carlos and making surrender more attractive, the government permitted the situation at the agency to deteriorate. The new agent was J. C. Tiffany from New York and, like Clum, also a member of the Dutch Reformed Church. When Juh and Geronimo warned him that additional outbreaks would occur if more beef was not issued, he tried to get additional appropriations for meat and took several superficial steps on the Indians' behalf, building a school, digging irrigation ditches, and allowing them to disperse more widely over the reservation. But he also, as several subsequent inspections revealed, indulged in extremely questionable practices in purchasing beef, thus reducing the amount that might have been obtained with the available money, and committed a number of other irregularities that left his honesty open to question.

Later a grand jury in Tucson had this to say about him: "For several years the people of this Territory have been gradually arriving at the conclusion that the management of the Indian Reservations in Arizona was fraud upon the government; that the constantly recurring outbreaks of the Indians and their consequent depredations were due to the criminal neglect or apathy of the Indian Agent at San Carlos. . . . Fraud, peculation, conspiracy, larceny, plots and counterplots seem to be the rule of action on this agency." With these strong words, the grand jury proceeded to accuse Tiffany of paying for supplies that were never received, charging the government for rations in the names of Indians who were not on the reservation, using government tools and wagons for personal gain, and hiring out Indians, at the government's expense, to work in privately owned coal mines.

If the agent himself was not doing much to solve the Apache problem, neither were the nearby settlers. Some of them upstream from the reservation diverted enough of the Gila River's water into their own fields to dry out those of the Apaches. And every time anyone suspected the existence of minerals on the reservation, the whites would claim the land. Usually these claims were admitted, because the boundaries had never been surveyed. Congress, in one of its niggardly moods, refused to pay the cost of a survey. This slight expenditure might, in the end, have saved hundreds of lives and thousands of dollars.

As a result of these abuses, many of the Apaches were growing restless, Geronimo and Juh among them. The white man's ways were not theirs, and conditions on the reservation offered them little hope. Tiffany was sitting on a potential explosion that would require only the slightest spark to set it off.

That spark was supplied by an odd mixture of a medicine man named Noch-ay-del-klinne and some badly taught Christianity. He had gone to school in Santa Fe, where he became interested in the white man's religion, particularly in the story of the Resurrection. The idea of the dead coming to life fascinated him, but he did not see why this remarkable phenomenon should be limited solely to Christ.

On his return to the reservation, he became a minor medicine man, a dreamy mystic, who spent much of his time alone in the wilderness but who was regarded by everyone as completely harmless. By June, 1881, however, he had gained a curious ascendancy over the Apaches. He made his home in the mountains at Cibicue Creek about forty miles beyond Fort Apache. To this lonely spot, the Indians flocked by the hundreds to see him, and Tiffany began to receive reports of strange activities. Noch-ay-del-klinne, he heard, was describing conversations he had had with long-dead chiefs and was promising to resurrect several of them.

Tiffany sent his Apache scouts to investigate what was going on. When they returned, they had a surly attitude toward white men, had either given away or lost their arms, and would not tell the agent what Noch-ay-del-klinne was doing. So Tiffany ordered the medicine man to report in person at the San Carlos agency. Noch-ay-del-klinne refused to come. General Eugene A. Carr, in command at Fort Apache, ordered him to report to the fort. Again Noch-ay-del-klinne refused. Angry and afraid,

Tiffany requested Carr to arrest the medicine man and bring him back dead or alive. Of the many mistakes Tiffany made as agent, this was probably the most serious. Noch-ay-del-klinne was certainly stirring up the Indians to some extent, but a direct confrontation between his followers and the Army was bound to result in trouble.

Because he questioned the loyalty of his scouts, Carr at first considered leaving them at Fort Apache but decided he could never find Noch-ay-del-klinne without their help. They, in turn, accepted the assignment of going with him but only with great reluctance. Carr was extremely nervous and, in addition to the scouts, took eighty soldiers with him to arrest the single Indian. As Clum could have told him, the presence of so many troops would not be reassuring to the Apaches.

After reaching the valley through which the Cibicue Creek runs, Carr divided his force in two and warily approached Noch-ay-del-klinne's dwelling place. About twenty warriors were standing around when Carr, speaking through his interpreter, announced he had come to take Noch-ay-del-klinne back to Fort Apache. The medicine man said he had no objection to going. He would have gone before, he quietly explained, except he had had a patient who needed tending. Now, however, the patient was cured.

Suddenly, without any apparent reason, the warriors grew tense. Perhaps the interpreter made some mistake in his translation. The soldiers thought a fight was about to start; but several of the scouts, in voices loud enough for the rest to hear, assured Noch-ay-del-klinne he would not be hurt. With their words, the Apaches relaxed, and the crisis passed.

In direct contradiction to his scouts' assurances, Carr almost immediately warned the medicine man he would be killed if he tried to escape or if the others attempted to rescue him. Then he did a curious thing. He departed with forty-six of the soldiers to make camp about two miles away, leaving the remainder of his men and the scouts to follow with Noch-ay-del-klinne. But Noch-ay-del-klinne was not finished eating. Finally one of the officers impatiently ordered the soldiers to bring Noch-ay-del-klinne along, whether he was ready or not. This command created resentment among the assembled warriors.

Hurrying down the trail, the scouts, troops, and their prisoner caught up with Carr just as he was making camp. Some of the Apaches were following, and what happened next occurred so quickly the sequence of events is not entirely clear. Shots were fired, the Apaches captured many of Carr's horses, which had been set out to graze, several scouts deserted to the other side, some soldiers were killed, and a fight was on.

Many Americans who were familiar with the Apaches' ways thought the battle must have started inadvertently. Some of the younger warriors had perhaps wanted only to come close enough to talk to Noch-ay-del-klinne before he left. Because of Carr's show of military strength and his abrupt manner, the Apaches had been upset, and their tension had spread to the soldiers. As the warriors had approached, someone had grown nervous and fired a shot. Certainly the Indians did not fight in deadly earnest. For if they had, as Crook commented when he heard the news, they would have wiped out Carr's command.

More and more Indians came down from the mountains to join the others. In the midst of the confusion, some of the soldiers noticed Noch-ay-del-klinne apparently attempting to crawl away from the camp. Instead of trying to halt him, they deliberately shot and killed him in spite of the scouts' earlier assurances that he would not be hurt. The battle lasted until dark. The next day, Carr returned to Fort Apache, but the outburst of violence at Cibicue Creek had ignited the tempers of the Indians. Past wrongs were recalled, and several bands went on the warpath. They ambushed four Americans close to Fort Apache, shot three soldiers only eight miles away, and raided at least one ranch, killing several of the white occupants and running off with stock. Among his other contributions to the troubles at San Carlos, Carr lost 3,000 rounds of ammunition to the Apaches.

Rumors flew everywhere. The report reached San Carlos that Carr and all his men had been killed. Orlando Willcox, commanding general in Arizona, fell into a panic and rushed as many soldiers as he could possibly spare to San Carlos and Fort Apache and brought others in from the east and the west. This show of strength impressed some of the Indians. Five of the mutinous scouts surrendered voluntarily. In return, the Army sentenced two of them to Alcatraz, then a military prison, and hanged the other three. But the presence of so many troops and Willcox's swift retaliation made many of the other Apaches more restless and nervous than ever before.

Juh, Geronimo, and Nachez were particularly disturbed by the large numbers of troops entering the reservation and wondered openly whether this show of force was directed against the Chiricahuas and the Warm Springs Apaches. When they mentioned their fears to Tiffany, he tried to explain them away. But the events that Carr and Willcox had set in motion could not be stopped.

A group of White Mountain Apaches, suspected of having taken part in the fight at Cibicue Creek, had been ordered to surrender. They did so and were given their freedom on parole. Suddenly and without apparent reason, the Army revoked the parole and sent three troops of cavalry to bring them back to Fort Apache. The band had moved to the subagency near the Chiricahuas, so Geronimo and Juh saw the soldiers ride up, armed and ready for battle. It was the day rations were given out, and the White Mountain Apaches asked the major in command for time to draw their supplies of beef and flour. The major refused this reasonable request and started to move against them with his troops. Some of the White Mountain Apaches ran to the camp of the Chiricahuas and told their confused version of what was happening.

Panic seized the Chiricahuas and Warm Springs Apaches. After hurried consultations, many of them prepared to flee south that night with Juh, Geronimo, and Nachez, although Loco, chief of the remaining Warm Springs Apaches on the reservation, refused to join them with his band. (The Indians called him Loco because he believed peace with the Americans was possible.)

Under starlit skies and moving rapidly but quietly, the

Apaches set forth on their race to the Mexican border. As soon as the Army learned of their departure, it tried to intercept them but met them only once. A large detachment of soldiers under the personal command of General Willcox caught up with the rearguard south of San Carlos shortly after they had attacked a wagon train and killed seven Americans. The Apaches scattered among the rocks and dared the soldiers to come and get them. In an effort to do so, the Americans lost three dead and two wounded without apparently inflicting a single casualty on the Indians. That night, the Indians pressed a vicious attack on Willcox's men, sometimes coming as close as ten feet from the Americans. It appeared to the soldiers to be a major assault, but it was only an effort to distract their attention while the women and children got away.

As soon as they had, the Apaches broke off the fighting, and in the night, they continued their race southward. Willcox was unable to stop them. Following their trails through the mountains and over the deserts, they avoided being seen by the Americans, crossed the border into Mexico, and reached the refuge of the Sierra Madres, where they joined Nana and his band.

They were glad to be back in their mountain fortress again, away from the heat and dust of San Carlos and the presence of the troops they hated so much. But they missed the families and friends they had left behind. In January, 1882, they sent messengers to Loco and the remaining members of the tribe saying they would soon come to get them. Loco was not disturbed, but some of the other Apaches, who were attempting to stay at peace, were nervous about the prospective raid on the agency.

They told Al Sieber, chief of the Apache scouts, and he told Tiffany. Tiffany did not think such an attempted rescue was possible and believed he exercised complete control over the Apaches. But he did tell Willcox, and the general did not share the agent's confidence. He alerted all the post commanders, sent two cavalry troops south to try to intercept them, and brought in troops from New Mexico.

The raiding party started north in April, slipped past the soldiers' patrols without being seen, and reached the vicinity of San Carlos on April 17. The next morning, they struck. One of the Apaches who was then a boy on the reservation later described the attack. "Just as the sun was beginning to shine on the distant mountain tops, promising a hot day," he wrote, "we saw a line of Apaches spread out along the west side of camp and coming our way with guns in their hands. Others were swimming horses across the river or pushing floating logs ahead of themselves. One of their leaders was shouting, 'Take them all! No one is to be left in the camp. Shoot down anyone who refuses to go with us! Some of you men lead them out.'

"The suddenness of the attack, its surprise effect, and the inhuman order from one of the chiefs calling for the shooting of people of his own blood threw us all into a tremendous flurry of excitement and fear. We did everything they told us to do. We were given no time to look for our horses and round them up but were driven from our village on foot. We weren't allowed to snatch up anything but a handful of clothing and other belongings."

During the raid, one American and one Indian lost their lives. They were Albert Sterling, chief of the San Carlos police, and one of his scouts, who made an abortive attempt to head off the Nednis and Chiricahuas. Some of the Warm Springs Apaches were saddened by the sight of a warrior holding Sterling's boots, for the police chief had been good to them.

The predicament of the captive Indians was described by the boy. "None of our Warm Springs Apaches had weapons. This, with the brutal shooting of the two scouts, convinced us that we were helpless in the hands of the Nednis. We told ourselves that our safety depended on keeping quiet and not trying to escape. We were filled with gloom and despair. What had we done to be treated so cruelly by members of our own race?

"Our outlook was all the blacker because we realized that the officers at the agency would blame us for the killings which had occurred there and would probably think that we ran away on our own accord. We felt we could not return to the agency even if we could get away from the wild Indians. So the future held for us only hard flight through the mountains and desert under constant pursuit by the troops."

While some of the warriors fell behind to serve as a rearguard, the leaders drove their prisoners quickly along the Gila River for a few miles and then turned north toward the Gila Mountains. Their trail brought them close to Fort Thomas, and the colonel in command sent two companies of cavalry on their track. The troops followed the fleeing Indians until the Apaches adopted their old tactic of making the pursuit more difficult by scattering in every direction. At this, the soldiers gave up and returned to the fort. They claimed they had run out of provisions after so short a time in the field, but the true reason for their negligence may have lain in the colonel's depressed state of mind. He had been in poor health and only eight months later committed suicide.

When the Warm Springs Apaches reached the mountains, the rearguard overtook them, and they all rested for a while at a spring. Then the leaders announced they would have to march overnight. At midnight, they came to another spring Geronimo knew about and stopped there to drink. None of the Indians had had anything to eat, so a party of warriors went off to raid a nearby sheep ranch. Ordinarily they would have contented themselves simply with stealing the animals they wanted, but they were angry and killed the seven white men, one woman, and two small boys they found. One small girl was spared only because the Indian wife of one of the Apache sheepherders pleaded for her life.

The next morning, the raiders rejoined the main party of Apaches, bringing with them several hundred sheep, which they promptly roasted and ate. The leaders then held a council to decide on the best means of getting back to Mexico. They had successfully fought off the Apache police from San Carlos and had evaded the troops from Fort Thomas, but they knew that soon the whole country would be up in arms against them and every soldier dedicated to their defeat. If they were to escape, they had to move much faster, and to do this they needed horses, particularly for the women and children.

Two more raids gave them enough horses to move faster. Their goal was to reach the wilderness of the Chiricahua Mountains, making the first part of the journey by way of the Peloncillos. The northern portion of these are known as the Steins Peak Range and end at the small Southern Pacific Railroad town of Steins. This was a familiar route to the Apaches, and it was in these mountains that they had scared Walker's party into turning east. Once they reached the southern tip of the Steins Peak Range, they could cross the San Simon Valley and be in the Chiricahuas.

But the Army, in spite of the public's denunciations of its ineffectiveness, was making an effort to cut them off before they reached the safety of the Mexican border. Lieutenant Colonel George A. Forsyth, with six companies of cavalry, had been ordered west from New Mexico. He went first to Lordsburg, New Mexico, and then on to the town of Steins, where the Army sent him a desperately needed tank car of water for his horses and men. All the time, he had been searching for signs of the Apaches' northward route, thinking they might follow the same course on their way home, but his scouts had found nothing.

On the morning of April 23, he decided to move north to the Gila River, taking the main body of his men up the more easily traveled Animas Valley, while a corporal and six scouts—two Mojaves and four Yumas—under Lieutenant D. N. McDonald, searched the southeastern end of the Steins Peak Range for signs of the Apaches. McDonald soon came across the trail of a small band moving northward and decided to follow it, thinking it had been made by a group of reinforcements coming to join the main body. The trail led through the heart of the mountains over rugged country and through narrow canyons. The chances of an ambush were so great that McDonald changed the usual order of marching. Instead of following the trail in single file, he ordered the best scout, Yuma Bill, to go ahead, while he followed close behind. His other scouts were sent out on either side as flankers. Although the terrain limited the distance the flankers could move from the trail, they at least offered some protection against an ambush.

After traveling about twelve miles, they came to a ridge capped by rock that lay directly across their path. The only way to get past it was to follow a narrow canyon that ran through it but whose steep sides eliminated all possibility of using flankers. McDonald was ready to run the risk of an ambush, but Yuma Bill pointed out some wisps of smoke hanging above the ridge. They were so faint that McDonald could barely see them even when Yuma Bill told him where to look, but they indicated the Apaches had camped on the ridge and had extinguished their fires on seeing the approach of the Americans.

A wiser man would have waited where he was while he sent word back to the main body of troops, but McDonald ordered his corporal to go and inform Forsyth while he himself prepared to advance, leading his handful of scouts. The scouts, however, had a different view of the situation. Even Yuma Bill, one of the bravest, refused to march on, so McDonald went by himself.

But the band of Apaches thought they had not put out their fires quickly enough and that the wisps of smoke still remaining would warn the soldiers and make an ambush impossible. So they retreated, and when McDonald came to their campground, he found it empty. Yuma Bill, who regretted having left the lieutenant alone, joined him and, after looking around, decided the Apaches had left the area.

On the basis of Yuma Bill's evaluation, McDonald persuaded the other scouts to continue to march. Because the land opened out again, McDonald was able to use flankers once more and proceed with greater safety. In three miles, the trail grew broader, and it was obvious more Apaches had joined the original band. The two Mojave scouts became so frightened that they would not keep up with the others but lagged in the rear. The corporal had now returned; but Forsyth, since McDonald was apparently following only a small band moving north, remained in the valley.

Continuing along the trail, McDonald came upon two prospectors who, he hoped, might be able to give him information.

But they were so overcome with terror as to be incoherent. McDonald advised them to go to Lordsburg and started on his way again. Because he had seen the general direction of the trail in the distance, he decided to take a short cut and pick it up later. But they did not rejoin it as quickly as they had expected, and Yuma Bill said the Apaches must have turned deeper into the mountains. Pointing to a large rock several hundred feet in length that lay at the foot of a mountain spur, he assured McDonald they would find the trail between the rock and where they were now standing.

McDonald would have liked to have resumed his former marching formation with flankers on either side, but his Indians were becoming more and more nervous, and he felt it important to show no signs of fear himself, so they rode grouped together, three scouts on one side of McDonald, Yuma Bill on the other, and the corporal in the rear, while the two Mojaves continued to remain far behind. At least, McDonald consoled himself, in the event of an enemy attack, the laggards might escape and ride to tell Forsyth.

The hot sunlight splashed on the mountains of the Steins Peak Range, as the eight soldiers and scouts rode toward the rock. Behind them, the Animas Valley stretched flat in the distance toward Lordsburg and Canador Peak, and its alkali flats shone bright under the desert sun. All was quiet except for the sound of the horses' hooves, the creaking of leather, and the occasional jangle of a bit when a horse tossed its head. War seemed far away, but on the top of that rock twelve to fifteen Apaches were waiting with their guns ready as the soldiers came nearer and nearer. In the foothills just behind them were an even larger number, and in a canyon deeper in the Steins Peak Range, but not far away, were yet more. For the Apaches McDonald had been trailing had met the main band returning from San Carlos.

The soldiers were within a few feet of the rock before they noticed the original Apache trail they had been following. It skirted the base of the rock and disappeared behind it. At this critical moment, their attention was distracted by the sight of two Indians who were walking together about a half mile off. Fearful of being seen by them and unaware of the greater danger closer by, the soldiers hid behind the rock and peered around the corner of it at the distant Apaches. Because their view was poor, Yuma Bill decided to look over the top.

As soon as he did, the Apaches hidden on top opened the fire they had held so long. Their bullets immediately killed the three Yuma scouts and wounded Yuma Bill. By pure luck, McDonald jerked his head just at the moment the Apaches began their volley, so their shots missed him. He turned and raced down the foothills at runaway speed, unable either to check or control his horse, while Yuma Bill managed to stay in the saddle and follow him. The corporal in the rear was in no immediate danger of being struck, and the two Mojaves were safely out of gunshot.

About fifty yards away, McDonald was able to check his horse and wheel around. At the same time, the Apaches who were hidden on the slopes behind the rock opened fire. One bullet passed through the lieutenant's hat and another scraped his chin, but he was unharmed. Notwithstanding the new volley, McDonald paused long enough to fire at the Apaches on the rock and drive them to cover. Although he was wounded, Yuma Bill turned his horse at the same time and stood up in his stirrups to fire one last shot at his enemies. Then he slowly fell forward on the neck of his horse and slid to the ground, dead.

McDonald and the corporal raced together down the slopes of the foothills toward the plains, rejoined the two Mojave scouts, and found the two prospectors. They mounted these two men on the horses of the dead scouts and told them to ride as fast as they could to the safety of Lordsburg. Then, determined to make a stand, the men began digging pits before the Apaches attacked them. Forsyth, who was still marching up the flat valley, had sent out additional scouts along the slopes. Some of these heard the sound of fighting and came to McDonald's aid. Although they were almost in a panic, McDonald quieted them and put them to work digging.

The Apaches did not attack immediately but paused long enough to mutilate the bodies of the three dead Yuma scouts. Then they dragged the corpses to the place where Yuma Bill lay dead, built a hot fire of dry brush, and burned the bodies in it. While they celebrated their victory, they gestured toward McDonald as though they were daring him to come and fight them.

McDonald had with him the fastest horse in his troop, so he told one of the Mojaves to ride to Forsyth as quickly as possible, while he remained behind and held the Apaches in check. The scout galloped off; and McDonald, wanting to set an example for his frightened men, climbed out of the rifle pits and crawled unobserved toward the celebrating Apaches. When he was within several hundred yards of them, he carefully piled some small rocks in front of his position to serve as a barricade. In a short time, two Apaches, who had detached themselves from the others, came riding in his direction. McDonald raised his sights to 500 yards, aimed carefully, and fired. One of the Apaches fell from his horse; the other turned and galloped back to his friends.

Because they knew about the presence of Forsyth's six troops of cavalry in the valley, the Apaches realized a major engagement was likely and that the killing of McDonald, since he had eluded their ambush, was relatively unimportant. Forsyth's scouts now knew where they were. Yet they could not retreat back to the Gila River, for the soldiers were out from every garrison, combing the country for them. So they sent the women, children, and old men to the crest of the Steins Peak Range, where they would be safe during the fighting, and took up a strong position in a U-shaped canyon, occupying the higher slopes where they could fire down on the Americans. Although they had left the reservation reluctantly, the Warm Springs Apaches were now so thoroughly implicated that they had to cooperate with the Chiricahuas and Nednis.

McDonald's scouts, anxiously awaiting help, became convinced that the first courier, in spite of his fast horse, had been intercepted, and they insisted that McDonald himself, along with the corporal, go in search of help. An Apache outpost spotted them and raced in pursuit. The two white men leaned forward in their saddles and urged their horses on. To the Indians' dismay, the Americans' horses were so much faster that the soldiers could even pause to breathe them and still stay ahead.

In the Animas Valley east of the Steins Peak Range are several alkali flats. In the rainy season, these depressed areas in the floor of the valley fill with water and become short-lived, shallow lakes. The rest of the year, they are dry and devoid of vegetation, so they offer no cover. The Apaches saw the Americans dash to the center of one of them and dismount, apparently prepared to kill their two horses and use their bodies as breastworks. Such a position in the barren flat could be a strong one, and the Apaches stopped to consider the best way to attack. As they did so, firing could be heard at the southern end of the flat, and the two Americans noticed the Apaches start withdrawing toward the mountains. In a short time, an Indian came riding in McDonald's direction, mounted on one of the few horses left at the rifle pits. McDonald at first thought the pits had been taken and the horse captured, but he then realized the Indian was one of the Mojave scouts he had left behind. Hearing the shooting, the Mojaves, having overcome their original cowardice, had decided to leave the pits and come to McDonald's rescue. The Apaches had pursued them, and had been fighting them at the southern end of the flat.

But the Apaches had quickly lost interest in both McDonald and his small band of scouts. The courier he had sent out earlier from the rifle pits had eluded them and reached Forsyth, who was now galloping to their rescue with his six troops of cavalry. To Geronimo and the other leaders, the time had come to assemble all the warriors in the canyon they had selected and make ready to defend their women and children against this larger number of soldiers.

With the arrival of so many men, the tide of battle had turned in favor of the Americans; and Forsyth took the offensive, advancing toward the canyon held by the Apaches. The terrain was so rugged he could not use his horses, so, well out of rifle range of the Apaches, he ordered his men to halt and dismount. One troop was to remain and guard the horses; two were to conduct a flanking operation on the left; two more were to flank on the right; the sixth and remaining troop was to advance up the canyon.

The Apaches had taken up a position on the left side of the canyon and on a tumble of rocks in the center of it, which was connected by a much lower ledge of rocks to the left wall. The desert heat was oppressive and the men were tired, but Forsyth, rather than let the Apaches escape under the cover of darkness, ordered an immediate attack. After an hour of strenuous climbing, the Americans outflanked the Apaches and forced them to abandon their position and move back up the canyon, where they took up another position. More fighting followed, and once again, the Americans outflanked the Apaches, who retreated higher into the mountains. The battle was one of maneuvers rather than spectacular charges. Forsyth had no desire to sacrifice his men needlessly and held them back until he commanded the positions the Apaches held. The Apaches were not willing to fight as long as they could still retreat. And so the battle raged all afternoon. In addition to the four scouts under McDonald, several other Americans were killed, and six or eight were wounded. The Apaches, too, suffered casualties, but not enough to impair their fighting strength.

Around five o'clock in the afternoon, the terrain had become so rough and the day so late that Forsyth decided to break off the fighting. His next move depended on the identity of the Apaches he had been battling. Some of his officers believed they were the main band under Geronimo, in which case he should turn south. Others thought it was a smaller band coming to Geronimo's aid, in which case he should turn north and try to cut Geronimo off from the border. Fortunately for the Apaches, he agreed with the latter opinion, largely because he had seen no trace of Loco's carefully hidden women and children. With that misjudgment, he handed the victory to the Apaches, for they had gained what they wanted—access to the Chiricahua Mountains.

That night, when darkness fell over the desert and the stars shone brilliantly in the clear sky, the Apaches began to move down the slopes of the mountains, headed in a southwesterly direction. Forsyth, meanwhile, was on the other side of the range, prepared to march north. When the Indians reached the San Simon Valley, they followed the tracks of the Southern Pacific Railroad west for eight miles and then turned south and entered the foothills of the Chiricahua Mountains south of the entrance to Apache Pass. Some of them appeared on the outskirts of the mining town of Galeyville, near present-day Paradise, killed a deputy sheriff, destroyed some tents, and threw the inhabitants into such a panic that the newspapers reported that thirty-five whites had been slain instead of the one.

From there, the Apaches continued south through the wild and beautiful country of the Chiricahua foothills, a land marked by strange rock formations, deep canyons, and the high ridges of mountain spurs. Al Sieber, chief of scouts, was close on their trail. Because he was accompanied by only one or two men, he could not attack the Apaches and grumbled that the Army never seemed to have enough men in the right place at the right time. Many miles behind him were Captain William A. Rafferty from Fort Bowie and Captain Tullius Cicero Tupper from San Simon Station. They had joined forces in the foothills of the Chiricahua Mountains, but the Apaches had already left in the direction of Cloverdale, New Mexico. And behind them was Forsyth, who had learned, while marching north in the Animas Valley, the true identity of the band he had engaged. On receipt of the news, he returned to Steins, where the railroad brought him two more tank cars of water for his men and horses. After a brief rest, he picked up the Apaches' southward trail. In the Chiricahuas, he was joined by another troop of cavalry under Captain Adna R. Chaffee. The Army now had enough soldiers chasing Geronimo and Juh, but as Sieber had commented so wryly, they were not in the right place, for the Chiricahuas had reached the Peloncillo Mountains near the Mexican border. In a short time, they would be across it and safe, for relations between the United States and Mexico were strained, and Mexico had expressly forbidden the entrance of American troops into its territory.

By forced night marches, the Apaches arrived at the border long ahead of the soldiers, crossed it, and began to relax their guard. Although they still moved only at nighttime, they did not go as fast and they allowed the younger ones to sing songs and race each other while they traveled. When they were about twenty-five miles northwest of Janos, they stopped to camp by a small butte near some hills. Close by was a marsh, where they could water their stock. The leaders decided to let their people rest after the long, hard journey from San Carlos, so they stayed for two days, spending much of their time in singing and dancing.

At dawn on the third day, they were awakened by the sound of shots. The warriors, taken unaware, grabbed their guns and rushed to the top of the butte to defend the women and children in the camp, now caught in the crossfire of their men and the enemy. In just a few minutes, hundreds of rounds of ammunition poured into the camp from a hill that was about 400 yards away, while the Apaches, to their dismay, saw a detachment of American cavalry charging toward them.

The sanctity of the border had been broken. On arriving at it, Tupper, who was senior to Rafferty, had decided to cross it regardless of the consequences to his career. As he saw it, the Apaches had killed numerous Americans and would eventually return to kill more. So why should he be stopped in his pursuit by an artificial line drawn on a map? He did not really have enough men to assault such a large band of Apaches, but he correctly guessed the Indians would not expect an American attack on the far side of the border and therefore he would have the advantage of surprise.

Their two-day rest gave him the opportunity to catch up with them, and he had arrived near the butte the night before. In the early morning hours, some of the scouts had climbed to a hill that overlooked the butte, while one troop of cavalry took up a position that would prevent the Apaches from escaping to the plains and the other made the first charge.

In spite of the heavy fire of the Apaches, Tupper's men kept advancing toward the camp. The Indians were so shaken by the unexpected attack that they shot too high. Otherwise they would have cut down the cavalry and demolished Tupper's command. As it was, his men almost reached the camp before the Apaches finally forced them to withdraw slowly and rejoin the other troop. Sieber and some of his scouts, however, climbed into a small sink about 150 yards from the camp, thinking they could hold this forward position.

The battle had now come to a standoff. The Americans lacked enough men to storm the Apaches' camp. The Apaches apparently underestimated Tupper's audacity and thought he had a stronger force than he actually did. So instead of launching a counterattack, they remained where they were, hoping for a chance to slip away to the hills to the west. For several hours, there was desultory fire on both sides. Loco called to the scouts, hoping he could persuade some of them to desert, but none did. One of the women among the Warm Springs Apaches mistakenly believed her son was among the scouts. She climbed to the highest point on the butte, where she was in plain sight, and cried out to him that the Warm Springs Apaches were prisoners, not willing participants in the battle. But the Americans did not understand her and shot and killed her.

They also made a daring raid on the Apaches' horses, which were at the marsh. Cutting between them and the butte, they were able to make off with more than seventy. This was a serious blow. But aside from the casualties inflicted on the Indians early in the fighting, this was all the Americans could do.

Several Apaches, remembering Al Sieber and his scouts in the sink, slipped away from the butte and attacked them. One by one, the scouts were able to run safely from the sink to the main body of soldiers, but the action diverted the attention of the Americans and permitted the Apaches in the camp to steal away in small groups toward the hills. As usual, they had previously designated the place they would meet in case of disaster —a small spring where they would at least have water. After drinking and eating what little food they had been able to bring with them, they counted their casualties. These amounted to several women killed and wounded. Although Loco had a slight wound, most of the warriors had escaped the battle unharmed. They were in a desperate plight, however, short of horses and food and hampered by the presence of so many women and children. Still unaware of the small number of Americans that had followed them, they continued their flight toward the Sierra Madres as soon as it was dark.

It was fortunate they did, because the Americans had suddenly been greatly reinforced. The trail of the Apaches had brought Forsyth, too, to the Mexican border, where he learned that Tupper had crossed it. Forsyth also had orders in his possession prohibiting him from entering Mexican territory, but he decided to follow Tupper's example and continue his pursuit of the Apaches regardless of international agreements. He caught up with Tupper's men that day and made camp.

The next morning, the Americans started again on the trail of the Apaches, who had been marching all night. By daylight, the Indians were still some distance from the mountains and so tired they stopped to rest for an hour or so. Some who still had horses pressed on, and three of them saw coming toward them the Mexican Sixth Infantry, under Colonel Lorenzo García, which was returning to Chihuahua from Sonora. They escaped being noticed by the Mexicans, but contrary to all Apache tradition, they failed to return and warn their friends.

Unaware of the danger ahead of them and certain the Americans were following close behind, most of the warriors stayed at the rear under the leadership of Geronimo and another Apache, Chihuahua, who was gaining a reputation as a war leader. They were prepared to fight off the Americans if they should overtake the Indians. Only a handful of warriors were on guard in the front. Within a few miles of the foothills of the

Sierra Madres, they stopped to rest; and the women and children, knowing of no reason why they should delay, passed them and marched right into an ambush laid by García.

The first shots killed some of the women toward the front. Then the Mexicans charged into the midst of the column. The air was loud with the cries of the wounded and dying, for these were largely unprotected women and children who were being slaughtered, persons who could not fight back. Some of them tried to flee from the Mexican bullets and gain the safety of the mountains. Among those who did, many were shot down as they ran. Sometimes whole families were destroyed at once.

When Geronimo and Chihuahua heard the Mexican gunshots, they and about thirty warriors who were with them came rushing to the women's aid. A few women and young children had remained with the rearguard, and while the men held off the Mexicans, some of these women dug a rifle pit in the sandy bed of an arroyo that ran near the scene of the ambush. Others dug additional smaller holes in the banks of the arroyo, creating a ring of outposts. A small amount of water seeped into the sandy bottom of the central rifle pit, so they had some moisture with which to quench their thirst, but little else.

The Mexicans charged, but the Apaches, keeping up a steady fire from their improvised fortifications, drove them back. The guns of the warriors became hot, and they were running short of ammunition. A weary Mexican soldier dropped a sack of 500 cartridges on the ground, and none of the other Mexicans noticed it. At this critical juncture, when every fighting man was needed, it was hardly worth a warrior's life to retrieve it, but one of the women volunteered to try. In the midst of the battle, she slipped from the rifle pit, reached the cartridges, and came back safely with the heavy sack.

Some of the soldiers recognized Geronimo and began to taunt him, calling him by name and warning him his day had come. But although they tried again and again, none of their charges succeeded in overrunning the rifle pit, and none of their bullets reached him. About noon, they disappeared. Everything was quiet, but Geronimo was suspicious, so the warriors remained where they were instead of leaving their holes and starting toward the mountains. A short distance off was a mesquite tree up which a young Indian woman climbed to look around her. Soon she called to the Apaches that the Mexicans had withdrawn and they were safe. But Geronimo did not recognize her voice and thought her action might be a ruse staged by the Mexicans to get them to leave the protection of their holes. The other warriors agreed with him, so they remained where they were.

It was fortunate they did, for soon the Mexicans were back and again surrounded the embattled Apaches. But the Indians still held them off. Nothing García did could dislodge them, and the fighting continued until after dark. In desperation, García ordered his men to start a grass fire on every side of the Apaches, hoping the smoke and flames would drive them into the open, where they could be shot. The flames curled upward in the desert night, and soon the grass was burning in the circle around the small group of Apaches. On every hand, it came closer and closer, surrounding them in a ring of flames. The situation was so serious they had to leave their holes. Yet they could not leave with the few small children they had with them, for their whimperings would reveal their movements. So the warriors asked the women permission to choke them. It was a cruel choice, but life for the Apaches was cruel. The women consented, and in the darkness the warriors killed the infants. They laid the small, lifeless bodies on the sandy floor of the arroyo, and one by one slipped quietly out of their holes and crept through the fire. So skillfully did they move that the Mexicans never saw them.

That night in the mountains, the scattered Apaches gradually found each other, gathering in small bands that became larger and larger as new groups of stragglers joined them. "All during the night in our camp on the cold mountainside," one Apache wrote later, "we could hear people mourning and wailing for their relatives who had been killed or captured. There was no help for the wounded, no food, no chance of getting reinforcements."

Although they were shattered by the battle, they had accomplished a remarkable feat in holding off the Mexicans. The Apache dead amounted to more than seventy, and another thirty were taken captive. But these were mostly unarmed women and children, those who had first walked into the ambush. García had suffered almost forty casualties, about half of them resulting in death. He had done well against the defenseless but not against the fighting men.

The next morning, watching from the mountains, the Apaches saw a curious sight. Across the plains came the American troops advancing toward the Mexicans. The two groups met, but instead of fighting each other, as the Apaches hoped they would, García merely challenged Forsyth's right to be in Mexico. Forsyth explained his mission, and García said it had already been accomplished by his battle of the day before. At Forsyth's request, García led Forsyth to the scene of the battle and showed him the dead bodies. Neither man seems to have taken into account the disproportionate number of female and child corpses, and Forsyth was satisfied and agreed to leave. García handed him a formal protest for his intrusion across the border, and Forsyth marched his troops back to New Mexico by a route that brought him close to the town of Janos. As he passed by, he could hear the bells of the church ringing in celebration of García's victory—a victory in which slightly more than 30 Apache warriors, short of ammunition, had held off about 250 trained troops. The sound of the bells echoed over the surrounding plains and in the thicket where the Apaches had gathered on the fatal day of the slaughter years before, while up in the mountains, the Indians continued on their sad way to join the other Nednis and Chiricahuas.

XVI
Invaders in the Sierra Madres

EXCEPT for the accident of the Mexican ambush, the raid on San Carlos would have been a brilliant operation. A handful of warriors, encumbered by the presence of many women and children, had outfought and outmaneuvered hundreds of well-equipped troops. If it had not been for the coincidence of the Americans crossing the boundary just as García marched back from Sonora, the Apaches would have completed the raid almost unscathed. As it was, the enemy had won a major victory; and if it had not been for the valiant rear-guard action of Geronimo and the other warriors, the Apaches' losses would have been even more serious. But he prevented the Mexicans from pursuing them and enabled them to reach the Sierra Madres.

Once there, they resumed their old way of life. As usual, they did not remain concentrated in one large ranchería but divided into smaller groups under various chiefs and other leaders. These bands, however, kept in close touch with each other and worked in concert for the benefit of the Apaches as a whole.

In the Sierra Madres, they had many of the things they needed—game, water, grass, and, above all, safety. No Mexican troops would dare follow them into that wild, unknown country, where every canyon offered a site for an ambush. But certain supplies, such as ammunition and cloth, could be obtained from only one source, the Mexican settlements and ranches.

The Apaches never fully understood the white men's form of government, and the conflicting policies they observed confused them even further. They had the idea that in Mexico each town acted as an independent unit, and this belief was reinforced by the attitudes of the Mexicans themselves. One community would offer them stiff resistance, while another would try to bribe them to stay at peace; Sonora would massacre them, while Chihuahua would give them presents. They, therefore, thought they could make a treaty with an individual community. If they could, this would be helpful to them in securing supplies.

After holding a large council, they decided to approach the officials of Casas Grandes in Chihuahua. Geronimo was a leader in advocating this course of action; and although some of the Indians believed he was largely motivated by his desire to obtain some of the white men's liquor, they decided to see if the town would make peace with them. About a third of the band agreed to go with him and Juh.

They left the safety of their mountain fortress and descended the eastern slopes of the Sierra Madres. About three miles from the town, they made a large, well-guarded camp and selected a Spanish-speaking woman to be their emissary. She went to the old city and entered it cautiously. The sight of a single Apache woman did not alarm the citizens, and they guided her to their officials, who listened to her and agreed to meet the Apaches halfway between their camp and Casas Grandes.

Geronimo and Juh played a leading role in the negotiations that followed. Accompanied by some of the warriors, they talked with the *presidente,* or mayor, of Casas Grandes, who, to show his trust, came with only a few soldiers. The *presidente* assured Geronimo and Juh that the people of Casas Grandes were just as anxious for peace as the Apaches. All past differences between them, he said, should be forgotten and an era of friendship should take the place of the past warfare. To demonstrate his sincerity, he told Geronimo and Juh the Apaches were free to come to Casas Grandes to talk with its people and trade with them.

Some of the Apaches remained in their camp, but others accepted the *presidente*'s invitation. When they first entered the city, they were alert, but the reception they received quickly assured them the *presidente* had meant what he had said. Everywhere they went, they were greeted by smiles and expressions of friendship, and no part of the city was closed to them. They lounged in the plaza, with its row of impressive government buildings, and peered through the doors of the church that stands at one corner of it. They wandered up the side streets, looking into windows and talking to their new friends. And to make the occasion of the peace more festive, the Mexicans even gave them liquor, which they drank greedily. When the sun dropped over the foothills to the west of the town, everyone agreed that, after years of fighting, the Apaches and the people of Casas Grandes had finally made a lasting peace.

The second day was better than the first. All suspicion of possible treachery had completely vanished. Some of the Apaches even brought with them goods they wished to trade and began bartering with their new friends. Once more the Mexicans brought out liquor and offered it to them. Any restraint resulting from fear had now completely broken down, and the Apaches drank more liberally than before. By sundown, many of them were thoroughly drunk, and the three-mile trip back to their camp seemed a long way to go, so they decided to spend the night at Casas Grandes. Most of them chose to sleep alongside the river that runs right next to the town, while a few others made their camp to the south. But they were in high spirits and, as they still had some liquor, they kept on drinking until late at night and entertained themselves by dancing and singing. Then, one by one, the liquor overpowered them, and they dropped to the ground in stupefied sleep. Overhead, the stars shone brightly, the cool of the desert night swept over them, and all was quiet. Geronimo's course, it seemed, had been the correct one.

Suddenly they woke to find the Mexicans among them. Guns were firing in the darkness and sabers were slashing through the air and falling on sleeping bodies. Defenseless and taken completely by surprise, the Apaches had no chance of fighting back. Those who could ran for their lives. One man, wounded in the leg, was unable to run, but he reached the riverbed and hid behind a piece of driftwood. Those who had camped to the south of the town had a better chance than the main body, because they were a little farther away, but even they had to race through a fusillade of bullets.

When the survivors reached the site of their old camp, they discovered that the other Apaches, hearing the sound of shooting, had started to retreat to the mountains. After traveling about ten miles, they had stopped long enough to roast some beef and leave part of it for any Apaches who might have escaped the massacre. The Mexicans' victory was almost complete. They killed probably ten or twelve warriors and captured twenty-five or thirty women, including one of Geronimo's wives. Geronimo and his cousin Juh were among those who sadly rejoined the others on their way back to the mountains. Geronimo's peace policy had proved a complete failure. From now on, nothing but warfare could exist between them and the Mexicans.

Back in the mountains, they debated what to do next and decided to revert to their previous strategy of taking what they needed by force. The main body of Apaches, along with most of the women and children, would remain in the Sierra Madres, while from time to time the warriors would raid the settlements, just as they had done for hundreds of years.

In the north, the Americans had begun to realize that their confused Indian policy was not succeeding. Profiteers were making money out of both the reservations and the military, for those represented big markets for beef and other supplies in the thinly populated territory. Many an American, however much he may have desired peace for his personal safety, was growing rich out of the unsettled situation. But most of them realized it could not prevail forever. The Apaches on the reservation, tired of poor treatment, were growing increasingly restless, and further outbreaks were imminent. Geronimo and Juh, in their raid on San Carlos, had demonstrated the Army's ineffectiveness. And the presence of the Nednis, Chiricahuas, and Warm Springs Apaches in the Sierra Madres meant that New Mexico and Arizona were always open to attack. As long as those warriors were free, no one in the two territories was safe; and one more outbreak like Victorio's could make the land unfit for settlement.

So in October, 1882, George Crook was sent back to take command in Arizona. His first move was to restore order on the reservations. In November, he held a council at which he explained to the Indians that many of the rumors they had heard were nothing but lies. The government, for example, was not planning to send them to the Indian Territory in present-day Oklahoma. Also, because much of the unrest came from the crowded conditions in which they had to live, he gave them permission to spread out over the reservation and, at the same time, reduced the number of roll calls that had forced them to stay close to the agency. In this way, he hoped to give them a chance to grow their own food and become self-sufficient. He also made it clear to them they were answerable to the Army and not to the civilian agents who had treated them so miserably. Among other steps, he reorganized the Apache police, whose morale and efficiency had been deteriorating, and issued regulations that positively prohibited the making of tiswin, their native liquor. This last order was unpopular with the Indians, but Crook knew drinking was a continual source of trouble with them. Once drunk, they were ready to fight each other or the Americans.

Crook next gave his attention to the Apaches in the Sierra Madres. He knew from long experience fighting them that he could not defend the border from their raiding parties with the number of men under his command. There were too many ways they could slip past his patrols. The only hope of subduing them was to launch an offensive and take the unprecedented step of invading their mountain fortress.

While Crook was making preparations for his new campaign, Geronimo and some of the other warriors were conducting a protracted raid in Sonora, striking several ranches and settlements. But they were running short of ammunition. Most of their guns were of American manufacture and the bullets they captured from the Mexicans would not fit them. So they decided to send a smaller raiding party into southeastern Arizona to replenish their supply.

As the leader of this raiding party, they chose Chato, whose name was the Spanish for flat-nosed. A Warm Springs Apache, he was unpopular with some of his fellow warriors largely because of his open ambition to succeed Nana. Geronimo was among those who disliked him and did not entirely trust him, but no one doubted his hatred of the white men or his ability as a fighter.

As Crook would have predicted, Chato had no difficulty in evading the small patrols guarding the border and, on March 21, 1883, attacked a charcoal camp at a town ten miles from Tombstone. The Apaches killed three men—a fourth escaped—and then attacked another camp. They killed one of its two occupants immediately. The other remained out of sight in his tent. Not knowing whether anyone was inside the tent or not, the Apaches took shelter behind a corral and called out to any possible occupant, but the American did not reply. They then fired a volley through the canvas walls. Somehow the bullets missed the lone white man. Two Apaches, noted for their close friendship, raced forward to see what was inside. The American coolly drew aim on one of them, and shot and killed him. The other turned and fled back to those waiting behind the corral, who withdrew to find less aggressive targets.

In the days that followed, the raiding party seemed to be almost everywhere. The Indians at San Carlos were in a state of panic, fearing another attack like the one carried out by Geronimo and Juh. But instead of driving north, the raiders turned east into New Mexico. About twenty miles from Lordsburg they found Judge H. C. McComas of the federal court, driving in a buckboard with his wife and his six-year-old son, Charlie.

They shot Mrs. McComas through the head, and she tumbled from her seat to the ground, dead, and they took Charlie captive. The judge tried to escape, but he got only 200 yards from the buckboard before he died with four bullets in him. The raiders then stripped the corpses of their clothing and continued on their wild way.

Feeling was already running high in Arizona and New Mexico, and it was further inflamed by the deaths of the prominent judge and his wife and the capture of their son. The soldiers and civilians, both American and Mexican, habitually killed women and children when they attacked an Apache ranchería and proudly reported the total number of dead. García, after his attack on Geronimo and Juh's band, had boastfully shown Forsyth the bodies of women and children. But because a white family was involved, this was different. To the settlers of the Southwest, the attack near Lordsburg was murder. The Army bore the brunt of the criticism, but Crook was philosophical about it and even sympathized with some of the complaints.

Before the raiders left Arizona, the warrior who had attacked the tent decided to give himself up. His name was Tso-ay, later called Peaches by the soldiers because of his light complexion. He had been so saddened by the death of his good friend that he did not want to continue fighting. The other Apaches did not object to his defection. According to their custom, each warrior had to decide for himself what he wanted to do. So he went north and they turned south, slipping through the Army's patrols and reaching their friends in the Sierra Madres. They had lost only two men, the warrior killed at the tent and Peaches. In less than a week, this small band of fewer than thirty warriors had killed twenty-six of their enemy, traveled some 400 miles, completely disrupted the countryside, and escaped with fresh supplies of ammunition.

Lieutenant Britton Davis, whom Crook had placed in charge of San Carlos, had gone to bed on the night of March 30, 1883, when he heard the hinges of his bedroom door creak. Standing in the entrance was an Indian with a gun. Because the raiders had just killed Judge McComas and were expected to turn back to the reservation, Davis picked up his revolver and covered him. The Indian turned out to be one of the agency's secret informers, and he brought the news that the raiding Chiricahuas had arrived and numbered as many as fifteen or twenty. They had, according to the Indian, gone to the ranchería of some White Mountain Apaches some twelve miles from the agency. In the darkness, Davis quickly assembled some thirty of his scouts, marched to the encampment, and surrounded it. Like many rumors on the reservation, this one proved an exaggeration, for the "fifteen or twenty Chiricahuas" was only Peaches, who gladly surrendered, giving up his weapons without the slightest resistance. Being uncertain of Peaches's sincerity, Davis placed him in irons. But Peaches was truly tired of war and desirous of being a friend of the Americans, and when Davis asked him if he would serve as Crook's guide during the coming offensive, he readily agreed.

Crook was then at Willcox in the Sulphur Springs Valley. Because the town was on the Southern Pacific Railroad and relatively near the border, it made an ideal staging point. As soon as Crook heard of Peaches's surrender, he sent for him. Peaches explained he had joined Geronimo and Juh unwillingly in the first place, that he had been badly treated, and that he wanted to demonstrate his friendship for the Americans. He would not only serve as Crook's guide into the mountains, he would give him full information about the enemy. They consisted of seventy full-grown warriors and fifty boys capable of fighting; there was dissension among the leaders; they were short of supplies, particularly ammunition; and many of the Apaches were ready to surrender. While Geronimo was happily raiding in Mexico and sure he could always take refuge in the mountains, the defector, Peaches, had revealed his whereabouts, his limited strength, and his great weaknesses.

The surrender of Peaches was a stroke of luck for Crook, but it did not clear away all the obstacles to his invasion. One of these was the interruption caused by a group from Tombstone, who organized a band known locally as the Tombstone

Toughs. Their avowed purpose was to march into the Sierra Madres and annihilate the Apaches. They loaded themselves and their liquor, of which they had a plentiful supply, into wagons and started off to the border. To their great surprise—and dismay—the Mexican officials raised no objections whatsoever to their crossing it. They had fully expected to be stopped, so they could return to Tombstone and spend the next months complaining about Mexican officialdom. Now they were in a quandary, for they certainly had no desire to risk their lives fighting the Apaches on unfamiliar terrain. So they decided to march north and kill a few of those living on the reservation at San Carlos.

When they reached Willcox, they stopped and made camp, apparently hoping Crook would halt them and give them reason for complaint. But Crook, realizing how quickly public opinion could be aroused on behalf of the Tombstone Toughs, paid no attention to them. Disappointed by this treatment, they left and went to Fort Thomas. The commander, who had been warned in advance of their coming, extended every courtesy to them and also abided by Crook's instructions not to interfere with them. So they marched up to the edge of the reservation. The Indians, who had also received warning, had posted guards around every encampment and were prepared to fight, knowing the Army was ready to come to their assistance. But the liquor and the inspiration of the Tombstone Toughs gave out at the same time, so they retreated to their hometown, where they announced they had personally inspected the reservation and found everything in order.

Another obstacle to the planned offensive was the agreement then in force between the United States and Mexico providing that the armed forces of one nation could enter the territory of the other only under limited conditions. The troops had to be "in hot pursuit" of a particular band, and they could not go closer than six miles to a town or encampment. If these provisions were strictly enforced, Crook's proposed campaign could not be carried out.

A request to Washington for amplification brought only

further confusion. Crook was ordered to pursue the Apaches without regard to boundaries and, at the same time, he was instructed to abide by the terms of the international agreement. He was, however, a resourceful man. Traveling by train, he visited the military and civilian authorities of Sonora and Chihuahua and found them in a mood to cooperate.

They themselves had recently launched an offensive into the Sierra Madres, penetrating the wild mountains farther than they had ever done before. But an advance guard of their scouts had been ambushed in a canyon by Geronimo's band. The Apaches had fired from the surrounding cliffs and rolled down large boulders that dealt death as effectively as the bullets. An attempt to storm the heights failed, and the scouts fled in complete rout. So heavy had their losses been that the regular soldiers had also withdrawn.

In light of this failure, the authorities were glad for American help and consented to Crook's entering their country as long as he did not do so before May 1, which would give them time to organize their own armies and have them in the field.

Precisely on May 1, 1883, Crook crossed over the border and entered Mexico. He had with him 50 American soldiers and almost 200 Indian scouts under Captain Emmet Crawford. As he had done ever since he first commanded in Arizona, he counted heavily on the Indians, knowing they were the only people who could travel and fight effectively in that rugged country. He had also recruited as scouts some of the Chiricahuas who had remained at San Carlos, hoping their presence among the soldiers would prove to Geronimo and the others that almost every man's hand was turned against them, even their friends'. He had enough supplies with him for sixty days, loaded on five packtrains of mules. Each American, including the packers, was chosen for his fighting ability and his endurance, for Crook knew this would be no easy campaign, and he wanted only the fittest and ablest.

They crossed the border into Sonora by way of the San Bernardino Valley and went south. Occasionally they stopped at small Mexican towns, where they were always received cordially, for the Mexicans were as anxious as the Americans to see the Apaches finally defeated. The area was not naturally rich, but its poverty had been increased by the desertion of fields and ranches. Few dared work them for fear of an Indian attack. On the evening of May 7, they turned eastward and entered the Sierra Madres. Darkness surrounded them as they ascended the canyon. Suddenly the scouts came to a halt, for an American soldier had caught an owl and tied it to the pummel of his saddle. The Indians explained to Crook it was foolish to go farther with a bird of such ill omen in their midst, because there would be no chance of defeating the Apaches. Eager to maintain the scouts' spirits, the Americans released the bird, which flew away into the darkness. Satisfied, the scouts started up again, and the column marched through the wilderness until midnight, when the tired men at last made camp.

On May 8, they continued up the canyon they had been ascending and knew at once that Peaches had proved a reliable guide, for they saw the tracks of numerous horses and cattle and came across some beef that had been freshly butchered. This was clearly one of the principal Apache trails. "The path wound up the face of the mountain," wrote Lieutenant John G. Bourke, who was with the expedition, "and became so precipitous that were a horse to slip his footing he would roll and fall hundreds of feet to the bottom. At one of the abrupt turns could be seen, deep down in the canyon, the mangled fragments of a steer which had fallen from the trail, and been dashed to pieces on the rocks below." They reached one summit only to discover another towering above them. Soon they passed the place where the Mexicans had camped before the ambush of their scouts.

The country, Bourke said, "seemed to consist of a series of parallel and very high, knife-edged hills—extremely rocky and bold; the canyons all contained water, either flowing rapidly, or else in tanks of great depth. Dense pine forests covered the ridges near the crests, the lower skirts being matted with scrub-oak. Grass was generally plentiful, but not invariably to be depended upon. Trails ran in every direction, and upon them were picked up all sorts of odds and ends plundered from the Mexicans—dresses, made and unmade, saddles, bridles, letters, flour, onions, and other stuff."

The trail became more and more narrow, steep, and dangerous. Even the surefooted mules were having difficulty staying on it. Six of them slipped off and rolled to the canyon below. Fortunately in each case, the grade happened to be slight, and the animals were not seriously hurt. At night, guards were set on every surrounding crest, no fires were permitted unless they could be completely concealed, and the medicine men among the scouts went through their ceremonies more and more devoutly.

The next day, they were in even more rugged country. Yet the column of men under Crook pushed forward. About noon, the trail turned down a narrow, rocky gorge that opened into an amphitheater high in the mountains. A stream ran through it with clear, sparkling water. Pines, oaks, and cedars grew on the sides of the ridges, and nearby were several peaks from which sentries could look out over the surrounding country. When Peaches had left on the raid into the United States, this had been the site of the Apaches' principal ranchería, but now it was deserted. The Apaches had moved even farther into the wilderness.

When the column made camp on May 10, the scouts under Crawford told Crook it was useless for the Americans to stay with them any longer. The packtrain simply could not keep up with their pace. Five mules had slipped from the trail the morning before. Three had broken their necks, and the remaining two had had to be shot. That morning, five more had fallen, but although they had not been seriously injured, they could not continue at that rate. The scouts proposed they go ahead while the white soldiers followed and tried to stay not more than a day's march away. However concerned he may have been about dividing his command, Crook saw that this was the only practical way to proceed.

If at all possible, he did not want open warfare in those

mountains. With their knowledge of the terrain and their mobility, the Apaches would have the advantage. On the other hand, if they started to lose, they could scatter in every direction. The Americans would have little chance of running down small bands among those ravines and peaks, where the Apaches knew every trail and hiding place. He instructed the scouts, therefore, to give the Indians every opportunity to surrender and to treat any prisoners well, so as to induce others to surrender also.

While his enemy was advancing against the ranchería, Geronimo was off fighting in Chihuahua, unaware of the approaching danger. He had not forgotten the prisoners—including his own wife—taken when the people of Casas Grandes had betrayed him, and he wanted hostages to exchange for them. Laying an ambush along the road outside that city, he captured six women, wives of soldiers stationed there. He sent one of them, an old woman, to Casas Grandes to tell the officials the Apaches were holding captives whom they would like to exchange. Meanwhile they laid another ambush, but to their disappointment, no one came along the road.

On their return to camp after this last effort, the boys who were with them roasted some beef. "We were sitting there eating," one Apache wrote later. "Geronimo was sitting next to me with a knife in one hand and a chunk of beef I had cooked for him in another. All at once he dropped the knife, saying, 'Men, our people whom we left in the base camp are now in the hands of U.S. troops! What shall we do?' This was a startling example of Geronimo's ability to tell what was happening at a distance."

Because he had some gifts as a medicine man, the Apaches took his premonition seriously and agreed to hurry back over the 125 miles of desert and tortuous mountains that separated them from their friends and relatives.

While Geronimo was racing to the aid of his people, the scouts had continued to push into the Sierra Madres and were finding more and more recent signs of the Apaches. Suddenly, on May 15, they came across two warriors and a woman. Disregarding Crook's instructions, they fired at them, but the three escaped.

Chato had built his band's ranchería some distance from the others. It consisted of thirty wickiups, arranged in two clusters, and it contained the loot they had taken in Mexico. Living there also was Charlie McComas, the young son of the federal judge. As they often did with boys, the Apaches had informally adopted him into their tribe and were making an Indian of him, a practice that increased their fighting strength.

The Apaches in the ranchería, never suspecting the white men would pursue them this far, were completely off guard. The first they knew that the scouts were near was when the scouts launched their attack. They killed nine Apaches and captured two boys, two girls, and a young woman, but the rest of the Indians escaped. The husband of one of the slain women was so infuriated by the sudden attack and the death of his wife that he grabbed some rocks and used them to beat Charlie McComas to death. Then he hid the body so the white soldiers would not find it.

After burning the wickiups and rounding up the livestock, the scouts talked to the woman they had captured. She told them the Apaches were astonished when they saw the scouts advancing, never thinking they would be attacked in these mountains. They would be even more upset when they learned that Peaches was acting as their guide, because he knew every one of their trails and hiding places. Loco, she was sure, wanted to return to the reservation, and so did Chihuahua, the Apache who had fought with Geronimo during the rearguard action against García. She was not certain about Chato and Geronimo. Juh, she knew, would not return, but he had lost so many warriors he was no longer a threat. If the scouts would permit her to leave for two days, she believed she could persuade all the Chiricahuas to surrender.

The scouts gave her some bread and meat, enough to last the time she had requested, and allowed her to take the oldest captured boy with her. They fed the other prisoners well and tried to make them think that surrendering to the Americans was worth their while. Soon the soldiers came up and joined them, and they all made camp together.

The weather was rainy and cold; water froze in their buckets and pails, and the smoke from the burned ranchería hung in the air. When the scouts moved forward later, they had to cross another of the high ridges of the Sierra Madres. On reaching the top, they saw a column of black smoke rising from a high knoll. The scouts immediately stopped and lit their own fire to answer it. Five miles farther on, they found an excellent campsite at the junction of two canyons, each of which contained a stream. Grass was everywhere, so here they had food for their livestock and water for both men and animals. The scouts sent up another smoke signal and immediately received an answer from the top of a nearby butte. Soon two women appeared, calling to the soldiers as they approached, for they were ready to surrender.

In a few hours, six more women came in. One of them was the sister of Chihuahua. She confirmed that her brother was willing to surrender, too, and was now trying to gather his band together, for they had scattered after the first shooting. Crook listened to them gravely and saw that they were fed and cared for. He was following a delicate strategy. If he proceeded against the Indians, he might suffer heavy casualties and fail to capture them. On the other hand, if he remained camped in the middle of their stronghold, they might believe that resistance was useless and surrender without bloodshed.

On May 18, his hopes were partly realized. Early in the morning, four more women came to the camp, along with a boy and one warrior, the first to appear. They were shortly followed by sixteen more Apaches in a group that included Chihuahua himself. He told Crook that most of the warriors were away raiding or hunting, but he was trying to persuade his own band to surrender and had sent messengers to them for that purpose. During the day, forty more Apaches came in, and Chihuahua asked for permission to leave with two of the younger men and try to hurry the others. Crook agreed to this request.

The next day, the soldiers moved their camp about five or six miles. Water was no problem in the Sierra Madres, but they needed a fresh source of grass. As they made the new camp, Crook called for a count of the Chiricahuas. They now totaled 70, and before nightfall the figure had risen to 100. By the following day, when Crook had ordered another count, the figure had increased again to 121. His strategy was producing the results he desired.

While the surrenders were taking place, Geronimo was racing back to the Sierra Madres, first meeting the women and the children he had left some distance from the ambush at Casas Grandes. That night he held a council, during which he said, "Tomorrow afternoon as we march along the north side of the mountains we will see a man standing on a hill to our left. He will howl to us and tell us that the troops have captured our base camp."

"We marched quite early the next morning," wrote one of the Apaches, "straight west through a wide forest of oaks and pines. About the middle of the afternoon we heard a howl from the hilltop to our left. There stood an Apache calling to us. He came down through the rocks to tell us that the main camp, now some fifteen miles distant, was in the hands of U.S. troops. . . .

"Thus the event which Geronimo foretold when we were still several days' journey away, and had repeated last night, came to pass as true as steel. I still cannot explain it."

Geronimo resisted his immediate instinct to fight or flee. He thought he should first try to talk to Crook. He, some of his men, and a few of the older women climbed to the pinnacles surrounding the soldiers' campground and called to them, asking if they would be harmed if they came down to talk. One of the scouts and one of the captive Indians went out to meet them and told them that Chihuahua had already surrendered and that all hostilities had ceased until he had had a chance to round up his band. With this assurance, the Apaches entered the camp in groups of twos and threes, and among them was Geronimo. He wanted to hold a council with Crook, but Crook refused. For the moment at least, the general held the psychological advantage, and he did not want to risk losing it by debating with Geronimo.

So he simply told the leader he could see for himself that by serving in the scouts many of the Apaches had shown they were against him. He pointed out that the Americans had already entered the stronghold Geronimo thought was impregnable. And he added that the Mexican armies were cooperating with the Americans during this offensive. In conclusion, he told Geronimo it was up to him whether he wanted to surrender or not.

Geronimo walked away, feeling angry and helpless. An hour later, he tried to speak to Crook again, but Crook refused to say anything further, treating him with considerable indifference. He was being careful not to get into an argument with Geronimo or to do anything that might increase his prestige among the other Apaches. Meanwhile, the scouts were circulating among the new arrivals and repeating the warning that Mexican soldiers from Chihuahua and Sonora might arrive at any time.

Geronimo was rapidly assessing his position and did not find it good. The presence of the troops in the Sierra Madres and the willingness of the scouts to work with them were both bad signs. No place was secure from the white men, and his own people were turning against him.

Finally, he returned to the camp and asked to speak to Crook again. This time he explained he had always wanted peace but that he had suffered many wrongs. He told of the treachery he had suffered from the Mexicans and how he was trying to negotiate with the officials of Chihuahua for the return of his people. And he related how he had been badly treated at San Carlos. If Crook would guarantee him better treatment in the future, he would agree to surrender and return to San Carlos. But Crook knew that if he bargained with Geronimo, every other Apache would demand the same privilege and he would lose his ascendancy over them. So he told Geronimo his choice was simply peace or war.

On May 21, Geronimo made up his mind. He could fight the Mexicans or the Americans or those of his own people who had joined Crook, but he could not fight them all at once. He was a defeated man and willing to surrender, but he requested permission to go in search of the scattered members of his band. He had been sending smoke signals to them, he said, but they would not answer, thinking the signals were made by the scouts in an attempt to entice them into an ambush. Crook postponed making a decision.

He was in a precarious position. Every day, more Apaches were coming into the camp, and he had no means of controlling them except through the force of his personality and the shock he had given them by invading their mountains. But he could only press his advantage so far. He did not, for example, ask the Indians to give up their weapons. Such a request might have scared them and started them fighting or running away. But he made the point to them that he was letting them keep their guns because he was so little frightened of them, thus impressing them even further with his supremacy. He also had kept in mind the international agreement he had violated. Even though he had received the cooperation of the Sonoran and Chihuahuan officials, he had to leave Mexico sooner or later, and the sooner the better for his future career in the Army. Furthermore, he was running short of supplies. He had brought enough for sixty days, but his own men had consumed a considerable portion of the food, some had been lost when the mules fell from the cliffs, and he was now feeding many more people than he had anticipated.

When Crook announced his intention of starting the march back to San Carlos, Geronimo objected and proposed they stay in the mountains a week longer. His own band was still scattered in every direction, they did not have enough food, and they had no means of transportation for the small children and the older women. Given more time, they could collect their people and their belongings.

Crook recognized the justice of Geronimo's objection but could not accede to it. He had to get out of those mountains, but he made an unusual agreement. He would leave with those who were ready to travel and permit the others, including

Geronimo, to follow after. It was a bold decision, but Crook was a bold man. Realistically, he could not guard that many Apaches anyway, as they worked back down the narrow, steep trail. He had to put his trust in the word of the Indians and the prestige he had gained among them.

By May 23, even old Nana had surrendered. Juh was the only important leader who had not showed up, but he had lost so many warriors with his incessant fighting that his band was no longer significant. And the time had come for Crook to leave.

The procession the general led down the mountains presented a curious sight. The younger children and the older women were mounted on horses or mules, whichever could be provided for them, and the rest were on foot. Because of the heat, most of them cut bunches of cottonwood foliage, which they wore on their heads to protect themselves from the sun. They had brought with them all the supplies they could carry, their cradleboards, their blankets, their guns, and the baskets they had covered with resin so they could be used to hold water. The Apache scouts mingled with them, their long hair held back by flannel headbands and their rifles always near at hand. In addition to the Army's supplies, the Indians drove some of their cattle down the mountains, and several donkeys were loaded with mescal heads, which they had gathered just before leaving. Along with the Indians were the fifty American soldiers, their uniforms dusty and soiled but their spirits high. Supervising all this was Crook, dressed, as always, in civilian clothes and alert for any signs of trouble.

Geronimo met with more delays than he had expected in collecting his band. They were all over that wild country. Many were difficult to locate, and some were reluctant to return to San Carlos. Fearful that Crook might think he was breaking his word, he asked Loco and Chato to go ahead to Crook's camp and ask him to wait there. But Crook could not do so and began the march back to the United States, leaving instructions for Geronimo to come as soon as possible.

Geronimo was having difficulty living up to his promise. Although some of the Apaches were reluctant to go back to San

Carlos, they agreed their decision did not have to be final. If conditions on the reservation did not improve under the Army, they could always break out again. So they left the mountains, but before giving themselves up to the Americans, they wanted to find horses. They conducted one last raid on the Mexicans, and although they failed to take many horses, they captured approximately 350 head of cattle. At least they would not return to the reservation poor.

Crook, on arriving in the United States, found Arizona in an uproar against him for bringing the fearsome Apaches back. It would have been far better, in the opinion of the settlers, to have killed them all or left them in Mexico. Knowing how the people had acted in the past, he was worried about the safety of his captives—not those under his immediate protection and custody, but those who would be coming in later alone. So he sent Lieutenant Britton Davis down to the border to meet them and escort them to San Carlos.

Davis made two successful trips with bands of Apaches and then returned to wait for Geronimo. Weeks passed, and there was no sign of him. Davis was beginning to wonder if Geronimo had broken his word, when he appeared with his Apaches and the 350 head of cattle. Geronimo was both surprised and angry to find the soldiers waiting for him. Davis tried to explain that the precaution had been taken for the Apaches' own safety, but Geronimo could not understand this line of reasoning. After all, he had made peace with the Americans. Why should he now be afraid of their attacking him? Davis said there were good Americans and bad Americans, just as there were good Apaches and bad ones. This argument was unconvincing to Geronimo, but he reluctantly agreed to accept the escort. Next, Davis protested against the 350 head of cattle, but he did not carry the protest far, because Geronimo began to show signs that he was sorry he had surrendered and might return to Mexico.

The cattle posed a major problem for Davis. Not only did they represent stolen property in the eyes of the white men's laws, but they would greatly slow down the march to San Carlos. On his two previous trips, Davis had moved quickly, thus avoiding any chance of the citizens attacking him or causing other trouble. But Geronimo refused to push his slow-moving herd. They represented the wealth of his people, and he was not going to run off their fat by racing them through a supposedly friendly country.

At a ranch in the Sulphur Springs Valley, he even insisted on stopping for several days to give the animals a rest. A fresh argument broke out between him and Davis, with Davis insisting they would have to move more quickly than that. "I had been holding in reserve one argument for just such an emergency," Davis later wrote, "and I now sprang it on him. He had seen General Crook in Mexico with American troops. The Mexicans had the same right to come into the United States. We were too near the border to risk stopping, as the Mexicans might be following us.

" 'Mexicans!' he snarled, 'Mexicans! My women can whip all the Mexicans in Chihuahua.'

" 'But the Mexicans have plenty of cartridges and you have practically none,' I argued, as I pointed to his nearly empty cartridge belt.

" 'We don't fight Mexicans with cartridges,' he replied contemptuously. 'Cartridges cost too much. We keep them to fight your white soldiers. We fight Mexicans with rocks.' "

But he finally consented to stay for one day only, instead of the three he had originally demanded.

Davis had finished pitching his tent, when two Americans came out of the ranch house and walked over to talk to him. They asked him casual questions about his name and his mission and then, having gathered the information they wanted, they told him who they were. One was the United States Marshal for the Southern District of Arizona and the other was the collector of customs at Nogales, the port of entry into the United States. The cattle were contraband, having been smuggled into the country without duty having been paid on them, and Geronimo and his band were wanted in Tucson on charges of murder. The marshal then wrote out an official order requiring Davis to help him arrest the Apaches and take them to Tucson.

This had all come about because of that slow-moving herd. For the marshal told Davis he had tried to intercept him before with the other bands, but he had traveled too fast. But now at last justice would be done. Davis thought quickly but could see no way out of his dilemma. If he helped the marshal arrest Geronimo, the Apaches would certainly break out again, even though the marshal was prepared to swear in Davis's packers, the cowboys at the ranch, and as many citizens as he needed from Willcox to outnumber the Indians three to one. In addition, Davis would have failed in his assignment. But if he did not obey the marshal, he himself might well go to jail, and the Apaches would certainly fight back anyway.

As Davis was desperately searching for an answer, Geronimo was settling down for a rest at the ranch. The warriors were herding the cattle nearby, and the women were getting ready to prepare their men's meal. At this moment, a scout reported seeing a small cloud of dust coming from the direction of Fort Bowie. Davis correctly guessed it must be a friend of his, Lieutenant "Bo" Blake, whom he had invited to meet him on the march and spend the night. The appearance of Blake gave Davis an idea. Blake had graduated a year ahead of him from West Point and therefore was technically his superior. Blake could supersede him in command and steal away with the Apaches under cover of night, while Davis remained behind in obedience to the marshal's orders. But could they persuade Geronimo to leave, and would they wake the marshal and the customs collector?

After supper, the two civilian officials came to visit Davis in his tent, largely to enjoy their victory over him. Blake, who had an attractive personality, began to ingratiate himself with them. Soon he suggested they all have a drink together and took out a bottle of scotch he had brought with him from Fort Bowie. The marshal and customs collector were delighted, and the bottle passed freely that evening. When it came their turn, Blake and

Davis were careful to drink as little of it as possible. They had only the one bottle, and they required a lot of it. It had to put those two officials to sleep. When the marshal and the customs collector got up to leave, Davis and Blake pressed them to take what remained in the bottle, assuring them they had plenty more and were glad to share it with their good friends. Soon the marshal and the customs collector were stretched out and snoring deeply.

Now Davis and Blake had to persuade Geronimo to move, and this was not going to be easy. When he was told he would have to head for San Carlos immediately, the Apache was furious. Davis had promised he could rest his cattle for a day, he said. Now he was breaking his word. In reply, Davis told him part of the truth. The men were officials who wanted a thousand dollars in customs duties or they would take the cattle off and sell them in Tucson. He was careful not to tell Geronimo they wanted the Apaches, too, for fear that would drive him into open warfare. While Davis talked, Geronimo's anger grew, his lips twitched, and he shifted his rifle nervously. Finally he exploded. He had come north from Mexico, he said, in peace, and all he had met with was trouble and threats. If the two Americans wanted to steal his cattle, let them try it in the morning. He himself was going back to sleep. He also said he intended to hold Davis to his promise to stay at the ranch for two nights.

One of the scouts intervened and began speaking to him rapidly without pausing to interpret. Geronimo tried to interrupt him, but the scout kept talking. Gradually Geronimo's spirits began to flag. Nobody seemed willing to support him. Davis then saw his opportunity and said he thought the reason Geronimo refused to follow their plan was his fear he would make too much noise. This annoyed him, but Davis followed up by telling him what a joke it would be when the marshal and the customs collector woke up in the morning and discovered they were gone. Slowly Geronimo began to smile, and the argument was won.

If anyone knew how to move cattle quietly, it was the Apaches. They made hardly a sound in the still night as they packed their belongings and herded their livestock in a northerly direction. Soon they were gone, and the marshal and customs collector were still sleeping soundly. Davis sat down on a box outside his tent and waited for dawn.

The customs collector was the first to awake. He rubbed his eyes, looked around, ran to the gate, and looked some more. Then he dashed back to the ranch house to wake the marshal. The two men brought out their field glasses and, still in their underwear, climbed a ladder to the roof of the ranch house and peered in every direction. There was no sign of the Apaches, the 350 cattle, or the scouts. The empty plains of the Sulphur Springs Valley stretched for miles in every direction.

"Slowly they climbed down the ladder," Davis wrote later, "and reentered their room. In a few minutes they came out again fully dressed and walked over to where I was awaiting them.

" 'Where are those Indians?' asked the marshal.

" 'They're gone,' I replied rather inanely.

" 'Cut out your impertinence and answer my question,' he demanded. 'Can't I see they're gone? What I want to know is, where they are gone.'

" 'That I can't tell you,' I replied. 'The officer I introduced you to last night is my superior. When I reported to him the condition of things he took the command away from me, ordered me to remain here in obedience to your subpoena, and left with the outfit about ten o'clock last night, ten hours ago. By now they must be forty miles from here. But whether they went toward Fort Bowie, or toward Fort Grant, or Geronimo lit out for Mexico as he threatened to do and Blake followed him, I don't know. Blake did not tell me his plans and it would have been an impertinence for me, his junior, to have questioned him.'

"The marshal looked me straight in the eyes.

" 'You're lying,' he said.

" 'Perhaps I am, but you can't prove it,' I replied with a smile, the first time I had felt like smiling in several days."

The marshal and the customs collector decided that no matter which way Blake might have gone, to Forts Bowie or Grant or to the Mexican border, he had too much of a start on them. So they admitted defeat, released Davis from the marshal's order, and they rode in together with Geronimo, his cattle, and caught up with Blake a few miles south of the reservation's border, and they rode in together with Geronimo, his cattle, and his band of Apaches.

But Geronimo's troubles were not over. The Mexicans complained to the American government about his cattle and came to examine their brands. There was no question they were stolen—under the white men's laws. To Geronimo, they were not. He had made peace with Crook and the Americans; he had never surrendered to the Mexicans, and they remained his traditional enemies. In fact, they still held the captives they had taken earlier in Casas Grandes. Those cattle belonged to him. They had been captured from his enemies by him and his warriors at the risk of their lives. Crook, however, could not agree, for he had to consider the United States' relations with Mexico. Furthermore, if he permitted Geronimo's band to retain their stolen livestock, he would be encouraging other Indians to steal, too. So he ordered the cattle confiscated. Geronimo was infuriated by this new injustice and resumed reservation life more bitter, resentful, and untrusting than ever.

XVII
At War Again

ALTHOUGH Crook confiscated Geronimo's cattle, he wanted the Apaches to be satisfied with reservation life. Therefore, he arranged to have them transferred from the area around the San Carlos agency to Turkey Creek in the White Mountains near Fort Apache. This was much higher land, covered with game-filled forests that more closely resembled the favorite haunts of the Chiricahua and Warm Springs Apaches. He also thought they should be herdsmen, not farmers, because riding horses and driving cattle were less alien to their normal way of life than sowing and reaping crops.

But now that the Apaches had been conquered, the Department of the Interior was reasserting its authority over them. It determined they should be farmers and issued them a dozen light wagons and a dozen plows. "Then," said Lieutenant Davis, "the fun began. The Indians' ponies would weigh some seven to eight hundred pounds; the harnesses sent them were for horses double that size. . . . [We] laughed till we ached over the efforts of the Indians to harness their ponies in harnesses big enough for two of them. None of the ponies had ever before seen such a thing as a wagon or a harness; many of them had never even been broken to a saddle. I honestly believe that some of them could have crawled through the collars put on them if given a little time.

"By stuffing the collars with anything available in the way of old rags, cutting the harness to shreds, and the assistance of half a dozen Indians to each pony, a wagon would finally be hitched up, the proud proprietor would mount it, seize the reins, and away he would go over the plains at full tilt, his erstwhile assistants scrambling into the tail end of the wagon as it passed them on the run. The Indians, whooping and laughing, were getting as much fun out of the circus as we were.

"Later some of them tried out their new plows in the San Carlos river bottom. The ponies, unaccustomed to a slow gait, preferred to trot or gallop, and the plow-points were oftener above ground than in it. Now and then a point would strike a hidden rock or stump; then the plowman would execute a sommersault over the plow handles, to the great delight of his friends. A furrow, when completed, had the regularity of the trail of a snail on a bat."

The Indians were having fun with this ill-suited equipment, but few of them had any intention of becoming serious farmers.

Britton Davis, with two assistants to help him, was detailed to supervise the move from the San Carlos agency to Turkey Creek and to remain with the Indians after they were settled. On their arrival at their new home, the bands scattered in different directions to start building their rancherías. Most of the more hostile Apaches, like Geronimo, chose sites several miles away from Davis's tent, but one did not. This was a minor leader named Ka-ya-ten-nae. He was a friend of Geronimo's and several of the other leaders, but many of the Apaches disliked him because he was one of the warriors who had seen García's troops advancing but had failed to turn back and warn the others. As a result, some of the Apaches rightly blamed him for the massacre in which so many women and children had been killed by the Mexicans. Ka-ya-ten-nae disliked reservation life just as much as Geronimo, but instead of building his ranchería at some distance from Davis's headquarters, he chose a ridge directly above it. In this way, he could always know what was going on.

By the time the Indians were settled it was mid-June, and they pleaded it was too late in the year to plant crops, because winter would come before they could be harvested. Davis, recognizing there was considerable truth in their argument, did not press them and accepted their promises that as soon as spring came they would start work in earnest. He was also doubtful whether the Apaches could farm successfully anyway. They had no inclination for this type of work, and the best farming lands near Turkey Creek had already been taken up by other Apaches who had been moved there earlier. All that was left were a few bottomland sites and some upland areas that might, with good luck, be dry-farmed.

The absence of any work was demoralizing. Most of the warriors spent their days loafing and gambling. Some of them traded their horses with other Apaches for supplies they wanted, and a visiting band of Navajos secured more of their horses in exchange for blankets. A principal source of discontent was Crook's order prohibiting the making of tiswin. The chiefs and other leaders protested strongly against this infringement on their personal rights, but Crook was adamant. Let the idle Indians start drinking, and no one could foresee what might happen.

Ka-ya-ten-nae paid no attention to the order, and one day he held a tiswin party on the ridge overlooking Davis's tent. Davis went turkey hunting that day and, finding no birds in the nearby bottomlands, started up the ridge in search of one. Ka-ya-ten-nae's lookouts saw him approaching and warned the warriors. Under the influence of the liquor they had been drinking, they decided the time had come to rid themselves of the white men's authority. Several of them laid an ambush and would have killed Davis, but as he was ascending the trail, he heard a turkey calling below him and turned back to shoot it. The sound of that bird was all that saved his life.

During the night, a stone struck the roof of his tent and

rolled down the side, which was the signal that one of his secret informers wished to talk to him. He crawled out under the back wall and went some twenty steps north, the procedure he followed when he met his informers. In the darkness, he found a woman waiting for him, and she told him what had happened at Ka-ya-ten-nae's ranchería. Davis decided he could not permit such large-scale drinking of tiswin and made up his mind to arrest Ka-ya-ten-nae the next day. "What would happen when I attempted the arrest," Davis later wrote, "no one could possibly foresee. Ka-ya-ten-nae had an immediate following of thirty-two of the most reckless of the young braves. They would stick by him I felt sure, but what the other Indians would think of his arrest I could not predict. It would be a stunning surprise to them and their reaction to it might be anything. . . . If the reaction of the majority was for peace, I could get away with the arrest. If, however, it was for war, I was determined that the Indians should not be the only ones to make a killing."

A friend was visiting Davis, so Davis roused him and asked him to ride to Fort Apache and request the commander to send four troops of cavalry at once. As daylight began to break, he ordered the scouts to assemble the chiefs. The troops arrived just as the chiefs were gathering 200 yards away from the hospital tent that Davis used for his meetings. At his bidding, at least twenty chiefs and leaders entered the tent while about forty warriors stood outside. All of them were armed.

Ka-ya-ten-nae had not appeared, so Davis sent for him again. At last, he came down from the ridge with his warriors, whom he stationed about 100 yards from the tent, and walked toward Davis, angrily demanding the meaning of this meeting. David told him tiswin drinking was forbidden and that as a punishment he would be sent to the commanding officer at San Carlos, who would decide what to do with him.

Without a word, Ka-ya-ten-nae turned around and walked back to his men, who spread out in battle formation, cocking their guns at the same time. Davis had enough troops to overpower the Apaches, but he and the chiefs would most certainly be caught in a crossfire if the soldiers and Ka-ya-ten-nae's band exchanged shots. The Apache met his warriors, talked to them briefly, and then came to the tent with his men. He was so furious he could hardly speak, but he demanded to know which of his people had reported him. His rage had been diverted from Davis to his own Apaches, and Davis had won.

Repeating what he had said before about sending Ka-ya-ten-nae to San Carlos, Davis reached forward and removed the leader's cartridge belt and revolver and told him he was under arrest. Two Apaches offered themselves as hostages if Ka-ya-ten-nae could be permitted to keep his weapons during the trip to San Carlos. A warrior should not be asked to submit to the indignity of traveling unarmed. This request was made with such sincerity that Davis agreed to it.

Captain Emmet Crawford, who was commanding at San Carlos, brought Ka-ya-ten-nae before the Apache court, which found him guilty. He was sentenced to five years in the military prison at Alcatraz. The arrest of Ka-ya-ten-nae and the penalty imposed on him made a deep impression on the Apaches. At least for the time being, the practice of making tiswin, if not stopped entirely, was continued only on a small scale.

Winter came to Turkey Creek, and snow covered the mountains. Finally the weather broke, and in the spring of 1884, a few of the Apaches made halfhearted efforts to clear some of the land. This work was not for warriors, however, and they delegated most of it to their women. On one of his rare visits to Davis, Geronimo, with great pride, showed the lieutenant a tiny blister on the palm of his hand as evidence he was working and invited the lieutenant to see his farm. When Davis visited him the following day, he found the Apache sitting in the shade, while one of his wives fanned him and his other two wives hoed a patch of not more than a quarter of an acre in which a few meager sprouts of corn were growing. His efforts were typical of most of the warriors'. Nothing about farming appealed to them, particularly in those unproductive lands.

Although many of the Apaches preferred this idle life to the dangers and sorrows of continued warfare, a sense of restlessness was pervading the reservation. A major disturbing element was the growing conflict between the Army and the Department of the Interior. In December, 1884, a new agent was appointed at San Carlos. He was a man who knew little about Indians but was greatly jealous of his own authority. Inevitably, he and Crook clashed. The Apaches, of course, sensed the interdepartmental wrangling and were quick to take advantage of it. If a request of theirs was turned down by the agent, they went to the military; and when a military decision bothered them, they appealed to the agent. Sometimes they gained a favor in this fashion, but the Americans' inconsistency created confusion and unrest.

At Turkey Creek, Davis noticed the Indians under his supervision beginning to change. They had been ordered to abandon the old custom of beating their wives, but a woman appeared at Davis's tent with her arm broken in two places and her shoulders covered with bruises. Davis arrested her husband and locked him up at Fort Apache. Several chiefs came to Davis to protest what he had done.

Tiswin was also being made again, despite Crook's orders. Davis arrested one Apache responsible for holding a drinking party and placed him in the guardhouse at Fort Apache. Although several chiefs protested his arrest, Davis kept him locked up for two weeks.

Shortly after, Davis arrested another Indian for the same offense and locked him up also. Chihuahua came immediately to Davis's tent and violently denounced the lieutenant's action. This did not surprise Davis, because Chihuahua was one of those who liked to drink. But he was astonished to find Chihuahua accompanied by Mangas, the son of Mangas Coloradas, for Davis regarded him and Loco as two Apaches loyal to the American cause.

But an action taken by Crook had had an unforeseen result. After the surrender, Crook had negotiated with the Mexicans for the return of some of their Apache captives. One of those released was a woman named Huera, who was a wife of Mangas. She was an expert at making tiswin, and she did not want the market for her product cut off. Because of her influence over him, Mangas had now joined Chihuahua in demanding the relaxation of the Army's regulations, and his shift contributed to further unrest among the Indians.

Davis listened to the two men argue but had neither the authority nor the desire to change Crook's orders. So after what they regarded as an unsatisfactory meeting, the chiefs and the other leaders conferred among themselves as to the strategy they should follow to have the restrictions on tiswin drinking and wife-beating rescinded. They decided the best way would be for a large number of the most influential men to drink and then confront Davis with the fact. What could the lone lieutenant do then? He certainly would not dare to arrest them all.

On the night of May 14, 1885, they held a tiswin party and at sunrise the following morning gathered at Davis's tent to report the fact. Loco began to talk first, but Chihuahua impatiently interrupted him. He spoke bitterly about the prohibition against wife-beating. After all, Apaches knew how to discipline their own people better than Americans did. Then he went on to condemn the order about making and drinking tiswin. They had all, he said, been drinking tiswin the previous night, and what was Davis going to do about it? Even if he could arrest them all, he did not have a jail big enough to hold them.

What Chihuahua said was true. The situation was far too serious for Davis to handle on his own, so he told them he would wire Crook for instructions. Protocol demanded that he send his telegram not directly to the commanding general but through the officer in charge at San Carlos, who would forward it with his comments.

Crawford had become so weary of the dissension between the civilian and military authorities on the reservation that he had asked to be replaced. The new commanding officer, Captain F. E. Pierce, knew nothing about the Apaches and had never even seen a Chiricahua, so he always relied on Al Sieber, the chief of scouts, to tell him what to do. Therefore, when he received Davis's telegram, he took it to Sieber. The night before, Sieber had been drinking and gambling and was still asleep—and probably suffering from a hangover—when Pierce woke him. He read the telegram sleepily and muttered it was just "another tiswin drunk," something Davis could handle by himself. In the light of this comment, Pierce filed the message away and did nothing further about it.

Back at Turkey Creek, the tension was mounting. Davis, not once thinking his telegram had never reached Crook, believed the general was making preparations for whatever course of action he intended to follow. To have sent another telegram would have been impertinent on the part of a second lieutenant. Friday passed, and then Saturday. Some of the Apaches, and especially Geronimo, were growing increasingly nervous over the delay in deciding their fate. Geronimo remembered the sentence given to Ka-ya-ten-nae for having a tiswin party and recalled his own experience when Clum had placed him in irons and carried him to San Carlos. As he thought of these events and recalled the injustices he had suffered from the Americans, his imagination ran riot. He pictured himself under arrest again with those humiliating irons attached to his wrists and ankles. He saw himself, like Ka-ya-ten-nae, locked in a cell in the island fortress in California. He became certain the soldiers would be under orders to kill him if he resisted arrest. Then he convinced himself they would not imprison him; they would hang him outright. Death at the end of a rope would be his reward for having lived at peace with the Americans and farmed his little plot of land.

He discussed his imagined plight and that of the other Apaches with several of the leaders. Some became convinced they should flee immediately; others preferred to remain on the reservation, arguing that even if the Americans punished them, the punishment would not be as bad as resumption of the endless warfare. Geronimo used all his great powers of persuasion and told them the soldiers were coming to remove all the Apaches, not just those involved in the tiswin drinking. On Sunday, he even said that Davis had been killed along with some of the most important scouts. Loco remained unmoved; he had always been less militant than the others. Chato, who had led the raid from Mexico into Arizona and New Mexico only a short time before, had become a firm friend of the Americans, one of the Apaches whom Davis trusted the most. On the other hand, Mangas had been influenced by his wife's desire to make tiswin and was ready to go. Nachez, Chihuahua, and Nana were also ready to flee. Altogether, they were able to muster thirty-eight warriors, eight boys old enough to fight, and approximately a hundred women and children. Inflamed by Geronimo's wild stories and his overworked imagination, they fled the reservation.

As they were leaving, they cut the telegraph line where it passed through the foliage of a tree. Then they cleverly tied the broken ends together with a leather thong and drew the line taut, making the break difficult to see and thus delaying the reports of their flight. Although Geronimo had told the others that Davis and Chato were already dead, they were not. But he had, however, laid a plot to have them killed. The only defections that had ever taken place among the scouts were during the arrest of Noch-ay-del-klinne, but Geronimo had now persuaded three of them, one his half brother, to turn on Davis and kill him in the confusion following the outbreak.

As soon as he heard of the Indians' flight, Davis ordered his scouts to meet him at his tent. On the reservation, they were ordinarily issued only four or five rounds of ammunition each, because cartridges served as currency and, as such, were worth twenty-five cents apiece. Before going in pursuit of Geronimo, Davis had to issue more. He was certain that if any of the scouts were going to attack him, they would choose this moment. So he selected three men in whom he had absolute trust as guards and ordered the others to ground their guns—that is, to keep the rifle butts on the dirt beside their feet. Quietly, he instructed the three guards to shoot any man who lifted his gun. As he entered the tent, Geronimo's three sympathizers, knowing they had lost their chance, disappeared into the bushes. They were, however, the only men who deserted.

Davis, with his scouts and some troops from Fort Apache, went in immediate pursuit of the fleeing Apaches, but he was too late. At sunrise the following morning, he saw the dust raised by the Apaches' ponies some twenty miles in the distance and knew he could never hope to overtake them. So he went back to Fort Apache and awaited orders from Crook.

Almost immediately dissension broke out among the fleeing Indians. Somehow they learned that Davis and Chato were not dead, and they saw no evidence of the soldiers coming. Nachez and Chihuahua accused Geronimo and Mangas of lying and were so angry they even threatened Geronimo's life. Finally, they contented themselves by splitting from the rest of the band. While the others went south, they turned north to the mountains of the Mogollon Rim, planning to hide there until they could decide whether or not they could risk going back to the reservation.

At Fort Apache, Davis received orders from Crook to recruit a hundred more scouts and take to the field. Crook also mustered all his other forces and put them on the alert. No one knew which way the Apaches had gone, and all New Mexico and Arizona was in a state of fear.

Davis and his scouts soon found the trail left, not by Geronimo, but by Chihuahua. So while the instigator of the outbreak escaped to Mexico, the lieutenant chased the band that was willing to surrender if they could only find some way of explaining to the Americans why they had fled. Davis finally located one of their camps and, knowing of no reason to negotiate with them, opened fire at a distance of 600 or 700 yards. The range was too far, and none of the Apaches was hurt. But with this demonstration of hostility, Chihuahua, who had been wavering between peace and war, made up his mind for war. He became the scourge of the Southwest, sweeping down on lonely ranches, destroying a small Army encampment, and collecting supplies. This was like the days of Victorio all over again. Posses of ranchers and miners and companies of scouts and troops were scouring the country, but they could not locate the elusive Apaches. Then Chihuahua vanished across the border back into the Sierra Madres, which Geronimo had reached before him. Once again the statistics are obscure, but altogether in those few weeks, Chihuahua probably killed at least seventeen civilians as well as several soldiers.

Back in their mountains, the Apaches took up their old life —only Juh was no longer there. About the time that the others had surrendered, he had gone to Casas Grandes and purchased some liquor. While riding away from the town along the edge of a river, his horse stumbled down the bank and threw him into the water. Two of his sons were with him, but they were not strong enough to lift so heavy a man. One of them held up his head, while the other raced for help. When Juh's warriors arrived, the chief was still alive. They built a shelter for him, but he did not survive the accident. His death, however, did not materially affect the strength of the Apaches, because his band had already become so weak.

Always ambitious, Geronimo's prestige among the Indians continued to grow and he was recognized as a principal leader by the group hiding in the Sierra Madres. They depended heavily on him to set up the strategy that would maintain their freedom, and the results of the next months of action proved his strategy was good.

The Apaches had always been accustomed to operating in small bands. This time, they worked in even smaller ones. One tactic they adopted was to make false camps. If their pursuers came close to them, they would pick out a location, build some small campfires, and tether one or two worthless horses nearby. Then, while their enemy waited to ambush them on their return at nightfall, they would press onward.

Realizing the Apaches had eluded him and that he faced another long campaign in Mexico, Crook organized two columns of scouts, one under Crawford, whom he asked to have recalled to his command especially for this purpose, and the other under Captain Wirt Davis. Crawford was to go down the western flank of the Sierra Madres in Sonora, and Davis was to parallel him in Chihuahua. If they came across any signs of the Indians, they were to follow them into the mountains.

Crawford's men marched under almost incredible conditions.

The country was wild and rugged, and at least once the temperature soared to 128 degrees. Mexican communications were poor, and although the soldiers and scouts were well received in the settlements where they could make their identity known, more than once the Mexicans mistook them for the enemy and shot at them from ambush. When a scout was finally killed by one of the settlers, the majority of the scouts were so enraged they decided to attack the Sonoran town of Oputo, wipe it out, and return to the United States. Others favored marching directly back to the border and, instead of bothering with Oputo, simply killing all Mexicans they found on their way. The argument lasted all night, and in spite of Crawford's pleas, they would probably have attacked the Mexicans if they had not just then come across the trail of some of Chihuahua's band. This diverted their attention and a detachment of thirty scouts set off in pursuit.

The following day, they located the Apaches' camp and attacked it, wounding one warrior and capturing fifteen women and children. But in spite of the sorrow they caused, they had not seriously impaired the Apaches' fighting strength. They remained a formidable fighting force, and Geronimo was determined not to surrender.

During this campaign, Crook learned the futility of attempting to use cavalry in conjunction with the scouts. Although he had relied heavily on the Apaches as fighters ever since he first came to Arizona, he had sent regular soldiers along with them to maintain their morale and protect the packtrains. But he now realized the scouts could take care of themselves without any help and could move more swiftly if they were not impeded by the cavalry. From then on, although they were still commanded by white officers, he allowed the scouts to operate without supporting troops.

While Davis and Crawford were marching through Sonora and Chihuahua in search of the elusive Apaches, a small band of them went north through Crook's defense lines and conducted a series of spectacular raids. Once again the press and the public rose up in anger at Crook and the ineffectiveness of the Army. Geronimo had chosen not to lead this small group—it was composed of less than a dozen warriors—and permitted it to be headed by an Apache named Josanie, who had previously been unknown to the Americans. In letting Josanie serve as leader, Geronimo had made a wise decision. Josanie's tactics were as successful as Victorio's and Nana's. In a two-month period, he killed about forty-eight white men, including soldiers and civilians, and stole about 250 horses. In turn, he lost only one warrior. But even this ratio was too heavy for the Apaches. The Americans could always find a hundred white men ready to take the place of those who had died; the Apaches had no substitute for the single warrior.

Crook was now fighting on two fronts at once, the Southwest and Mexico. North of the border, he could only follow in almost hopeless pursuit of Josanie's small band. South of it, he was pressing against the main body of the Apaches.

The Sierra Madres were no longer the impregnable fortress they had once been. They still presented some of the roughest terrain to be found in North America, but Crook's initial campaign had stripped them of some of their mystery and made them more familiar to the Americans. Also, his use of Apache scouts gave him troops capable of traveling where few American soldiers could venture. Crawford's column actually crossed the mountains from Sonora to Chihuahua, a feat considered so remarkable that many Mexicans refused to believe he had done it. When he arrived on the other side, some thought he was a bandit making up an implausible story to cover up his wrongdoings and his tattered appearance and the worn looks of his men furthered their suspicions. They even threatened to put him in jail.

A detachment of Captain Wirt Davis's scouts, approaching from Chihuahua, also surprised an encampment and killed a woman and a boy and captured fifteen women. But Geronimo and the warriors eluded the Americans, for they were too wise to waste their lives and their limited supply of ammunition by hurling themselves against superior forces. While the Americans and the scouts wore themselves out, climbing one mountain crest after another, the Apaches hid in their canyons and waited for the Americans to leave. Sooner or later, they were certain, the Americans would give up.

But Crook did not. As soon as the enlistments of the scouts ran out, he brought Davis and Crawford back to the United States, reequipped them, enlisted fresh recruits, and again sent them south across the border. Davis was ordered to go to Casas Grandes in Chihuahua and seek out a band that was reported to be nearby, while Crawford was to go to Oputo, where a rumor had it that another band lurked. At the least, this strategy would flank the Sierra Madres again and perhaps prevent the Apaches from striking the Mexican settlements to obtain more supplies.

The constant pressure was beginning to tell on the Apaches. They were so few, and their enemies were so numerous. They could elude the Americans during one vigorous campaign, but no sooner was it over, than the white men started another. On every side they were surrounded by their foe. Both the Mexicans and the Americans were determined to capture or kill them, and although cooperation between the two white nations was not of the best, they were now willing to work with each other, and the Mexicans no longer insisted on the sanctity of the international border. Some of the Apaches began to talk about the futility of further resistance. Chihuahua, for example, had had second thoughts about their initial outbreak almost as soon as it had occurred. His doubts were returning. Geronimo, however, remained firm. He did not want to try to make peace with the Americans again. Although he continued to maintain control over the Chiricahuas, his influence was decreasing.

In early January, 1886, Crawford found a trail left by some of the Apaches near Oputo and followed it as rapidly as he could. Deeper and deeper into the mountains he led his men, up one crest after another, moving cautiously but rapidly. He was in such a hurry that he marched for eighteen hours straight, and on the morning of January 11, he located their ranchería and attacked. The mountains and the forests echoed with the sound of shots as his men poured bullets into it. But although the Apaches were completely surprised, Crawford's scouts inflicted little bodily injury. They had to flee so quickly, however, that they could not take their supplies with them. Crawford captured most of their horses and other belongings, which was a demoralizing blow and proved to many of the Apaches the pointlessness of fighting on. Choosing one of their women as a messenger, they opened negotiations for peace and agreed to conclude them the following morning, which would give them time to hold the necessary council. Even Geronimo, in the face of this fresh attack, was beginning to weaken.

The American forces had been concentrating their attention on the Apaches and did not realize that another potential enemy was also tracking the Indians. This was a detachment of Mexican soldiers, accompanied by Indians who had been selected for their hatred of Apaches. A mist had fallen over the mountains, and in the uncertain light, the Americans thought the Mexican detachment must be Davis's and that he had crossed the Sierra Madres. The Mexicans, however, mistook the American scouts for the enemy Apaches and, without asking any questions, began shooting. In self-defense, the scouts returned the fire. Crawford and the two Americans who were with him stepped forward and called out their identity. The firing continued. Crawford sent the other two back to calm the scouts, while he himself climbed a boulder where he could be better seen. A Mexican bullet struck him in the head, and he fell mortally wounded.

While Geronimo and the Chiricahuas watched in amusement, the battle between the Mexicans and the Americans became more general. Lieutenant Marion P. Maus succeeded to Crawford's command and was finally able to restore order, but the Americans had suffered one dead and four wounded. The Mexicans had lost about four men and an almost equal number wounded and were in an evil temper. They demanded that Maus provide them with mules for carrying their wounded back to civilization. In the interests of international harmony, Maus gave them some.

In addition to the dead and wounded, the battle had seriously affected the negotiations with the Apaches. A short while before, most of them had been ready to surrender to Crawford. Now they were not so sure they wanted to. Finally they agreed to come north and talk with Crook personally, but they insisted Crook must not bring soldiers with him to the conference. Because they needed time to collect supplies from their scattered caches, they set a date several weeks away.

Under the circumstances, these were the best terms Maus could hope for. The Apaches were now alert to the presence of the Americans and ready to fight or run farther into the Sierra Madres. So his chances of capturing them would be slight, at least without heavy casualties among his own men. On the other hand, they seemed truly willing to make peace.

By March, 1886, the Apaches had finally come north and met with Maus, who had been waiting for them. He notified Crook that they were ready to talk. The general had enough troops available for a full-scale battle, but he wisely abided by the Apaches' wishes and did not bring them with him. If he had done so, he knew the Apaches would have noticed them from a distance and would have disappeared into the mountains again. He had with him only a handful of people, including a few staff assistants and several Apaches. Among these were Chiricahua women with news of the Apaches' friends on the reservation and Ka-ya-ten-nae. Crook had had his sentence reduced to eighteen months and granted him permission to return to Fort Apache. As a result of Crook's kindness and the impression made on him when he saw the size of San Francisco, Ka-ya-ten-nae had become a firm friend of the Americans and a loyal supporter of Crook.

The place Geronimo had chosen for the parley was the Canyon de Los Embudos in northeastern Sonora, several miles below the border. Crook quickly saw why the Apaches had selected this site. Maus was camped on a small mesa overlooking the plentiful supply of water in the canyon, and there was also enough fuel and grass at hand to last through long negotiations. The Apaches had made their camp on a small conical hill only about 500 yards away. The hill, however, was surrounded by several steep ravines, and, as Crook commented, it would have required a thousand men to have stormed it. By that time, the Apaches would have been gone. Nor did they ever relax their guard, for they came into Maus's camp only in small groups. The other Indians remained on the hill to guard it.

Crook had three principal leaders to deal with. In the democractic fashion of the Apaches, none of them could speak for the band as a whole. Any final decision had to be debated in council. Furthermore, the influence of these leaders varied according to the particular circumstances at a given time and the mood of the band as a whole. Geronimo was not a chief, but his prowess in battle had won him a reputation as a war leader. He commanded a small personal following, but the others would be guided by him, especially if they were preparing to fight. Second, there was Chihuahua. He had a larger personal following than Geronimo but was less well regarded as a warrior. Last, there was Nachez, son of Cochise and the hereditary chief of all the Chiricahuas. But he had never attained the position his father had had. He had a small personal following and little influence in council. Of the three, Crook was most concerned about Geronimo because he was least disposed to be friendly to the Americans.

As soon as Crook had eaten his lunch, Geronimo asked to talk to him. From the American point of view, this was a poor sign, for the Apaches' choice of Geronimo as a spokesman indicated they were in a belligerent mood. Otherwise they would have selected a less warlike leader to negotiate with the Americans. Geronimo came to Crook's camp, accompanied by Nachez and Chihuahua, and met with Crook in the shade of some cottonwoods and sycamores growing in the bottom of the canyon.

Geronimo began speaking. "I want to talk first of the causes which led me to leave the reservation. I was living quietly and contented, doing and thinking of no harm. . . . I was living peaceably and satisfied when people began to speak badly of me. I should be glad to know who started those stories. . . . I was behaving well. I hadn't killed a horse or a man, American or Indian. I don't know what was the matter with the people in charge of us. They knew this to be so, and yet they said I was a bad man and the worst man there; but what harm had I done? . . .

"Some time before I left, an Indian . . . had a talk with me. He said, 'They are going to arrest you,' but I paid no attention to him, knowing that I had done no wrong; and the wife of Mangas, Huera, told me that they were going to seize me and put me and Mangas in the guardhouse, and I learned from the American and Apache soldiers . . . that the Americans were going to arrest me and hang me. . . .

"I have several times asked for peace, but trouble has come from the agents and interpreters. I don't want what has happened to happen again. Now, I am going to tell you something else. The Earth-Mother is listening to me and I hope that all may be arranged that from now on there shall be no trouble and that we shall always have peace. . . . From this time on, I hope that people will tell nothing but the truth. . . . There are very few of us left. We think of our relations . . . living on the reservation, and from this time on we want to live at peace just as they are doing, and to behave as they are behaving. . . ."

Crook carefully watched the stocky, powerful Apache with his scarred face but said nothing. Suddenly Geronimo broke off and asked him, "What is the matter that you don't speak to me? It would be better if you would speak to me and look with a pleasant face. It would make better feeling. I would be glad if you did. I'd be better satisfied if you would talk to me once in a while. Why don't you look at me and smile at me? I am the same man; I have the same feet, legs, and hands, and the sun looks down on me, a complete man. I want you to look and smile at me."

Crook, however, insisted on hearing him out before saying anything.

". . . While living I want to live well," Geronimo continued. "I know I have to die sometime, but even if the heavens were to fall on me, I want to do what is right. . . . Every day I am thinking, how am I to talk to you to make you believe what I say; and, I think, too, that you are thinking of what you are to say to me. There is one God looking down on us all. We are all children of the one God. God is listening to me. The sun, the darkness, the winds, are all listening to what we now say.

"To prove to you that I am telling the truth, remember I sent you word that I would come from a place far away to speak to you here, and you see us now. Some have come on horseback, and some on foot. If I were thinking bad, or if I had done bad, I would never have come here. . . . Now what I want is peace in good faith. . . . I have finished for today."

Crook replied, ". . . why did you kill innocent people, sneaking all over the country to do it? What did those innocent people do to you that you should kill them, steal their horses, and slip around in the rocks like coyotes. . . . You promised me in the Sierra Madres that peace should last, but you have lied about it." He also accused Geronimo of having lied to the Indians about the deaths of Davis and Chato, thus driving the other Apaches into flight.

The two men went over the same topics again and again, neither yielding to the other, for, to an extent, they were both bluffing. Geronimo knew that his band was shattered and discontent. Many of them would desert him if he went on the warpath again, and Crook, that master of Indian fighters, would be on his trail with the Apache scouts. On the other hand, Crook knew that any time he wanted, Geronimo could take off for the mountains again; and although the Americans would eventually catch him, the desperate Apache would demand a high price for his life. So they sat and talked under the trees and, at the end of the first day, reached no conclusion.

That night, the next day, and the next night, the Apaches conferred. Chihuahua and Nachez had already weakened and were now ready to surrender. Although he tried to, Geronimo could not persuade them to continue demanding the best possible terms. He also knew that if they gave themselves up, they would take most of the band with them, so he would have to surrender, too.

At the next meeting, Chihuahua, reflecting the wishes of the council, replaced Geronimo as the principal spokesman. Crook had offered the Apaches two choices, but during the negotiations, they developed another alternative. The Apaches said they would agree to be sent East as a punishment, provided the period of their exile was not longer than two years. They would also expect that those of their friends and relatives who wished to join them would be permitted to do so. In addition, they made an exception of Nana. He was an old man and should be allowed to go directly back to the reservation.

Crook was wise enough to withdraw his demand for their unconditional surrender and accept these terms. After his experience with Ka-ya-ten-nae, he was certain that two years away from their homeland would subdue the Apaches, the fighting would be ended, and peace would be restored to the Southwest. The three leaders shook hands with Crook, Geronimo being the last to do so.

"We are all comrades, all one family, all one band," Geronimo said. "What the others say, I say also. I give myself up to you. Do with me what you please. I surrender. Once I moved about like the wind. Now I surrender to you and that is all." With those words, he shook hands with Crook again. Reluctantly, he had followed the wishes of the other Apaches and given up his freedom.

Crook made no attempt to disarm the Indians. With the few scouts he had and his own small personal escort, he could not have done so. And if he had tried, they would have either fought with him or fled back to their mountains. So in the evening, the Americans and the Apaches returned to their separate camps.

The fires had been lighted, and all was peaceful in the Canyon de Los Embudos, when a white man entered the Apaches' camp. To the great pleasure of Geronimo and the others, he had brought with him demijohns of mescal that he was willing to sell them. Unable to resist the chance to get drunk, the Apaches bought his liquor and listened to the stories he had to tell them. These were about the horrors that awaited them once they were firmly in the Army's custody. The man was Bob Tribolet, a Swiss-American, who lived just south of the Mexican border. At his place, he sold mescal and whiskey, and he probably also engaged in smuggling. That night, he was apparently acting as an agent of the war contractors. Once hostilities ceased, their profits would diminish, so they were anxious to see the fighting continue.

The following morning, Nachez was so drunk that he had passed out on the ground. Everything at the Apache camp was in confusion. Four or five mules were wandering around saddled but without riders. Geronimo and four other warriors were trying to ride two mules between them. The American officers were furious at Tribolet, and some of them wished they could hang him. But although they could see the damage he had done with his liquor, they did not know the wild rumors he had started among the Apaches. So they smashed the five demijohns they found undrunk and thought the problem was over.

Crook, anxious to get back to Arizona and file his official report to Washington, hurried ahead. The Apaches, whose mules were tired after their journey, were to follow him north more slowly, with Maus and his scouts serving as their escort.

His imagination inflamed by Tribolet's liquor and stories, Geronimo began to regret having come to terms with Crook. The general, he recalled, had once stolen his cattle from him. He may well have been responsible for the rumors that led Geronimo to leave the reservation. Perhaps, he thought, Crook was not as trustworthy as he appeared.

That night, Tribolet got more liquor into the Apaches' camp. As a result of the drinking, shots were fired. Geronimo heard the sound and thought the Apaches were being attacked. In a frenzy of terror, he went to Nachez, who shared his alarm. Chihuahua did not, and he remained in camp; but the other two leaders, hastily gathering approximately eighteen warriors and nineteen women and children, fled toward the mountains. The Apaches were on the warpath again.

XVIII

A Lie Is Mightier Than a Sword

MAUS sent word to Crook of Geronimo's flight and, with some of his scouts, went in pursuit of him, while the remainder of his men escorted the other Apaches north. Crook was disappointed by the news but not dismayed, for he was certain that as soon as Geronimo's band became sober and he could open communications with them, they would return. His hopes were confirmed by the almost immediate surrender of two of the warriors, who gave themselves up as soon as they recovered from their hangovers.

But when Crook made his report to Washington, the officials were stunned. Philip Sheridan was the commanding general, and because he had once fought the Plains Indians, he thought he knew how to fight Apaches. Sitting at his desk in Washington with little knowledge of either the terrain or the Apaches' tactics, he constantly demanded that the troops win an immediate military victory in the classical European tradition, and no amount of explanation could persuade him this was a different type of war.

When he learned Geronimo had escaped, he completely forgot that Crook had subjugated all but a small band of approximately twenty warriors from one tribe and began barraging Crook with questions and criticisms. He could not understand why Crook had ever bargained with the Apaches and settled for anything less than unconditional surrender. In fact, he wanted Crook to rescind his agreement with those already in his custody. Most of all, Sheridan could not believe that Geronimo could have escaped without the connivance of Crook's Apache scouts. He had never really approved of their use in the first place, and now he was certain they were treacherous and untrustworthy.

"Your dispatch of yesterday received," he wired Crook. "It has occasioned great disappointment. It seems strange that Geronimo and party could have escaped without the knowledge of the scouts."

Crook had long since learned that regular soldiers were almost useless against the Apaches and had based his entire strategy on employing other Apaches to fight them. In view of Sheridan's condemnation, which struck at the basis of his entire strategy, and also Sheridan's insistence on considering Chihuahua's band prisoners of war in spite of Crook's agreement with them, Crook wired in reply, "That the operations of the scouts in Mexico have not proven as successful as was hoped, is due to the enormous difficulties they have been compelled to encounter from the nature of the Indians they have been hunting, and the character of the country in which they have operated, and of which persons not thoroughly conversant with both can have no conception. I believe that the plan upon which I have conducted operations is the one most likely to prove successful in the end. It may be, however, that I am too much wedded to my own views in this matter, and as I have spent nearly eight years of the hardest work in my life in this department, I respectfully request that I may now be relieved of this command."

Sheridan was glad to comply with Crook's request and promptly transferred him to the Department of the Platte. In his place, he appointed Nelson A. Miles. Miles had an excellent reputation as an Indian fighter, a reputation gained partly by his performance in the field and partly by his skill in taking credit for himself. In most respects, he was the antithesis of Crook. Crook was modest; Miles was vain. Crook had the moderate ambition of a career officer; Miles secretly hoped to become President of the United States. Crook liked to be with his soldiers in the field; Miles preferred the comforts of posts and cities. Crook fought the Apaches hard, but he respected them; Miles disdained them as ignorant, vicious savages. "They excelled," he later wrote, "in strength, activity, endurance, and also in cruelty. They were cruel to everything that came within their power. . . . Their atrocities are simply too horrible and shocking to write out in words." So little did he understand the Apaches that when he retold the story of Eskiminzin, he said, "There is an Indian by the name of Schmizen [Eskiminzin] still living in that Territory who, for a number of years was in the habit of traveling past a certain white man's dwelling and on these occasions was always treated kindly, given food, and made comfortable whenever he cared to tarry. One morning after having stayed there long enough to secure a good breakfast, he picked up his rifle and killed his benefactor, and then went away boasting of what a strong heart he had. 'Why,' he remarked, 'a weak man or a coward could kill his enemy or any one who had done him an injury; but it takes a man of strong heart to kill a friend or anyone who has always treated him kindly.' This," Miles added, "is a specimen of Apache reasoning." He made no mention of the sad reasons why Eskiminzin had killed Charles McKinney or the massacre at Camp Grant. To Miles, Apaches were vicious brutes and should be treated as such.

As one of his first moves, he disbanded most of the Apache scouts, including all the Chiricahua and Warm Springs Apaches who had served Crook so well and faithfully. From then on, he intended to use Indians only in small groups of threes and fours, primarily as trackers. All the actual fighting was to be done with regular soldiers.

Next, he set in motion the most elaborate military preparations ever undertaken in Arizona. At great expense, he constructed and manned a complex network of heliograph stations. These were placed on some of the highest peaks, where their crews, using mirrors, could flash sunlight from one station to another and transmit signals by Morse code. They covered southeastern Arizona and part of northern Sonora. Under Miles's command were several thousand soldiers, to fight less than twenty Apaches. He organized these men in an intricate pattern of patrols, hoping to guard every water hole and every pass, thus making travel for the Apaches almost impossible.

Geronimo and Nachez concentrated their first efforts on evading Maus and his scouts. After they had done this and spent a few safe weeks in the mountains, they raided across northern Sonora, and in April, 1886, shortly after Miles took command, they crossed the border and stole some horses from Calabasas, a small town just north of Nogales. They next rode to the Peck ranch, only a few miles away, where they surprised and killed Mrs. Peck and her thirteen-year-old child and captured her ten-year-old niece. (When the Apaches killed women and children, it was murder; when the Americans did so, it was a victory.) After mutilating the two corpses, the Apaches ransacked the ranch house and took what clothing they wanted.

Peck and his helper, Owens, were two miles away, taking care of a sick bull. Geronimo led the Apaches in search of them and was able to surround them without their knowing it. Owens was mounted on a fast horse, and when he looked up and saw the Indians, he drove his spurs into its flanks and raced away, hoping to escape. Peck had no such chance and was taken prisoner immediately. Owens rode several hundred yards with some of the Apaches chasing him. Then their bullets brought him down. They salvaged his saddle and came back to join the others. Peck saw that his niece was a captive and, recognizing Owen's saddle, knew his helper was dead. Stricken with grief, he began acting like a crazy man. At least, that was the only way he could later explain Geronimo's action. For instead of killing Peck, the Apaches took away his boots and let him go free. The Americans thought Indians respected the insane as being possessed. It never occurred to them that Geronimo might have let Peck go because the cattleman was entirely defenseless.

Peck limped his way over the rough ground to his ranch,

where he found his dead wife and child. He put on a pair of slippers the Apaches had left as useless and walked another nine miles to Calabasas. The people of Nogales had already heard of the first raid, and a posse of eighty civilians arrived at the town just about the time Peck did.

Captain Thomas C. Lebo of the Tenth Cavalry was also alerted. With a detachment of troops, he was the first to arrive at the Peck ranch. His men wrapped the bodies of the woman and the child in blankets, buried them, and then picked up Geronimo's trail and started in pursuit.

Alarm spread across the country. Rumor was added to rumor. The number of dead Americans was three, but the newspapers carried the news that eight had been slain. The size of the Apache band also constantly grew. By May, it was reported that at least 150 warriors were ravaging the country, which was a tribute to Geronimo's fighting ability. Miles's heliographs flashed their messages from peak to peak. Geronimo saw the lights and thought they must be some sort of magic. So with typical Apache caution, he carefully avoided the mountaintops on which they were located as he led his warriors on their wild race.

He also avoided the American Army. In spite of his intricate preparations, Miles could not find the Apaches. Early in May, however, Lebo's troops discovered Geronimo's trail going into the Pinto Mountains of Sonora. Since his warriors and mounts were both weary, the troops began to overtake them for the first time. Rather than continue to race, he turned to fight. Choosing a steep slope up which he thought the soldiers would be foolish enough to charge, he hid his warriors, taking full advantage of all the cover available. Just as he had expected they would, the Americans tried to storm his position. The Apaches' guns fired, and the sound of shots rang in the air. One soldier slipped from his saddle, dead, another lay wounded on the ground, and the remainder turned their horses and dashed downhill to safety. In spite of the Apaches' bullets, a lieutenant ran forward, picked up the wounded man, and carried him back. While the Americans were busy caring for their casualties, the Apaches quietly slipped away, and Lebo's men did not attempt to follow them farther.

Miles now had several commands on Geronimo's trail—the men under Lebo and additional troops under Lieutenant H. C. Beson and Captain C. A. P. Hatfield. Probably never before in American military history have so many men pursued so few. But Geronimo dodged, turned, and twisted in the tradition of Nana and Victorio. His knowledge of the country and the tremendous endurance of his warriors gave him an advantage. Except for that one encounter, which had resulted in an Apache victory, the cavalry was having difficulty catching up to him.

On May 10, the Apaches killed two prominent citizens of Nogales and again fled. Captain Hatfield was ordered east of Santa Cruz, Sonora, as the Indians were expected to move in that direction. Hatfield located their camp and attacked. The Apaches were caught by surprise and fled, suffering only one casualty, a warrior named Ki-e-ta, who was wounded. He could not keep up with the others and, tired of warfare, hid until the American soldiers left. Then he traveled the long distance to Fort Apache and gave himself up.

Rounding up the Apaches' horses and collecting their belongings, Hatfield started west to Santa Cruz, proud of the victory he had won. But Geronimo was not giving up that easily. He and his warriors raced ahead, outflanked Hatfield, and laid an ambush in a narrow canyon through which they were certain Hatfield would march. One by one, the confident Americans entered the canyon. All was quiet except for the sound of the horses' hooves and the jingling of their bridles. When the Americans were well within the ambush, Geronimo's warriors began shooting. One of the soldiers fell to the ground, wounded. Two of his companions went to rescue him, but even as they were carrying him to safety, another Apache bullet struck and killed him. Hatfield's command, trapped in the narrow canyon, was in confusion. Suddenly, the Apaches swooped down on them and recovered their horses and most of their supplies. Then they were off again, leaving behind several more names to be entered on the American casualty lists.

Sometimes Geronimo's band, when hotly pursued, would scatter in typical Apache fashion, and the soldiers would not know which trail to follow. Sometimes he would lead the troops up into a range of mountains. When the terrain became too rough for horses or mules, he would abandon his mounts and proceed on foot across the crest and down the other side, where he would steal more animals and ride away. Meanwhile the troops, who were far less flexible, would travel the long way around the range, occasionally marching eighteen hours or more at a stretch in their hopeless effort to keep up.

Rumors grew, caused by the hysteria that gripped Arizona and New Mexico. It was said that signal fires had been lighted near the Mescalero reservation as a sign to the Mescalero Apaches to rise up and join Geronimo. Stories spread that the Chiricahua and Warm Springs Apaches remaining at Turkey Creek might break out. Reports flashed along the wires and over Miles's heliograph that the Apaches were here and then were there. Posses rode over the country. The Mexicans recruited Papagos, the Indians who had helped deal such a tragic blow to Eskiminzin, armed them, and sent them against the small band of Apaches. They could not find them either.

Some of the rumors were spread deliberately. A prospector near Prescott, Arizona, came running out of the mountains to report the presence of a large band of enemy Indians. In substantiation of his story, settlers had seen numerous signal fires burning. The sheriff organized a large posse to pursue the Apaches and discovered the truth. The prospector and his partner had discovered an unusually large lode of ore. Wanting the entire claim for himself, the prospector had murdered his companion and lighted the fires to prevent anyone from entering the mountains until he had hidden all traces of his crime and entered his claim. There were also truths that were never reported. Lonely miners and cowboys, both Mexican and American, were shot down, but their presence was never missed. During these hectic weeks, one Mexican herdsman had a lucky experience. Geronimo captured him in Sonora but, finding him unarmed, told him he was a good man who obviously meant no harm to anyone and released him. The newspapers reported the story with incredulity, although this was the second time during his raid that Geronimo had shown mercy to the defenseless.

In June, Geronimo was attacked by a detachment of Mexican soldiers. Several versions of what happened found their way into print. According to one, the woman charged with guarding Peck's niece was sleeping a short distance from the others at a point toward which the Mexicans were approaching. A warrior warned her to draw closer to the others, but she remained where she was with the white girl to guard that fringe of the camp. In the subsequent fighting, she was killed and Peck's niece was rescued. In another version, the white girl was being carried by a warrior who was wounded and whose horse was killed. He stood off the Mexicans but was finally forced to abandon the girl. In any case, she was actually recovered and turned over to the American troops in Mexico, who sent her home.

The reports of the casualties suffered by both sides in the battle varied greatly, as they so often did. One said the Mexicans suffered three dead and one wounded. Another claimed the Mexican dead totaled seven. As for the Apaches, the reports went from a minimum of a woman killed and one warrior wounded to a high of seven warriors dead. Add those last figures to the many other Apache casualties reported, officially and unofficially, and Geronimo's band of less than twenty warriors was wiped out many times over during the spring and early summer of 1886. In actuality, however, he broke off the fighting in July and disappeared into the mountains almost unscathed. Miles's thousands of regular soldiers had not inflicted a single fatal casualty on the small group.

Geronimo's decision to retreat to the Sierra Madres was entirely his own. Neither the Mexican nor the American armies had driven him there. He had been campaigning for months at a speed that exhausted the troops trying to keep up with him.

Now he and his warriors thought the time had come to take a rest themselves.

As part of his strategy, Miles had assigned a column of men under Captain Henry Lawton to flank the Sierra Madres on the west. The men were chosen for their physical strength and their ability as Indian fighters, and they endured unbelievable hardships as they marched back and forth through the wild, inhospitable lands of eastern Sonora. Many of them became so exhausted from this arduous work that they had to be replaced.

In assigning these men to this duty, Miles was following Crook's strategy, but not his tactics. Crook's various columns had been largely composed of Apache scouts, who were capable of picking up the enemy's trail and tracking them into the Sierra Madres. Miles's column was mostly made up of regular soldiers, and they did not pose much of a threat to Geronimo. If he wanted to raid into Sonora, they might come after him, but he had had enough of raiding for the time being. As long as he remained high in the mountains, he had little to fear from Lawton.

Geronimo's raids had now given Miles second thoughts about the Apaches. His personal popularity in Arizona and New Mexico remained high, higher than Crook's. Crook had fought and captured Apaches without much fanfare and with the quiet, unspectacular use of his small number of Apache scouts. Miles had regular troops massed here and there where the public could see them. In the opinion of many people, Miles was a general who was at last doing something about the threat to their homes and lives. They missed the point that all this activity was producing extraordinarily little in the way of results, particularly considering how few of the enemy were left.

Miles himself, however, was gaining new respect for the fighting capabilities of the Apaches. Originally he had believed he could defeat them as easily as he had beaten the other Indians against whom he had fought. Now, as he watched the futile maneuvering of his troops, he was beginning to realize he could not. He became so obsessed with Apaches that he began to worry even about those who were living peacefully on the reservation, particularly the Warm Springs and Chiricahua Apaches, who had demonstrated their faithfulness to the United States by refusing to accompany the others when they fled and by serving in the Army under Crook. The more he thought about them, the more concerned Miles became. If they should decide to break out, too, the war would be uncontrollable.

Chihuahua and his band were at Fort Marion, Florida, which was a relief. But why not ship the others away, also? Miles asked himself. Although he was violating the treaty the Americans had made with the Apaches, Miles began to make plans to send them at least as far east as Fort Sill in Indian Territory. As a first step, he selected a delegation headed by Chato and had them go to Washington. He hoped they would be impressed by the sights and persuaded to negotiate their own removal. The Apaches were interested in what they saw but had no desire to leave Arizona. On their return trip, they stopped at Fort Leavenworth. To their surprise, the government held them there, while Miles went ahead with his plans to transfer the others. He later wrote that Chato and the delegation "became defiant and exceedingly troublesome," as well they might have. Once again, the Americans had broken their word.

On the other hand, he made one wise, unspectacular move in Crook's tradition. Among the officers who had worked with the Apaches was Lieutenant Charles B. Gatewood. Unlike many of the officers, Gatewood liked the Apaches and, when he had been living at Fort Apache, had had an Indian nurse for his son. The Apaches, in turn, liked and respected him. He had met Geronimo personally several times, and Geronimo knew the high esteem in which the White Mountain Apaches held him. Although he was in bad health and had been transferred to New Mexico, Miles asked him to return and attempt to open negotiations with the enemy. Gatewood, who was noted among his fellow officers for his courage, accepted the assignment. According to Miles's plan, he was to be accompanied by two Chiricahua Apaches, Ki-e-ta, who had defected from Geronimo's band, and a warrior named Martine. He was also ordered to obtain an escort of twenty-five regular soldiers and not go near Geronimo without it. Because the commanding officer at Fort Bowie, where Gatewood prepared for his trip, could not spare that many men, Gatewood set off without the escort.

He traveled south through Sonora without obtaining any information concerning Geronimo's whereabouts, for the Apache was staying deep in the mountains. After covering more than a hundred miles, Gatewood joined Lawton's column. But Lawton did not know where Geronimo was either and was simply patrolling in the hope of picking up a trail.

Although he was safe in the mountains and leading the life he loved, Geronimo kept wishing he had some mescal. Raids provided ammunition and guns, but it was only good fortune when the Apaches came across substantial supplies of the white men's liquor. The only sure way to obtain it was by trading. With this in mind, Geronimo opened up negotiations for "peace" with the Mexican town of Fronteras, which is south of Douglas, Arizona. Neither side was truly interested in stopping the fighting, but Geronimo wanted mescal, and the Mexicans thought they might have a chance to get the Apaches drunk and kill them all. So they responded favorably to the overtures of the women Geronimo sent to treat with them and also began to arm themselves heavily for the slaughter they hoped would follow.

Times had changed without Geronimo's realizing it. In the old days, the people of Fronteras might have given him mescal to prevent his attacking them, or they might have attempted to massacre his warriors. He was prepared for either of these possibilities. But instead of following the traditional pattern of dealing with the Apaches by themselves, the people of Fronteras spread the news of Geronimo's presence, and troops began to converge on the small town. Gatewood and Lawton received the report and, in the middle of August, 1886, raced back north, for Fronteras is only about thirty miles below the border. The going was rough and slow, and when they were close to the town, Gatewood went ahead while Lawton followed close behind. Arriving at Fronteras, Gatewood discovered that Lieutenant Wilbur E. Wilder, with a detachment of troops, had reached it before him. From the officer, he learned that two women from Geronimo's band had been in the town shortly before but had left, taking some mescal with them.

The Mexican officials had their plans all laid. They had brought in 200 Mexican troops and intended to entice Geronimo into Fronteras, get the Apaches drunk, and then massacre them. This was the old trick they had used so many times before, but Geronimo was alert and suspicious. He had trusted the Mexicans too many times before with fatal results, and he was not going to fall into one of their traps again. Although he would send his women for liquor as long as the Mexicans would give it to him, he did not approach the town himself or let any of his warriors do so. They remained a considerable distance away, where they could either defend themselves or escape to the mountains.

The arrival of Gatewood disturbed the people of Fronteras. Although they had not yet succeeded in luring Geronimo into their town, they were still hopeful and were afraid that Gatewood might upset their plans by alarming the Apaches. So they begged him not to follow the women or try to talk to the Apaches. But Gatewood was determined to carry out his assignment. With his two Apaches, Ki-e-ta and Martine, and eight men from Wilder's command, he left Fronteras, going south as though he intended to join up with Lawton. But once he was out of the Mexicans' sight, he circled to the east and soon picked up the women's tracks.

To show his friendly intentions, he tied a white rag torn from a flour sack to a stick and had one of his men carry it high, so the enemy could see it. In taking this action, he was deliberately disobeying orders, for he had been firmly instructed not to approach Geronimo with an escort of less than twenty-five men. But Gatewood understood Apaches better than Miles did. If he had gone anywhere near Geronimo's camp with that many soldiers, the Apaches would either have laid an ambush for them or disappeared into the mountains. In that terrain, the Apache leader held the upper hand, and he was not going to lose it by letting a large number of soldiers get close to him.

Ki-e-ta and Martine went ahead of the others, because Gatewood thought they would have a better chance of finding Geronimo if they were by themselves. On the third day, they located Geronimo's camp. Since there were only two of them, Geronimo let them enter it unharmed and asked them what they had to say. They explained Gatewood's mission, and Geronimo listened with interest. He remembered and liked Gatewood and saw nothing to fear in the small number of men he had brought with him. He also thought he might just as well learn what Gatewood had to say. So he asked Ki-e-ta to remain with him and sent Martine back with the message that he would meet with Gatewood on the following day.

That evening about thirty men from Lawton's command joined Gatewood. Geronimo spent the night with the other Apaches, drinking the mescal the women had brought from Fronteras. The next morning, although he had a hangover, he had not lost his sense of caution. When he learned Gatewood was advancing toward his camp with Lawton's men accompanying him, he sent four warriors to warn Gatewood that the soldiers could come no closer. Although the conference was taking place under a flag of truce, Geronimo was taking no chance that such a large force might surround him.

He waited until Gatewood had been conducted to the meeting place and the other warriors had assembled. Then he walked up, his rifle in his hands. Twenty feet away, he laid his rifle on the ground, greeted Gatewood, commented on his ill health, shook hands with him, and sat down so close that Gatewood could feel the pressure of his revolver touching his right thigh. As a peace offering, Gatewood passed around fifteen pounds of tobacco he had brought with him. Each Apache took his share, and the council opened.

Geronimo asked Gatewood what message he had brought from Miles. Gatewood replied he was authorized to offer these terms of surrender: The Apaches would be sent to Florida with their families. The President of the United States would then decide what to do with them. If they did not accept this offer, the Americans would wage war against them until the bitter end.

Geronimo was astonished at the severity of the conditions. When he had surrendered to Crook in March, Crook had told him he would have to go East for two years only, after which he would be able to return to the reservation and resume his former life. He was suffering from his drinking bout of the night before, and his hand shook. He asked Gatewood for some mescal, but wisely Gatewood had brought none with him.

The two men argued. As Crook had predicted he would, Geronimo was willing to surrender. With such a small band, he could not fight off the white men forever, but he wanted to return directly to Fort Apache. Gatewood, however, had no authority to offer him such terms. During the argument, Nachez kept silent. As the day wore on, the discussion continued to be inconclusive, for neither the American officer nor the Apache leader would budge from their original positions.

While Gatewood was talking with Geronimo, Miles was proceeding with his plan to send all the Chiricahua and Warm Springs Apaches on the reservation to Florida. This act was in complete violation of the terms under which they had originally surrendered, but Miles cared little for America's honor. Unfortunately, the officials in Washington, both military and civilian, including President Cleveland, cared as little as he did and encouraged him. Gatewood knew about Miles's plan and thought it had already been carried out. So toward the end of the discussion he told Nachez there was no point in talking further about going back to Turkey Creek, for his mother and daughter were already on their way to Florida. This news stunned Geronimo and Nachez. The announcement of Miles's action swept away all the reasons for their return to the reservation and the whole assumption on which they had based their decision to talk.

The lieutenant went back to his camp, where he found that Lawton himself had arrived with the rest of his men. In the Apache camp, the warriors sat up late discussing their new problem. Nachez undoubtedly led the talk for peace and Geronimo the talk for either war or flight. But Geronimo was interested in knowing more about Miles. Apparently he did not understand that the general was personally responsible for the treachery in moving the Chiricahua and Warm Springs Apaches to Florida and thought he might be a man who could be trusted. So they agreed they would meet with Gatewood again in the morning.

After daybreak, Geronimo and two or three of his warriors came within a few hundred yards of the Americans' camp and signaled that the Apaches wanted to talk to Gatewood. In response to their request, Gatewood returned to the meeting place to hear what Geronimo had to say. Geronimo questioned the lieutenant closely about Miles. He wanted to know what kind of a man he was, what he looked like, whether he could be trusted, and what authority he had. Gatewood extolled his commanding general and told Geronimo the President of the United States had personally sent him to Arizona to deal with the Apaches.

Geronimo listened carefully to everything Gatewood said. He had decided not to surrender to Gatewood, but he thought it might be worthwhile to go north and talk to Miles himself. But he laid down several conditions. The meeting place had to be at Skeleton Canyon on the western slopes of the Peloncillo Mountains. This was close to the north-south travel route of the Apaches, and if anything went wrong, Geronimo could retreat into the mountains he knew so well and escape back into Mexico. The warriors were to be allowed to keep their arms during the trip north, so they could defend themselves against any attacks. Lawton was to provide a loose escort to protect them from either Mexican or American troops, but he was not to come too close. And, as a final condition, Gatewood personally was to travel with them.

These terms were not what Gatewood would have liked and were far from the unconditional surrender he had first proposed. But he decided to take the risk of accepting them. He knew that if the Apaches broke away, he would receive the same censure that Crook had for not disarming them and making them prisoners. And he also knew he was risking his own life. For if the Apaches became nervous, he would be the American easiest to kill.

On the morning of the second day of the trip, a party of almost 200 Mexicans approached the Americans. One of Lawton's officers and his chief of scouts rode out to meet them. The Mexicans, all well armed, were prepared to attack the Apaches' camp and insisted they had a right to do so. Lawton moved quickly. He sent word to Geronimo to break camp immediately and start north. Run from the Mexicans? That was not Geronimo's way. He replied to Lawton that he was ready to attack the Mexicans in the rear while Lawton attacked them in the front. Caught between the two forces, the Mexicans would be annihilated. But Lawton persuaded him to give up this bloody plan and start moving north again ahead of the American soldiers.

With Geronimo out of the way, Lawton told the Mexicans the Apaches were now on their way to surrender and that the Americans would protect them. This made the Mexicans furious, but they finally accepted Lawton's proposal that ten of their men come with the Americans, and in the evening, when they caught up with the Apaches and made camp, they would see for themselves the Indians were peaceful.

Before nightfall, Geronimo learned about the ten Mexicans and suspected treachery. He sent a message to Lawton, demanding to know what their presence signified. Lawton assured him the American soldiers would guarantee his safety, and the two groups of men continued north.

After stopping for the day, Geronimo received word Lawton wanted him to come to the Americans' camp and talk to the Mexicans. He picked up his gun, told his warriors to arm themselves, and went with them to see Lawton. If the Mexicans wanted a fight, he would give them one. As he advanced toward the tree under which the Mexicans were waiting, one of them nervously touched his revolver. Immediately, the Apaches raised their guns, and a general battle might have broken out if the Americans had not jumped between the two hostile groups with their hands in the air. The tension eased, and the Mexicans, satisfied by what they saw, left.

The next day, several of the officers, including Lawton, rode with Geronimo's band to prevent any more threats from Mexicans, while the rest of the command followed behind. During the day, the men in the rear became lost. Lawton, anxious about his troops and scouts, arranged a camping place with Geronimo and left to find the rest of his command. When he did not reappear, Gatewood sent his interpreter after him. He, too, became lost and spent the night wandering around on his exhausted mule. Gatewood and two other Americans remained alone with the Apaches that night when they made camp. If Geronimo wanted to change his mind about meeting Miles, this was the opportunity to do it. He could easily overpower the three white men and take to the mountains again. But instead he told them that they had kept faith with him, so he would keep faith with them. The Apaches' camp, he said, was their camp, and he gave them the best the Indians had to eat.

But when they reached Guadelupe Canyon just north of the border, he became greatly alarmed. Lawton was temporarily absent, and some of the Americans, without the restraining influence of their commander, decided to shoot the Apaches. Geronimo learned what they were planning—he was quick to know everything that was going on in the soldiers' camp—and he began to move his band away from them. Gatewood heard what he was doing and galloped after him. Geronimo and Nachez tried to persuade the lieutenant to leave Lawton's escort and join them in going to Skeleton Canyon by themselves. This was a greater risk than Gatewood dared take, not for fear of Geronimo, but because he needed the soldiers to protect the Indians from Americans, both military and civilian.

Although Gatewood calmed the soldiers, two days later the same talk started up again. Once more Geronimo learned about it. In the few days since he had agreed to make the trip to talk to Miles, he had been threatened three times, once by the contingent of Mexicans and twice by his own American escort. This was a repetition of what always seemed to happen to him when he dealt with the Americans. He was still willing to meet Miles, but he suggested doing it by himself without Lawton's troops around. Once again, Gatewood, with great difficulty, persuaded him not to leave. But the lieutenant, already in poor health when he undertook this assignment, had become exhausted by the great responsibility he bore with so little support and asked Lawton to relieve him of his duty. Recognizing his dependence on Gatewood, Lawton refused.

While Geronimo was traveling to his meeting with Miles, the general was executing his other plan to rid the country of Chiricahua and Warm Springs Apaches. The Indians near Fort Apache were asked to report for a roll call. Not suspecting any treachery, they came in as usual to be counted. Some troops were drilling nearby, but the friendly Apaches paid no attention to them. When they had gathered in a group, the troops suddenly surrounded them, and the commanding officer abruptly told them they were prisoners and would be sent East. The women and children were immediately separated from the men, and all of them were placed under guard. Shortly afterward, they were marched to Holbrook, Arizona, and placed on a train for Florida. Never again would they see their native land or the small farms they had started to work. Every Chiricahua and Warm Springs Apache was sent into exile, including the scouts who had fought so well and courageously for Crook. Even they, after their long months of hard service under the American flag, were considered enemies. This was their reward for believing the Americans.

While this sad betrayal was taking place, Geronimo and his band reached the Peloncillo Mountains. Skeleton Canyon runs deep into the western side of the mountains, and in the rainy season the water from it pours into an arroyo in the broad San Bernardino Valley. Geronimo had chosen this place for the meeting because of the security it offered him. He knew this country; he had traveled north and south through those mountains many times. He was close to the Mexican border, so he could flee to the Sierra Madres. Failing that, he could cross the valley and lose himself in the Chiricahua Mountains, where he had lived with Cochise. Or, to the east, he could reach the Animas Mountains of New Mexico, which the Nednis had visited so often. For his campsite, he carefully selected a rocky mountain spur above the canyon. From that position, he could repel an attack or flee to the mountains as well as overlook the valley and Lawton's campsite below.

He kept watching for the cloud of dust that would indicate Miles was arriving, and from time to time, he went down to Lawton's camp to ask for news. On one occasion while he was there, two cowhands from a nearby ranch rode up to visit the soldiers. Immediately suspicious, Geronimo demanded to know their identity. Reassured by the soldiers' explanations, he rode with them, unarmed, part way back to his own camp. Not until years later did he learn that one of them had seriously considered shooting him on the spot.

Lawton had advised Miles by heliograph of the success of Gatewood's venture and Geronimo's desire to talk to the general personally. But Miles refused to come unless Geronimo sent a hostage to Fort Bowie as a sign of his sincerity. The Apache had complied with this condition, but the sun rose and fell over the San Bernardino Valley and still there was no sign of Miles. The general, who had been so energetic in organizing all those patrols and the complex heliograph network, was considerably less energetic about coming to terms with Geronimo now that Gatewood and Lawton had accomplished the difficult task of persuading him to discuss surrender. Miles, it was rumored later, was delayed by a dinner engagement in Tucson, which he found of greater importance than the end of the Apache wars.

Unlike Crook, who had tracked the Apaches himself into the depths of the Sierra Madres, riding his mule and sharing the hardships of his troops, Miles set out for Skeleton Canyon well equipped with saddle horses and wagons. Although the journey from Fort Bowie was not a long one, for greater comfort he would switch from a horse to a wagon and back again. He also brought with him a heliograph operator and constantly sent messages to Lawton, cautioning the captain not to let himself be captured and taken as a hostage and warning him against letting his men be surprised by an Apache attack. Considering what Gatewood and Lawton had already accomplished on their own, this additional advice from their commanding general was insulting. Rather than new instructions, they needed the presence of Miles himself soon, before Geronimo changed his mind and the wild chase started all over again.

On September 3, 1886, Miles finally arrived at the foot of Skeleton Canyon. Geronimo saw him from his lookout on the rocky spur and rode unarmed to the camp to meet him. Dismounting from his horse, he walked up to Miles and shook his hand.

"The general is your friend," the interpreter told him.

Geronimo quietly replied, "I never saw him, but I have been in need of friends. Why has he not been with me?"

Geronimo opened the conference by recounting the grievances he had suffered in the past and explaining why he was reluctant now to make peace and surrender to the Americans. Miles answered that he would be treated well. He told Geronimo that Chihuahua was in Florida and that the other Chiricahua and Warm Springs Apaches were being sent there. He drew a line on the ground.

"This represents the ocean," he said. He placed a small rock beside the line. "This represents the place where Chihuahua is with his band." He picked up another stone. "This represents you, Geronimo." He placed another stone a little distance off. "This represents the Indians at Fort Apache." He then moved Geronimo's stone and the other alongside the stone representing Chihuahua. "That is what the President wants to do," he said. "Get all of you together."

As Miles continued talking, Geronimo gained the impression that Florida was a land with water, timber, and grass. The Apaches would all live there together in safety and, instead of being considered prisoners of war, they would be given a reservation large enough for them to exist in comfort. Geronimo himself would receive a house and livestock and would not have to work his farm, for the government would supply the labor. And in the winter it would give him clothing and blankets.

Geronimo listened and then said, "All the officers that have been in charge of the Indians have talked that way, and it sounds like a story to me. I hardly believe you."

Miles assured him he was telling the truth. If these were really the conditions of surrender, Geronimo thought, peace was better than war. He had never liked the restrictions of living under the white men's rules with military officers and civilian authorities telling him what to do. On the other hand, he had been fighting for years against hopeless odds, for the white men were endless in number. No matter how many the Apaches killed, there were always others to take their places. Man to man, the Americans could not win, but the war was not man to man. Years ago, Cochise had pointed that out. In spite of his warriors' gallant struggle and the casualties they had inflicted on their enemy, their tribe decreased, while the white men grew ever stronger. Geronimo was also moved by his desire to see his friends. Almost all of them had surrendered, and all he had left was his tiny band. Soon he would be a renegade among his own kind.

Miles, trying to impress Geronimo with the Americans' superiority, told him about the heliograph system. Geronimo had noticed the flashing lights but had not known what caused them. As a demonstration, Miles sent a message to Fort Bowie, inquiring about the welfare of the Apache hostage. In a short time, he received a reply. Geronimo became so interested that he sent for Nachez, who had remained in the Apache camp, probably to protect it from an attack by the Americans.

Nachez came down from the rocky spur. He, too, was interested in both the heliograph and the terms of surrender that Miles had offered. But neither he nor Geronimo could speak for the band. Each individual warrior had the right to be heard in council before any decision was made.

That night, they lighted their campfire and sat overlooking Skeleton Canyon and the wash cutting into the plains of the

San Bernardino Valley. Each warrior had the right to speak, the oldest and best fighters first. Their choice was not easy. Behind them lay the mountains to which they could retreat if they desired. But retreat to what? Freedom, yes. But for how long? A handful of warriors, no matter how brave and skillful, could not survive forever against the continual harassment of thousands of troops. In the person of Miles, sleeping in his blankets in the valley below, was the hope of a better future—a reservation where they could live in comfort and safety with their relatives and friends. If Miles was speaking the truth—and Geronimo thought he was—acceptance of his offer was the better course to follow.

The following day, September 4, 1886, Geronimo returned to the Americans' camp. The morning had started fair, with sunlight splashing over the Peloncillo and Chiricahua mountains and bathing the San Bernardino Valley with desert heat. In the Americans' camp along the wash, the soldiers sweated as they went about their duties, and those who were not working hid in the small amount of available shade. But as the day wore on, the clouds piled up over the mountains and plain—heavy, ominous clouds that blocked the sun.

Geronimo was busy gathering his warriors and consulting with them and Miles. For this was the moment of final decision.

At last, he said to Miles, "I will quit the warpath and live at peace hereafter."

A crack of thunder echoed over Skeleton Canyon, followed by flashes of lightning. The rain came down in torrents, filling the mountain streams with water and drenching the men in the Americans' camp. Geronimo, Nachez, and Miles huddled together in a canvas-covered wagon. The other Indians and Americans hid under the wagons, crawled inside them, or grabbed a few odd pieces of canvas and used them as protection against the rain. Then the clouds rolled back and the sun burst forth again. The Apaches and the white men were at peace.

The next day, they began the journey to Fort Bowie. Geronimo, Nachez, and four other Apaches rode ahead with Miles, while the others followed behind under Lawton's escort. On the trip, three men and three women changed their minds and slipped away, but without a leader like Geronimo to guide them, they posed no real threat to the Southwest. Sooner or later, they would be caught.

The news of Geronimo's surrender caused a flurry of governmental telegrams and memorandums. President Cleveland had wanted the Apaches' unconditional surrender. General Sheridan, believing that was what Miles had obtained, thought they should be turned over to the civil authorities, which would have been the equivalent of murdering them. Just as Crook had been confused by Howard's treaty with Cochise, official Washington could not understand exactly what terms Miles had made with Geronimo. All the telegrams and memorandums and subsequent investigations never completely cleared up the question.

Cleveland specifically ordered Miles to keep the Apache captives in the nearest jail or prison. Miles just as specifically disobeyed those orders and made arrangements to ship them to Florida. He later explained he had no prison or jail large enough to hold them. On September 8, he assembled the Apaches on the parade ground at Fort Bowie, which was now a large and comfortable military installation compared to the fort Carleton had established so many years ago. The sky was bright and clear overhead and the weather warm. Not far away was the spring Cochise had defended and the ruins of the stage station, which, no longer used, had fallen into decay.

The band marched out and sarcastically played "Auld Lang Syne," while the troops laughed and the Apaches looked at them in wonder, for they could not understand the white men's joke. At an officer's signal, the small band of Apaches with its military escort started the trip to the railroad town of Bowie. They descended the trail into the San Simon Valley, through lands the Apaches had freely roamed for so many years. This was the trail Cochise had permitted the stagecoach to use. This was country that Mangas Coloradas had allowed Bartlett's commission to reach without harm. If the Apaches had attacked the first Americans that came into their land, they could easily have defeated them, and the history of the Southwest would have been different. For although the Americans would certainly have come in greater strength later, their settlements would have been much delayed. But the Apaches had treated the first Americans reasonably, and now there were no longer any Apaches in that land except a few individuals who, sooner or later, would be hunted down.

At Bowie, the citizens assembled to see the Indians board the train. One man traded a pair of boots for Geronimo's moccasins. The Apache was pleased with the gaudy new footwear he had purchased. Then the whistle blew, smoke belched from the engine, and the wheels began to turn. Slowly the train started East, gathering speed as it went.

Behind the Apaches lay the Chiricahua Mountains, where the snows would soon fall, and the tall peaks of the Dragoons, where Cochise lay buried in an unknown cave. They went through the pass in the Peloncillo Mountains. To the south of them was the route they had taken so often, to the north lay Steins Peak, where Geronimo, although greatly outnumbered, had held off Forsyth's troops. Those days were over now, never to occur again.

Ahead of them lay the East and the future. It was not a bright one. They thought they were going to a reservation in a land of timber and grass and plentiful water, where they could be at peace but otherwise live as they always had. But there was no reservation waiting for them. Already the government considered them prisoners of war and was preparing room for them in an Army camp. They had thought they would soon see their families and friends; they did not know they would be kept separate from them for many months in contradiction to what Miles had promised. At Skeleton Canyon, Miles had placed the three stones side by side. He did not say the Apaches would be held in three different places in Florida and not allowed to visit each other. He had pictured Florida as a land in which they could live happily. He did not tell them that for Apaches the climate was even worse than at San Carlos.

But such had usually been the case when the Apaches had

dealt with the Americans. They had agreed to live at Cañada Alamosa in peace, but the Americans had broken their word. They had agreed to live on the Chiricahua reservation in peace and had done so. Then the government had ordered them to leave. They had agreed to settle peacefully at Turkey Creek, but those who had kept their word and even fought on the side of the Americans were now condemned to live in Florida. Chihuahua had agreed to go there, thinking he would be allowed to return to Arizona in two years. He was not. Geronimo had surrendered believing he was going to a large reservation. He was not. Always had it been the same. The white men were not to be trusted.

Peace from the Apaches had come to the Southwest, but it had been bought at a high price—the lives of many soldiers, civilians, and Apaches, and a stain of dishonor on a nation's record. In the end, lies accomplished what the Army could not.

Epilogue

THE epilogue was as inglorious as the means by which victory was gained.

Geronimo's surrender, as Tribolet had foreseen when he sold him the mescal, spelled economic problems for many of the war contractors, and some of them fell on hard times. But land values boomed, and in spite of the cut in the Army's expenditures, there was more prosperity for more people than before.

The bloodletting, however, did not stop. Now that the Apaches were conquered, the Americans began shooting at each other. In the sheep and cattle wars around Ganado, Arizona, almost 300 lives were lost; and many parts of the Southwest became as unsafe as they had been before. Sometimes whole families were destroyed in the feuds that took place. And years later at the White Sands, past which Victorio rode when he left the Mescalero reservation to go on his famous raid, the Americans exploded the greatest death-dealing weapon the world has ever known. With it, they later killed far more women and children in a few moments than the Apaches did in hundreds of years of fighting.

As for Miles, he refused to give credit to Gatewood for his part in Geronimo's surrender, would not accept the lieutenant's report of what actually had occurred, and criticized him for disobeying orders by approaching the band of Apaches without the escort of twenty-five men. The city of Tucson held a gala dinner at which Miles was given a ceremonial sword in commemoration of his victory over fewer than twenty warriors. Gatewood was invited to be a guest of honor, but Miles assigned him to some routine clerical duties to prevent his attendance.

Gatewood received a year's sick leave to recover his health. Shortly after his return to duty, a fire broke out at the fort to which he was assigned. In attempting to dynamite one building to save the others, he shattered both arms. Because of this disability, he was retired on the half pay of a first lieutenant. In less than nine years after Geronimo's surrender, he died. The government gave his widow a pension of seventeen dollars a month on which to raise their children. Miles, on the other hand, although he never became President of the United States as he had hoped, did become commanding general of the entire Army.

Mangas had never rejoined Geronimo after their initial quarrel following the outbreak. He stayed farther south in Mexico, but because his band was so small, he did not present much of a threat to either the Mexicans or the Americans. In October, 1886, he raided the Mexican ranch managed by Britton Davis, the former lieutenant, and stole some livestock and wagons. Davis sent word to Miles, who ordered a detachment of twenty men to go in pursuit. They caught up with the Apaches, who were slowed by the wagons they had taken, and captured them easily.

One Apache escaped from the train on the way to Florida and returned to Arizona to lead a lonely life among the mountains, tracked by the white men and without friends. A few other Apaches, who had not joined any of the bands, still remained at large, but they were considered renegades even by their own people.

Eskiminzin became a successful farmer. Many of the merchants at Tucson so trusted him that he could draw on several thousand dollar's worth of credit with them. But Congress failed to appropriate the funds for a survey of the Indians' lands, and Eskiminzin's, which was on the edge of the reservation, was found to contain minerals. The miners took his farm away from him.

Although there were considerable misunderstandings about the terms on which Geronimo had surrendered, everyone agreed Miles had promised him that when they went to Florida, he and his warriors could live with their women, children, and friends. Chihuahua's band was held at Fort Marion; Geronimo and his warriors were taken to Fort Pickens; the women and children were sent to St. Augustine.

The close confinement and the hot, humid climate took its toll of Apache lives, and by 1887, public opinion had become somewhat aroused on their behalf. They were reunited and moved to Mount Vernon Barracks in Alabama. This was an improvement, although not much.

Five years later, they were moved again, this time to Fort Sill in Indian Territory. Once again this was better, but many of them yearned to return to their homeland. No one in Arizona or New Mexico, however, would permit that, so they remained hundreds of miles away from the mountains they loved so well and which they had defended so gallantly.

Geronimo lived what almost amounted to two lives. The Americans were too afraid to permit him and his people to return to Arizona or New Mexico, but he rode in President Theodore Roosevelt's inaugural parade and appeared at the St. Louis Exposition. He sold pictures of himself for twenty-five cents—fifty cents if he signed them in large block letters. But back at Fort Sill, he was just one more Indian, liked by some, disliked by others. At least once more, the Apaches held a puberty ceremony. He loved it, because it brought back memories of those free days so long gone. But the dancers did not come down from the mountains, for there were no mountains to come down from. At times, as he had always done, he would get drunk. If he became too boisterous, the soldiers would throw him into one of the cells in the guardhouse. It is still known as Geronimo's cell and is a cheerless place with a barred door and a window so high that even the tallest man cannot look out of it.

In a newspaper interview in 1908, he said, "I want to go back to my old home before I die. Tired of fight and want to rest. Want to go back to the mountains again. I asked the Great White Father to allow me to go back, but he said no." On February 17, 1909, he died and was buried in the graveyard at Fort Sill.

A few years later, the Warm Springs and Chiricahua Apaches were given the choice of remaining near Fort Sill or going to the Mescalero reservation in New Mexico. Some had small farms in Oklahoma and now did not want to leave them. Many of the others, however, were glad to go. They have since intermarried with the Mescaleros and consider themselves one people. Officially they have named themselves the Tribe of the Mescalero Reservation.

At Geronimo, Oklahoma, I stopped to talk to one of the older and most respected citizens and asked him how the town had received its name. According to his researches, he said, the Indian had been running around that part of the country until the soldiers finally caught him there. So much for local history and local fame.

At Fort Sill, few of the soldiers knew the way to the Apache cemetery. They were too busy fighting today's wars to remember yesterday's. But a sergeant at military police headquarters was able to give me directions.

The heat was intense and the sound of artillery fire rumbled through the air as the men engaged in their daily practice. Geronimo's white marker showed clear and bright in the burning sunlight. Around it were the markers of his family and friends, so he was not alone. At the top of the stone, someone had attached a small, purple artificial flower. He was remembered personally by the living, too, and I was glad of that as I walked away from the old warrior's grave and turned back to the bustle of Fort Sill.

Yes, by American standards, he did sometimes break his word, but hardly as often as the Americans broke faith with him. And even though the Americans did not keep their agreements, he was willing to make new pacts with them again and again. Yes, he did get drunk on mescal, but no more often than many of the soldiers who pursued him. He killed women and children, but the Americans killed just as many or more, and as long as the victims were Apaches, they did not consider it a crime.

But above all, he fought, with skill and courage, as few men ever have against overwhelming odds. And he fought, not for greed or profit or empire, but only for the two causes Americans respect the most—his homeland and his freedom.

General Nelson A. Miles. Appointed to succeed General Crook, General Miles led the final campaign against Geronimo. Although eventually Geronimo surrendered voluntarily, Miles's strategy was relatively ineffective against the Apaches.

Eskiminzin. Chief of a band of Aravaipa Apaches, Eskiminzin voluntarily made peace with the Americans. A posse from Tucson attacked his encampment and slaughtered more than a hundred women and children.

Apache Pass. Because of its plentiful spring, Apache Pass was the most practical route for east-west travelers to take before the advent of the railroad. Control of it was essential to control of southeastern Arizona.

Skeleton Canyon. At the foot of this canyon, which runs into the Peloncillo Mountains from the west, Geronimo negotiated his surrender with General Miles

Loco. On the death of Victorio, Loco became chief of the Warm Springs Apaches. Although he wanted peace with the Americans, Geronimo forced him to leave the reservation and flee to the Sierra Madres.

Dragoon Mountains. These mountains in Arizona were one of the strongholds of the Chiricahuas. Terrain such as this provided the Apaches with many opportunities for ambush or flight.

Fort Bowie. Located in Apache Pass in the Chiricahua Mountains of Arizona, the fort gave the Americans control of the important east-west route used by the stagecoach and most travelers.

Apache Scouts. This photograph, taken around 1883, shows a group of typical Apache scouts, the men on whom General Crook relied to carry out his successful strategy against the Indians.

General George Crook. Of all American generals, General Crook most respected and best understood the Apaches. His strategy proved eminently successful, but misunderstandings with Washington made him ask to be relieved of his command.

Peaches (Tso-ay). The death of a friend made Peaches despair of warfare with the Americans. To prove his friendship for the whites, he served as General Crook's guide in the Sierra Madres.

Mangas. The son of the great chief Mangas Coloradas, Mangas never achieved his father's stature. But he fought resolutely against the Americans and was one of the last to surrender.

John Clum. One of the most effective Indian agents, Clum maintained order with the help of Apache police, some of whom are shown with him. Bureaucratic wrangling finally drove him to resign.

Chato. Although he was disliked by some of the other Apaches, Chato was chosen by them to lead a raid into the United States in search of ammunition. He inflicted heavy casualties and escaped back into Mexico.

Victorio. Chief of the Warm Springs Apaches, Victorio desired peace, but the demands of the Americans for his native lands caused him to wage spectacular warfare against them.

Cochise. Chief of the Chiricahuas, Cochise was one of the most respected of the Apache leaders. At first friendly to the Americans, he took to the warpath when an Army lieutenant tried to arrest him on false charges.

Army packtrain. Unlike the Apaches, who could live off the country, the Americans were dependent on outside sources of supplies. The terrain made wagons useless, so they relied on packtrains.

Fort Apache. Troops from Fort Apache arrested the medicine man at Cibicue Creek, an event that led to another Apache outbreak. Troops from this fort were also the first to pursue Geronimo on his final flight from the reservation.

Nachez. On the deaths of his father, Cochise, and his brother, Nachez became hereditary chief of the Chiricahuas, but he never exhibited his father's unusual qualities of leadership.

Acknowledgments

Many people have assisted me in the preparation of this book, and I wish to thank some of them specifically for their help.

At the Mescalero reservation in New Mexico, Hopkins Smith, Jr., Fred Hickman, and Judge Richard Magoosh received me cordially and gave generously of their time. At the White Mountain reservation, Mr. and Mrs. Edgar Perry of the White Mountain Apache Culture Center spent considerable time with me. They deserve particular praise for their efforts to preserve the Apaches' traditions and history. At the San Carlos reservation, Ted B. White, superintendent, and Colonel Frank A. Wilson, administrative assistant, made the agency's records available and talked to me about the past and present of the Apaches. I also wish to thank Emmanuel Victor, the Reverend Walker Tonto, and Alec David of the same reservation, and their families and friends, for the hospitality they extended.

The Arizona Pioneers' Historical Society, Tucson, Arizona, deserves particular mention for the excellence of its collections about the Southwest. I am appreciative of their permission to quote from the material they possess. Also, all the illustrations in this book came from their files and, too, are printed with their permission. The research librarian there is Miss Margaret J. Sparks, and her cordiality and interest make the library a delight to work in. At Fort Sill, Oklahoma, Gilette Griswold, who directs the museum, and Mrs. Turk, the librarian, were also helpful.

I would also like to thank the following for permission to quote from books or articles they have published: Cooper Square Publishers, Inc., the present publishers of *An Apache Life-Way,* by Morris Edward Opler; Eve Ball, *In the Days of Victorio,* Tucson, University of Arizona Press; the Stackpole Company, *I Fought with Geronimo,* by Jason Betzinez with Wilbur Sturtevant Nye; University of Oklahoma Press, *General George Crook: His Autobiography,* and *Joseph Reddeford Walker and the Arizona Adventure,* by Daniel Ellis Connor; Yale University Press, *The Truth About Geronimo,* by Britton Davis; and *Army,* the successor to *Infantry Journal,* "The Apache Pass Fight," by B. J. D. Irwin.

William Targ of G. P. Putnam's Sons has been in this, as in other books of mine, all that an editor should be. And that is saying a great deal.

I also owe thanks to Mrs. Bryan F. Peters of Tucson, not only for years of friendship, but also for letting me practically convert her house into my office while I sorted out and edited the notes I had collected in months of travel.

Superintendent David G. Stimson of the Chiricahua National Monument made available to me material collected by the National Park Service in connection with Fort Bowie and Apache Pass and arranged to have Robert Gamer and George Durrin of the National Park Service guide me around those historic sites.

Thanks of a special sort are due the members of the Douglas, Arizona, Police Department who so quickly recovered the equipment stolen from my car just before I was leaving for a trip into Sonora. They saved me a loss of time, as well as a financial loss, that I could have ill afforded.

There are many others, too, such as Bryan F. Peters, who years ago shared with me his two great loves: the Southwest and good books. His friendship is one of the warmest recollections of my youth, and I learned much from him that has stood me in good stead all my life. Some played a far smaller but still important role: the trader in Tucson who first taught me some understanding of Indian arts, the *vaquero* who so graciously allowed me to camp on his ranch overlooking the Sonora River, the *patrón* who gave me directions when I was lost near Aconchi, Sonora, and . . . But if I were to thank them all, these would cease to be acknowledgments and would turn into an autobiographical sketch of considerable length. And this is not the place.

As usual, however, I want to thank Mrs. C. R. Horton, Jr., for her loyal help in reading this manuscript and letting me have the benefit of her comments. Finally, I am grateful to George W. Adams both for his helpful suggestions and for drawing the map which appears as endpapers to this book.

Notes

Chapter I

Several accounts of the massacre of the Apaches exist, most of them varying in detail because they were based on hearsay. The episode was often discussed around campfires, and the Apaches many years later still cited it as a reason for not trusting the Mexicans. All the versions agree that the architect of the plan was James Johnson, although some say he was an Englishman rather than an American. All are also agreed that he fired on the Apaches with some sort of heavy weapon, whether it was a six-pounder, a howitzer, or what one of them called a "blunderbus." And there is no disagreement that the attack was launched after the Apaches had been invited to receive meal as a present and that the gun was aimed at the place where the meal was piled. The early settlers liked to talk about "Apache massacres," but they failed to mention that the massacres were more often *of* than *by* Apaches.

The practice of genocide was not uncommon in the Western Hemisphere, and the Americans later resorted to it with the same lack of success as others encountered earlier. Not only was it unjust and inhuman, it usually produced results that were opposite to those intended. It simply made the objects of the genocide policy so angry that they became more relentless than ever. On page 620 of J. P. Dunn, Jr.'s book appears a drawing entitled "Effect of Extermination Policy on Arizona Settler." It shows the settler in tatters, his hands raised in abject hopelessness, and an arrow sticking out of the lower part of his rear. This, even if it says nothing about the inhumanity of the practice, nearly summarizes its ineffectiveness.

Juan José was chief of the Mimbreños Apaches, who were named after the Mimbres River. The Americans later referred to them as the Copper Mines Apaches. They were an important and powerful group and are often considered as a separate tribe, but in time they became indistinguishable from the Warm Springs Apaches.

Today the name of Santa Rita del Cobre has been shortened to Santa Rita. The Americans conduct a large open pit operation there and have done so for many years. The historical markers, however, make no reference to the massacre of the Apaches and their subsequent victory beyond a brief mention that the mines were closed in 1837 because of "Indian troubles." This is certainly insufficient commemoration of an extremely brilliant military campaign. It is not difficult to imagine what the plaques would be like if the victory had been won by the Americans over the Indians.

Those who know that Hermosillo is the capital of Sonora may be surprised at the reference to Ures. In 1832, the capital was moved from Arizpe to Ures and later to Hermosillo. Today Ures is a large but relatively quiet center, some distance from the highway leading north and south through Sonora. The roads to it are good, but tourists come only rarely.

Mangas Coloradas's participation in Johnson's party was told to Eve Ball by the Apache James Kaywaykla. He said that he had heard about it from the son that Mangas Coloradas rescued. Miss Ball says this was corroborated by several other sources.

Chapter II

Many historical factors have conspired to obscure our knowledge of Apache traditions and customs. The early Spanish, and later the Mexicans, can hardly be blamed for their failure to conduct anthropological studies of Indians who lived in widely scattered and small groups and who were among the most implacable of enemies. The missionaries never lived among the Apaches as they did with the Pueblos, and the military and civilian authorities rarely saw them except during brief trading encounters or over the sights of a gun.

Some of the Americans who later moved into the Southwest attempted to learn more about them. Cremony, who served with the commission that surveyed the boundary between Mexico and the United States and was later assigned to Fort Sumner when the Mescaleros and Navajos were held there, made a serious effort to study the Apaches. He even developed an Apache grammar, which he sent to the Smithsonian Institution for publication. Unfortunately, the Smithsonian lost the manuscript, and Cremony did not possess another copy. Others, like Lieutenant Bourke, also studied the Apaches on a systematic basis and added much to our understanding of them. Many of these men, however, had full-time careers to follow, and their anthropological studies had to come after their regular work was done. Furthermore, they were handicapped by some additional problems. The Apaches had no written language; everything they knew was handed down by word of mouth, a procedure that may lead to discrepancies in a short period of time. As far as history is concerned, much was lost because of the Apache custom of never uttering the name of a dead man; many a great chief must have existed who is unknown to us because of this rule of Apache life. Also, the tribes were intermingled by our reservation policies, and this most certainly broke down cultural differences.

A growing interest in Indians has recently stimulated many fresh studies, and anthropologists flock to the reservations in such numbers that "anthropologist" is almost a bad word on some of them. Indians, like white men, do not necessarily relish spending hours having their lives and customs probed by an endless succession of graduate students and other scholars. Nevertheless, some excellent work has been and is still being done to document the customs and traditions of the Apaches as well as other Indians. In writing this chapter, I have drawn on many sources, the three principal ones being Geronimo's and Jason Betzinez's accounts of their lives and Morris Opler's book, *An Apache Life-Way.* This book, incidentally, is also well regarded by many Apaches, which is high praise indeed. Considerable details about Geronimo's early life were recorded both by himself and by Betzinez. It is also reasonable to assume that his family followed the usual Apache customs.

I have used the birthdate of 1829, which is given by both Geronimo and Betzinez. There is reason to believe, however, that Geronimo may have been born earlier than that, at least judging from his account of some of his experiences during his early life.

The shaman's song appears in Opler's *An Apache Life-Way,* page

108. The two quotations from Geronimo himself appear in his own story, pages 19–20 and 20–21.

Chapter III

There is a close parallel between the behavior of the early settlers in what later became Texas and the first Americans to arrive in the territory of the Apaches. In each case, the Americans were certain their laws and customs were vastly superior to those of the original inhabitants and insisted on their adoption. Regardless of the merits of the American tradition—and I believe they are many—this parochial attitude has made many enemies for the United States and has resulted in much bloodshed. Unfortunately, even today the United States has not overcome this habit of forcing its opinions on others, and the results are no better now than they were then.

During the conferences between Bartlett and the Apaches, Bartlett gave particular instructions that the remarks be taken down as accurately as possible. (They appear on pages 312–17 and 334–39 of the first volume of his book.) There is every reason to believe that, aside from some bias in favor of the American point of view, they reflect both what was said and the bewilderment of the Apaches at the Americans' concept of justice. The Apaches simply could not understand why they had to abide by American law just because they had permitted the Americans to enter their territory without fighting them. The logic is difficult to deny, and even Bartlett had great trouble doing so.

The reader should not be surprised at the articulateness of the Apaches. The motion picture and television stereotype of an Indian saying nothing but "ugh" simply does not apply to the Indians of the Southwest. Although they do not, like white men, feel compelled to talk when they have nothing to say, they can be extremely vocal when they do. In addition, they are excellent linguists. I remember one Pueblo Indian joking with me because he could easily converse with me in fluent English, his Spanish was better than mine, and I could not speak Tewa, the language of many of the pueblos. He was a man without much formal education but with an extraordinarily good ear. This is common among the Indians. Before the arrival of the Americans, many of them had learned to speak relatively good Spanish and were able to converse with white men in it.

There were at least five Apache chiefs in the vicinity of Santa Rita del Cobre at this time: Mangas Coloradas, Delgadito, Cuchillo Negro, Poncé, and Coletto Amarillo. The two largest bands camped near the town were led by Mangas Coloradas and Delgadito. The two principal spokesmen for the warrior's widow were Delgadito and Poncé. The Apaches' informal structure operated in such a way that each chief was independent of the others except in matters of mutual interest. It was then that Mangas Coloradas provided the leadership. But otherwise he had no control over the actions of the lesser chiefs. White men had difficulty in understanding this, and it complicated their relationships with the Indians.

The Americans referred to Santa Rita del Cobre as the Copper Mines. To avoid confusion, I have retained the older name because it is the one that appears on modern maps, although shortened to Santa Rita.

Bartlett's statement about the peaceful attitude of the Apaches appears on page 321 of the first volume of his book.

Chapter IV

As in Chapter II, I have followed Geronimo's own story and Betzinez's book closely and also have drawn heavily on Opler's *An Apache Life-Way* and Cremony's *Life Among the Apaches,* as well as on a number of other sources, for details concerning the process of growing up among the Indians.

Geronimo did not mention the route his mother took to Mexico, but it is not difficult to surmise what it was. Old settlers in the Southwest usually knew what route the Apaches would take if they knew their destination, for the Indians almost always went the same way. The problem was not so much knowing how they would travel but how to stop them.

Betzinez says that Geronimo married a Nedni, but Geronimo says Alope was a girl from his own group. This is further substantiated by his adding that he built their home near his mother's. He could not have done this if the girl had been a Nedni, as he would have been required to move to the Sierra Madres to be near her family.

Cremony wrote the description of the Apache hiding. It appears on pages 290–91 of his book. His description of their caution is on pages 214–15. Irving Dodge describes the Indians' problem with liquor, and the quotation comes from page 333 of his book.

Chapter V

Both Betzinez and Geronimo fix the date for the massacre at Janos as 1858, but the evidence seems strong that it occurred several years earlier. When Cremony was a member of the Bartlett Boundary Commission, he went to Fronteras, Mexico, and there talked with the military governor of Sonora, General Carasco. Carasco told him about leading an expedition against some Apaches who were at Janos to receive rations. The military governor of Chihuahua was so angry over this intrusion into his territory that he reported Carasco's action to the federal government at Mexico City. An investigation followed, but after what Carasco considered an unnecessary delay, the federal government exonerated him. It hardly seems likely that two such similar massacres took place at the same spot. Furthermore, Cremony noted the fear of the people of Arizpe at the presence of Apaches. This might well have resulted from the subsequent attack led by Geronimo.

Further evidence of an earlier date is offered by Geronimo. In his account of his life, he says he saw his first Americans about this time. Considering the numerous occasions on which Mangas Coloradas and other Apaches had talked to them, it does not seem possible that he could have avoided meeting them until 1858.

If the date is earlier than 1858, however, Geronimo must have been born before 1829. He was not only a warrior and married at the time, but he also had three children, according to his own account. Pregnancies did not occur in rapid succession among the Apaches, because the men were forbidden to have intercourse with their wives until the latest baby had been weaned. It seems likely that Geronimo was several years older than he believed himself to be and that his chronology of his early years was somewhat foreshortened.

The actual date, however, is not as important as the occurrence itself. Whether it was earlier or later, it deeply affected Geronimo's feelings toward the Mexicans and launched his aggressive career against them. It also accelerated his assumption of a role of leadership. If he had not personally suffered such extreme losses during the massacre, it is doubtful that the Warm Springs Apaches would have appointed someone so young and relatively unknown to be their emissary to the other tribes. Nor it is likely they would have later permitted him to lead them at Arizpe.

For the physical description of Geronimo, I have drawn on what Charles F. Lummis wrote in *The Land of Poco Tiempo,* a book that is a classic of the Southwest. The personal attributes that I have mentioned are obvious from his subsequent career.

The two quotations are from Geronimo's story and will be found on pages 44 and 45.

Chapter VI

For this account of the battle at Arizpe, I have relied on Geronimo's own version, although it contains some apparent but minor discrepancies. Before going on the warpath, he speaks of the Apaches' "scalp-locks." Actually he means their long hair, for they did not shave their heads. At the conclusion of the battle, he says that he ordered the Apaches to scalp the dead Mexicans. Ordinarily the Warm Springs, Chiricahua, and Nedni Apaches did not take scalps, and it is unlikely that they did so in this instance. More probably, in recounting the story, Geronimo was affected by the white men's expectation that Indians always scalped. He also says that he was chosen as war chief of all the Apaches following the battle. There seems to be little question that he distinguished himself in the fighting; and because of the losses he had suffered at Janos, it is likely that the three chiefs let him lead the fight on the last day. But there is no evidence that Mangas Coloradas, Cochise, or Juh surrendered any of their authority to him. For a number of years to come, although he waged relentless war against the Mexicans, he would remain a minor figure among the Apaches compared to men like Cochise and Mangas Coloradas. Toward the end of his career, however, he seems to have gained an ascendancy over Juh among the Nednis.

In his account, Geronimo does not mention a war dance, but this was the customary practice. The dance could have lasted anywhere from one to four nights. I have drawn on Opler for the description of it.

Even today, Arizpe, one of the loveliest of the northern Sonora towns, is difficult to reach from the south. The road leads part of the way along the end of the canyon wall, and a driver does well if he averages eight miles an hour. From the north the going is somewhat easier.

Chapter VII

The chronology of Geronimo's life continues to be somewhat obscure during this period. Betzinez says he married a Chiricahua woman and lived with that tribe for a while. Because of the close relations between the Chiricahuas and the Warm Springs Apaches, this is certainly probable. In a footnote to his own story, Geronimo also says he had two wives and speaks of Mangas Coloradas as his chief. Thus he must have returned to the Warm Springs Apaches, probably in connection with his third marriage. As an Apache warrior relating his exploits at war, he would not think such personal questions a matter of general interest and thus would not discuss them at any length. But his reticence should not mislead anyone into thinking that he did not care about his family. Apaches are an affectionate people.

In his story, he makes no mention of ever attacking the Americans during this period, although he was allied with Mangas Coloradas. It may well be that Geronimo never did, concentrating his considerable capacity for hatred on the Mexicans, at whose hands he had fared so badly. Or it may be that he did join in attacks on the Americans but wisely thought mention of the fact might create further problems for him.

In his story, dictated so many years after the events, two small details seem implausible. In describing the journey he made to warn the ranchería of the approaching soldiers, he says that he and his friend traveled for three days and arrived only three hours before the Mexicans. While this adds some drama to the tale, the

Apaches must have traveled much faster than that. Also, after the battle in which he was wounded, Geronimo says the Apaches scalped their dead enemies. This again was contrary to their custom, and the inclusion of the statement must have been a concession to the expectations of his American readers.

The account in this chapter is based largely on Geronimo's own story. The quotations appear on pages 57, 63, and 64–64. In the last, I have changed the word "warpath" to "raiding," which is more accurate.

Chapter VIII

There are several versions of what has become known as the "Bascom affair," but they are not in agreement in all details. The action was fast, and none of the participants was in a position to observe it all. Also, some of the accounts were written long after the event. Dr. Irwin, for example, wrote his in 1887, twenty-six years later. But they are not in disagreement over the substance of what happened.

Several people have attempted to combine the versions into a single chronological account. Because of the absence of data, this is not entirely possible to do; but I have been helped by the accounts of Robert Utley and R. A. Mulligan.

Much controversy has centered around Lieutenant Bascom, who with the passing years has come to be regarded as less and less of a hero. It is certainly apparent that he was not equal to his assignment. His abrupt seizure of Cochise and the others as hostages was a reckless and impetuous act that enraged the Indians and brought about many deaths. And he seemed to be utterly indifferent to the safety of the other white men at Apache Pass, including the men at the station. The brash, arrogant, inexperienced second lieutenant is an all too familiar figure in military history and a source of many problems.

When he denied any knowledge of the raid on Ward's ranch, Cochise was speaking the truth. The kidnapped boy, Mickey Free, later became a scout for the Army, and he was able to verify what Cochise had said. He was not captured by the Chiricahuas but by an entirely different tribe and was taken to the White Mountains, far from the home of the Chiricahuas.

On the other hand, it is probably not fair to blame Bascom for all the later troubles between the Chiricahuas and the Americans. Cochise did not attack any of the stages going through Apache Pass until the Bascom affair; he did cut wood for the Butterfield company; and he was on friendly terms with the men at the station. But there is evidence that even then he was not above attacking Americans when he thought the circumstances warranted it. After the Bascom affair, however, he made no effort at all to be friendly with them.

Bascom was killed the following February. He was fighting on the Union side at Valverde on the Río Grande.

For many years, the historic sites at Apache Pass—the station, the springs, and the two Fort Bowies that later were established there—were in private ownership. Indeed, Apache Springs was the principal source of water for a nearby cattle ranch. This area has now been made a national historic site and is administered by the National Park Service.

Although passengers often complained about the discomforts of riding in stagecoaches, the driving of them was a great art. The driver held six reins in his hands, one leading to each animal, and, with these and the use of his brake and whip, kept the team in harmonious motion. Some drivers were so skillful that, on approaching a curve, they would set the reins beforehand in such a manner that on entering the curve itself, they had only to apply a slight pressure to the brake in order to create the proper tension on the reins. Unknowledgeable onlookers would think the team had turned by itself. The driver who took the stagecoach that night past the rocks and the Apaches and over the bridge was a man of tremendous skill.

Only one account describes the stage going over the bridge on its axles. But it certainly could have happened.

The quotation from B. J. D. Irwin is on page 374 of his article.

Chapter IX

Cremony, having taken part in much of the fighting and having heard about the rest of it firsthand and shortly after the event, provides an interesting description of the Battle of Apache Pass.

His comments are particularly valuable because of his continued interest in the Apaches themselves. In later years, he talked to them about their side of it and picked up a considerable amount of information that would otherwise have disappeared. His informants, however, told him that sixty-three Apaches were killed by the howitzers. This does not seem probable. It is doubtful that so many Apaches would have remained so long in one place with the shells bursting about them.

It is difficult, once again, to determine precisely the chronology of some of the events, particularly the deaths of the miners from Pinos Altos. The soldiers came across their bodies on the way to the San Simon River. Because the Apaches had left the bodies where they had fallen, the evidence of what had happened was clear, but not the exact date.

No one knows for certain how many Apaches were gathered at the pass. They themselves were probably not sure, and the military was given to overestimating the number of enemies it defeated. This was simply human nature. But there is no question that both chiefs were there and that they were accompanied by one of the largest concentrations of Apache warriors in history.

When John Teal reported back to the wagon train, he said that his horse had been killed. He had crawled toward it, the horse had licked his hand, and this had determined him to kill at least one Apache before he himself was killed. The tale is romantic and touching, but John Teal also kept a diary. I have not been able to examine it personally, but those who have tell me that he states explicitly that the horse was not killed. In some accounts, he is reported to have said that he had with him three bottles of water. But according to the diary, they were not water bottles but whiskey bottles. And they were filled with whiskey. Life in the Army in the Southwest was hard, and drinking was about the only relaxation. The number of bottles of whiskey sold at Fort Bowie was prodigious. They are still being uncovered. But dead horse or live horse, whiskey or water, John Teal seems to have been a man of unshakable nerve. Even with a carbine, he exhibited extraordinary courage in holding off the Apaches and finally escaping from them. None of the accounts seems to indicate that he was in the least shaken by the experience or accepted it with anything but good nature.

Both Utley and Mulligan have done excellent work in correlating the various accounts and providing guides to them.

Roberts's victory at Apache Pass and Carleton's decision to build a permanent fort were important blows against the Chiricahuas. The east-west route was still far from secure, but the most dangerous point was in Union hands.

Geronimo's activities during this period are obscure. In his own story, Geronimo tells about his raid into Mexico and the subsequent defeat of the Mexican soldiers. He then says that because of the supplies they captured, the Apaches of Mangas Coloradas had an easy winter. Either he was mistaken in this, or the raid occurred earlier than 1862. Actually, Mangas Coloradas and the Warm Springs Apaches were hard pressed, which was the reason the chief sought to make peace with the Americans.

Also in his story, Geronimo says that after Fort Bowie was established, he, Cochise, and Mangas Coloradas made peace with the soldiers stationed there, doing so by shaking hands with them. The fort was not built until the summer of 1862, and Mangas Coloradas died the following winter. It seems unlikely that he quickly went back to shake the hands of the men who had wounded and defeated him. Probably Geronimo was referring to a later meeting.

He also relates a story about Mangas Coloradas being taken captive in a tent at Apache Pass and cutting his way out. Most likely, he was thinking of the first episode in the Bascom affair. General Oliver Otis Howard in his book *Famous Indian Chiefs I Have Known* says that Cochise told him Mangas Coloradas was present at that time, but there is no other evidence to support this contention. At least one white chronicler would have noted him, for Mangas Coloradas was not someone to pass unobserved. Many years had passed between the event and Geronimo's dictating the description of it, and he was probably confused.

The two quotations from Cremony appear on pages 166 and 164 in his book.

Chapter X

In describing the capture and murder of Mangas Coloradas, I have relied on Geronimo's account of Mangas Coloradas's early negotiations with the whites at Pinos Altos. It seems extremely likely that he had been led to believe the white men would make peace with him before he started those final conversations from the hillside.

For the remainder of the story, I have depended largely on David Connor's version. He is sometimes vague about his geography, and his account of the travelers' wanderings through New Mexico is occasionally confusing. For example, he does not adequately explain why, having reached Steins Peak, they went back to Pinos Altos. In other respects, however, his account is logical and straightforward. General West's reports, as the reader will learn in the next chapter, were fabrications. In 1915, having read what General West wrote, Connor was willing to make an affidavit that the statements were false. West was later charged with brutality but was apparently cleared on the basis of his own lies.

The quotation from Connor will be found on pages 36–37 of his book.

Chapter XI

For the initial portion of this chapter, I have continued to rely on Connor, whose account appears accurate and who is substantiated by other sources. The miners, of course, did not let the War Department know what had actually transpired. As they would see it, it was none of their business, they had other worries to occupy them, and they would not want to make enemies of the soldiers on whose protection they had to rely. But it is no wonder that the government in Washington made so many mistakes when the information it received from the field could be this inaccurate.

For Geronimo's story, I have depended on his own account, although his chronology indicates he may well have lost his sense of time with the passing years. He gives specific dates for certain of his adventures, but if these are matched against the dates of events that were known to the Americans, they often do not fit. Although annoying to an historian, this is not an important point. It is clear that during this period, Geronimo was engaging in minor raids, mostly against the Mexicans, and contributing to the general disorder that prevailed in the Southwest. It is his mode of life that is significant rather than the specific timing of each event.

In his autobiography, Geronimo states flatly that after the death of Mangas Coloradas, he was elected tribal chief. Of course, he was not. Victorio became chief of the Warm Springs Apaches, and numerous other chiefs, like Loco and Mangas, worked with him. Although Geronimo became more and more respected as a warrior, as a man with ideas, and as a leader on raids, he did not become a chief in the accepted Apache use of that word.

In his own narrative, Geronimo talks about fighting the Mexicans but not the Americans. As earlier, this may have been due to his unwillingness to get himself into more trouble. On the other hand, his original hatred of the Mexicans was so great that he may really have concentrated all his efforts against them. Most of his raids followed a similar pattern. A small group of Apaches would cross the border and steal what they could, sometimes successfully and sometimes unsuccessfully. Many of these raids were relatively uneventful, and yet on some of them the Apaches met stiff opposition from the Mexican soldiers. On one point Geronimo's narrative can perhaps be questioned. That is the frequency with which he tells of Mexican attacks on the Apaches in their rancherías. Presumably, unless he had gone to live with the Nednis, these took place on American soil, which does not seem likely.

In his pages covering these years Ralph H. Ogle gives a graphic picture of the Americans' vacillating policies. Connor (pages 306–8) presents a dramatic picture of corruption in the Army. He also (pages 333–35) tells about the bill introduced into the Arizona Legislature in 1866 for the professed purpose of defending the citizens but for the actual purpose of benefiting a profiteer.

Geronimo's sad comments about Mangas Coloradas are from pages 120–21 of his book.

Chapter XII

Did or did not the Indians at Camp Grant continue their raiding after they placed themselves under the protection of the Army? That was the central issue in the trial that followed the federal government's indictment of the participants in the massacre. The defense presented evidence they had and argued, in effect, that the massacre had been in self-defense. The jury, after deliberating for about nineteen minutes, agreed and returned a verdict of not guilty. But no Tucson jury would have convicted the defendants in any case.

The defense's evidence was somewhat tenuous, consisting of the identification of a dress, some saddles, and livestock in the possession of the Indians and recaptured at the time of the raid. The cross-examination of the United States attorney was something less than piercing, and he often did not call the original owner to the stand but depended on hearsay. On the other hand, it was clearly evident from Whitman's testimony that he was unable to prove the whereabouts of the Indians. He had only a handful of men under his command and no means of watching the Indians continually.

Probably the truth lay somewhere in between the two extremes. Some of the Indians at Camp Grant undoubtedly continued their old practices and when they were hungry went out and stole a white man's cattle. But if the depredations had been severe, Whitman would have known it. If nothing else, he would have noticed the unusual amount of loot in the Indians' camp. But he did not, and it is likely that the attacks that most hurt the settlers came from other tribes.

Although the citizens' attack on the Aravaipa Apaches did not directly affect the Chiricahua, Nedni, and Warm Springs Apaches, with whom this book is chiefly concerned, it contributed greatly to the distrust that surrounded all dealings between Indians and whites. By the white men's standards, the Indians were often treacherous. But so were the white men, and little faith could be placed in their word.

There are numerous accounts of the tragedy. One of the most touching is Whitman's report, which Colyer reproduced in his own report. Don Schellie, in his *Vast Domain of Blood,* has done a good job of drawing all the threads together.

Camp Grant should not be confused with the present Fort Grant, whose old buildings still stand and are utilized by the state as a school. The site of the original Camp Grant, where the massacre took place, proved so unhealthy that eventually the post was moved.

Eskiminzin later surrendered to the white men, who asked him about the murder of McKinney. The various versions of what he said differ in wording but not in sense. The one I have used was the one that Britton Davis thought the most likely to be accurate.

Camp Apache, an important base for fighting the northern

Apaches and the center of a large reservation, went through several changes of name: Ord, Mogollon, Thomas, and, finally, Apache. In 1879, it became a fort. Many of the old buildings still remain and are well worth visiting. In the one that General Crook often used as his headquarters the White Mountain Apaches have formed a cultural center under the direction of Edgar Perry. Perry and his wife are attempting to preserve the cultural traditions of the White Mountain Apaches before they disappear altogether. Among their many interesting projects is an attempt to record on tape the stories told by the older Apaches.

Colyer's report contains Whitman's account of what happened. I have drawn on this for Whitman's eyewitness statements.

Chapter XIII

In the first part of this chapter, I have relied heavily on both Howard's and Crook's versions of their activities. Naturally, their accounts differ on several points because of their differing attitudes. Both were admirable men. Howard, in spite of his love of speech-making and the fault of taking himself too seriously, truly desired and hoped to make peaceful friends of the Indians. And to an extent he succeeded with some of them. Crook was a practical soldier who was convinced that fighting was necessary first and wanted to get around to doing it before anyone else got killed.

Therefore, when they met with Eskiminzin, for example, Crook saw only Indians; Howard saw men who could be converted to the white men's ways with kindness and without the necessity of battling them. Obviously, Crook thought Howard something of a fool, and he expressed himself accordingly. One thing that particularly irritated him was his conviction that Howard was offering some of his officers the inducement of a transfer East, where Army life was easier, in return for supporting the peace policy. If this was so, Crook certainly was justified in his anger with Howard.

Ogle provides a comprehensive picture of the fluctuations in American policy toward the Indians, particularly during this period. The country was divided into two camps. Howard represented one, but Crook did not represent the other. He was far more moderate than many of the Westerners, who would have liked to have seen a war of extermination. Crook believed in treating the Indians fairly, and he issued orders that none of his men was to make promises that they did not have the authority to keep. His difference with Howard was over the fundamental question: Could an Indian be trusted before he had learned the white men's strength?

The delightful scene of Howard opening the meeting by praying and thereby scaring the Aravaipas away can be found in Dan L. Thrapp's *The Conquest of Apachería.* He discovered a document describing it in the New York Public Library. It was written by a woman who knew Whitman in Washington and wrote down what he told her.

Dealing with the peace that Howard made with Cochise, in the second part of this chapter, I have relied on Howard's own account and on the comments made by Frederick Hughes. These appeared as a series of letters to the Arizona *Daily Star* and were published early in 1886. Transcripts of them are contained in the Hayden Collection at the Arizona Pioneers' Historical Society. Hughes, who had a long and distinguished career in Arizona, worked with the Warm Springs Apaches and also with Jeffords at the Chiricahua reservation. He was not at the peace negotiations, but he heard about them directly from Jeffords. He is responsible for my statement that the treaty did not permit the Chiricahuas to raid in Sonora. This later became a subject of dispute, for many of the white men, knowing that at least some of the Apaches were conducting such raids, blamed the Chiricahuas and openly wondered whether Howard had not agreed to let them continue. If Howard had, Jeffords would have been the first to say so, for it would have relieved him of much criticism.

Jeffords, about whom relatively little is known, was one of the most extraordinary figures in Southwestern history. There is no doubt about the unusual friendship that developed between him and Cochise. No one knows exactly how it started. Malicious tongues whispered that Jeffords had gained the confidence of the chief by selling him guns, but no evidence supports this. In accepting the agency, Jeffords did himself a disservice. Large sums of money could be made by a dishonest agent, but for an honest one the job was miserable. A good agent usually found himself caught in a crossfire between the Army, the civilians, and the Indians and was blamed by all parties for what they thought had gone wrong. If Jeffords had been seeking fame and fortune, he could have found them in far easier ways.

The quotation describing Crook's arrival in Tucson is taken from Bourke, page 108. Bourke was a great admirer of Crook's, but he did not exaggerate the man's modesty. The direct quotations from Howard are as he gives them in *Famous Indian Chiefs I Have Known.* The resolution adopted by the New Mexicans appears in Colyer's report, and the statements by Crook are contained in his autobiography, pages 167–68 and 170.

Chapter XIV

For the part of this chapter describing the early days on the Chiricahua reservation, I have followed Hughes's description in the Arizona *Daily Star.* The quotations appeared in the issues of January 27 and 28, 1886. Governor Stafford's description of Cochise was published in the Arizona *Citizen* on December 7, 1872.

Geronimo was certainly at the conference with Howard. He says so, and so does the general. But his own story becomes confusing after that. In one place he states specifically that he went to Mexico in 1873 and spent the year there. In another, he says he left the Chiricahuas shortly after the signing of the peace and returned to Victorio. Soon after that, Clum arrived and put him in irons, according to his version. Actually, as the reader will discover, several years elapsed between the treaty made by Howard and Clum's action in removing the Warm Springs Apaches to San Carlos. It seems likely that Geronimo did go to Victorio shortly after the treaty was made and then down to Mexico.

In the narrative of his life, Geronimo equates himself with Cochise by saying that Jeffords issued equal rations to Cochise and to himself to distribute among their respective bands. At no time in his life did Geronimo have nearly as many warriors under him as did Cochise, and most certainly not at that point. This was the boasting of an old man looking back on his youthful career.

In describing the negotiations with the Chiricahuas, I have followed Hughes's account. He knew these Indians well, conducted the original talks with them before Clum's arrival at Fort Bowie, and went to the relief of Taza when he was under attack from the other Chiricahuas. There seems to be no reason to believe that his description of the events is inaccurate. Clum's account gives a bit more credit to Clum than is perhaps due him.

But there is no question he was a remarkable man. Although he was hard on Geronimo and made a serious mistake in moving Victorio—a mistake which later spread the Apache wars because he converted Victorio from a friend into an enemy—he understood the Apaches and their desire to govern themselves. He believed in punishing the bad and rewarding the good, and he tried to be fair to them. He was constantly irritated by the typical settler's attitude that all Apaches were bad. Those who want to know more about him may be interested in reading the biography written by Woodworth Clum, based in large part on John Clum's own records. I am indebted to the book for a graphic description of the capture of Geronimo.

Ogle relates in detail the difficulties at San Carlos and also unearthed the fact that Geronimo was put in charge of the Chiricahuas. Betzinez has a good description of Geronimo's flight from the reservation, which I have drawn on. He puts it, however, before, not after, the Warm Springs Apaches left.

The Mexicans were secretive about the death of Victorio. They gave the reward they had placed on his head—3,000 American dollars—to an individual and did considerable celebrating afterward, but the full story will probably never be known. An Apache's account is given in Eve Ball's book *In the Days of Victorio,* which contains an excellent description of life under Victorio. It is the story told by James Kaywaykla. Curiously, his account of the battle at Tres Castillas differs in some important aspects from what Betzinez says he was told by him. The description of Nana talking to the survivors is contained in Ball, pages 100–1.

CHAPTER XV

For the first part of this chapter, I have followed Eve Ball's book. Its subject and narrator, James Kaywaykla, was a small boy at the time, and much of what he knew he learned from hearing the warriors speak. He is responsible for the statement that Victorio committed suicide. This does not quite jibe with the Chihuahuan government's giving a reward to a specific individual for the slaying, but there are many possible explanations. The individual, for example, may have provided the information that led to the ambush.

Conditions on the San Carlos reservation are well described by Ogle in his book. The text of the grand jury's findings appeared in the Arizona *Weekly Star* of October 26, 1882. A copy of it is in the fine collection of the Arizona Pioneers' Historical Society.

The Cibicue affair (I have used the modern spelling of Cibicue with a final "e") is extremely complicated, and no one really knew what took place. I have heard at least one old Apache claim the Indians were merely indulging in harmless religious practices and the Americans tried to interfere. I am strongly inclined to share his point of view. Noch-ay-del-klinne waited peacefully for the soldiers' arrival and agreed to go along with them just as soon as he had finished his meal, certainly a reasonable request. It is also true that the Apaches could have annihilated Carr's command, particularly if there were as many of them around as the military later reported. Thrapp, in *The Conquest of Apachería,* has done an excellent job of taking the various accounts and correlating them.

In describing the raid on San Carlos, I have primarily used Betzinez's and Forsyth's accounts. Betzinez was one of the San Carlos Apaches who was forced to go with the Nednis and Chiricahuas. He was too young to engage in the fighting at the Steins Peak Range, but shortly thereafter he became an apprentice to Geronimo. He tells about the puberty ceremony held during the raid on the ranch. Even as an Apache, he was impressed by the importance the family attached to this rite. He also explains where the women and children were hidden and thus why Forsyth never saw them.

Forsyth includes a direct narrative by McDonald of his encounter with the Apaches. This adds value because, as a result, the entire account is firsthand.

The question of how often the Apaches engaged in torture again arises. The small girl who survived the raid on the ranch said, according to newspaper reports at the time, that the Apaches tortured her father before killing him, but she gives little in the way of detail. Whether they actually did, whether in her fright she thought they did, or whether a newspaper reporter led her to believe they did, remains a question. McDonald actually saw the Apaches mutilate and burn the dead bodies of his scouts. Mutilation of corpses is so foreign to the white man's mind that an American coming upon the remains would have immediately assumed the men had been tortured while still alive. Undoubtedly, mutilation of bodies occurred many times and led to the conviction that the Apaches often tortured prisoners.

At the time of the raid, many white men questioned whether Geronimo was present; and Tom Horn, who served in the scouts under Sieber, says he talked to some of the Apaches remaining at San Carlos and they assured him that Geronimo was not among the raiders. Betzinez, on the other hand, specifically lists these leaders among the group: Nachez, Chato, Chihuahua, Loco, of course, and Geronimo, and he says Geronimo played a leading role. Although Betzinez's relationship to the warrior may have given him some reason to overstate Geronimo's part, his account seems to be accurate. In every instance that he reports an event that is also described by reliable white sources, the two accounts concur.

The description of the fight with the Mexicans is taken from Betzinez. He was not present at the rifle pit in the arroyo but heard about it as soon as the warriors reached the mountains. One point on which he is somewhat confusing is the number of warriors involved. His totals come to approximately fifty altogether. This seems somewhat low considering that the Nednis and Chiricahuas were joined by Loco's Warm Springs Apaches. It may well be that some of the warriors left the main band about the time they reached Mexico.

When Forsyth passed by Janos, a courier rode out to meet him with another formal protest for his invasion of Mexican territory. This was from the colonel commanding at Janos. On his return to New Mexico, he filed a written report with his commander telling what he had done. His commander gave it back to him with the advice that, unless the Mexican government protested officially to the Secretary of State, it would be wiser to say nothing. Not until 1900, when he published his book, did Forsyth again admit publicly what he had done.

An excellent overall account of the raid is contained in Thrapp's book about Al Sieber. The two quotations from Betzinez will be found on pages 56–57 and 74 of his book.

Chapter XVI

The general conditions of the Apaches in the Sierra Madres were described by the scout Peaches when he finally decided to join the Army in its offensive. Bourke, in *An Apache Campaign . . .* (page 33), reports what he had to say. Peaches believed the Indians might be starved out of the mountains. Betzinez (pages 77–81) describes the massacre at Casas Grandes. He was present at the time, helping a woman who was trying to sell a horse, and was among those who slept at the southern edge of the town. Casas Grandes still exists but is no longer the bustling trading center it once was. The advent of the railroad in the flatter land to the east resulted in most of the activity being moved to Nuevas Casas Grandes, which is many times its size. Walking through the now-quiet plazas of Casas Grandes and talking to its pleasant inhabitants, it is difficult to envision the slaughter that once took place there.

The various raids undertaken by the Apaches in Mexico are described in detail by Betzinez (pages 81–109). He was with Geronimo at the time. He also tells about the fight with the Mexican soldiers (pages 111–12) and later on about the surrender of Peaches and his reason for doing so. Thrapp has an excellent summary of Chato's raid in *The Conquest of Apachería.*

Davis (pages 57–59) describes the surrender of Peaches, and Bourke, in *An Apache Campaign . . .* (pages 30–33), repeats the information that the defector gave to Crook. Lummis, in *General Crook and the Apache Wars* (pages 71–73), gives a delightful description of the Tombstone Toughs. In the West, as elsewhere, the bravest men were not the loudest talkers. Bourke, in *An Apache Campaign . . .* (pages 34–36), tells about the international difficulties Crook encountered.

Betzinez (pages 112–21) tells about Geronimo's life in Mexico and his activities just before the surrender. Not much is known about Geronimo's power as a medicine man, but some of the older Apaches interviewed by Opler in *Apache Odyssey* made mention of his magic. The two quotations describing Geronimo's premonitions appear on pages 113 and 115 of Betzinez's book.

Bourke's *An Apache Campaign . . .* is devoted entirely to this campaign. His description of the country in the Sierra Madres can be found on pages 77–78. Davis (pages 82–101) gives a firsthand description of meeting Geronimo and getting him safely to San Carlos. The two quotations by him are taken from those pages.

Chapter XVII

For the first part of this chapter, my most important source is Davis, who supervised the Apaches at Turkey Creek and went on the first campaign into the Sierra Madres. When he returned to the United States, he resigned from the Army to take a civilian job, but his interest in the Apaches continued, and he followed their activities closely. The Apaches, of course, did not write down their side of the outbreak, but Davis and Crook learned what had happened from some of the Indians who remained on the reservation. This information was useful to Crook when he was treating with Geronimo, because he was able to demonstrate that he was well informed on Indian affairs.

The description of Juh's death is taken from Eve Ball's book. Her narrator does not say that Juh was drunk, but nothing else could explain his inability to move himself from the water. Certainly a hardy Apache would not normally have been stunned by such a fall. His recent visit to Casas Grandes gives added credence to this interpretation.

Crawford's second campaign into Mexico is well described in both Bourke and Davis; and Thrapp, in *The Conquest of Apachería,* quotes directly from the pertinent government reports on the tragedy of Crawford's death. Bourke was at Crook's meeting with Geronimo and made a summary of the conversation between the general and the Apaches. Crook wanted no misunderstandings later. Both Bourke and Davis include in their books parts of the summary as well as Crook's reports to Washington.

Tribolet remains a shadowy figure in history, one who emerged briefly to work his evil and then retreated into obscurity again. Lummis, in *General Crook and the Apache Wars,* says that he had been tried earlier for stealing barley from Fort Huachuca. There is no question that he dealt in whiskey and mescal and that probably he also engaged in the extensive international smuggling that went on. In addition, it was rumored he traded with the enemy Apaches, selling them guns and ammunition. There is no direct evidence that he had connections with the "Tucson Ring," as the war profiteers were called. But all the indirect evidence points in that direction.

One American informed Bourke that Tribolet had sold thirty dollars' worth of mescal to the Chiricahuas and had boasted he could have sold them more. He certainly knew the potential danger of his action, and it hardly seems likely he would have run so great a risk for so small a profit. His only motivation must have been to stir up trouble and continue the war. Crook himself admitted that he could not understand all the economic crosscurrents at play in the United States and Mexico. Many people were benefiting from trade with either the Army or the Indians.

To the reader who would like to learn more about Crook and his campaign against the Apaches, I recommend Lummis's *General Crook and the Apache Wars.* This short book is composed of some dispatches Lummis wrote for the Los Angeles *Times.* He was a perceptive reporter and gives an excellent picture of Crook and the Apaches.

The quotations describing the Apaches with their wagons and the arrest made by Davis appear in Davis's book on pages 103–4 and 126.

Chapter XVIII

Although my remarks about General Miles may seen severe, I believe the reader of this chapter will agree with them. Miles's ambition to become President of the United States is generally accepted by historians and is probably the reason why he published his autobiography. That book is invaluable in a study of the Apache wars. It reveals Miles's attitude toward them, and it contains the texts of a number of official reports and the personal narratives of men like Maus and Wood. I have drawn on it, too, for Miles's attitude toward the Apaches, which appears early in his story of his campaign. It is also important because of the information it does not contain, particularly any significant reference to Gatewood's role. The general impression that Miles tries to give is that Crook had fought the Apaches for years without being able to conquer them, while he, Miles, cleaned up the problem in a few months.

He does not emphasize that all he faced was a tiny remnant of once powerful people. Lummis, in *General Crook and the Apache Wars* (pages 140–48), describes Miles and the early days of his campaign. Lummis liked and admired Miles but points out that he lacked the prestige among the Apaches that Crook enjoyed and was not nearly so effective in fighting or controlling them.

For the account of what took place at the Peck ranch, I have drawn on the narrative of T. D. Casanega that is in the collection of the Arizona Pioneers' Historical Society. He was a member of the posses organized in Nogales and he talked directly to Peck after the event. William Mullane (pages 72–90) contains a collection of the newspaper accounts that appeared in the Silver City *Enterprise* during this period and gives a sense of what the press was saying. John Bigelow, Jr., served as a lieutenant under Lebo, and he presents a good description of the futility of chasing Apaches with regular troops. Miles also has a fairly detailed account of Geronimo's raid but tries to lead the reader into believing that it was more or less a victory for the Americans.

There is some difference of opinion about Ki-e-ta's desertion. Miles says he was wounded during the fighting and made his way north alone. Others assert that the raiding party came close to Turkey Creek and that he deserted then. If the raiding party had come that close, it seems likely they would have created a greater disturbance on the reservation and perhaps have caused some Apaches to join them. On the other hand, Miles's account seems to be likely. Ki-e-ta might well have preferred to surrender to the authorities at Fort Apache, some of whom he must have known, than to the unfamiliar combat troops in the field. This would have been typical Apache caution. The place of his defection, however, is not important. His subsequent service to the Americans is.

There are numerous sources of information about Lawton's column and the service it performed. One of the best is Leonard Wood's narrative, which is contained in Miles's autobiography. Much controversy developed over Gatewood's role in inducing Geronimo to treat with Miles. Some gave most of the credit to Lawton, while others claimed the major credit for Gatewood. Miles almost completely disregarded Gatewood and would not accept Gatewood's official report as to what had happened. Gatewood's son later spent much time vindicating his father by obtaining statements from some of the men who knew what was occurring. Here is what one of them said: "I think Miles, Lawton, and Wilder, and several more, were looking for a cheap reputation at the expense of your Dad. I don't think there was one of the bunch that had the guts to go into Geronimo's camp." And another remarked: "Gatewood was the only man in the U.S. Army who could have gone into Geronimo's camp at the time. He knew nearly all the Apaches personally. He had an Apache nurse for his boy at Fort Apache and was respected and held in very high esteem by the Apache Indians. They considered him their friend and he was." Such remarks are typical. A review of the Gatewood Collection in the Arizona Pioneers' Historical Society leaves little doubt as to Gatewood's role, and I have drawn on it heavily for the description of Gatewood's activities.

Geronimo's surrender is described in a number of sources, including Geronimo's narrative and Miles's autobiography. The Senate Executive Documents, Second Session, Forty-ninth Congress, 1886–87, Volume II, Nos. 111–25, contain the pertinent reports as well as the many telegrams and memorandums sent and written following Geronimo's flight.

Judging from them, there is no question that there was confusion about the terms of surrender. President Cleveland expected them to have been unconditional and so did General Sheridan. Most of the witnesses on the spot were not paying much attention to the specific details. They all emphasized that Miles promised Geronimo safety for all his band, but they became vague about almost everything else except that the band would be kept together. Geronimo definitely thought he was surrendering under the condition that the Apaches would be given their own reservation. This is shown not only in his own narrative but in statements he made to civilian authorities at Fort Bowie as revealed in the Senate Executive Documents to which I have referred. It seems likely that Miles promised, at least by implication, more generous treatment than Geronimo and the other Apaches received. He was naturally anxious to make peace and may well have given assent to some question of Geronimo's without thinking what it meant when considered from the Apache's point of view. There was also the problem of interpretation. Much of the conversation between Geronimo and Miles was from Apache to Spanish to English. This certainly presented a possible reason for misunderstanding. All the evidence indicates that, whatever was actually said, Geronimo believed he was surrendering under different terms than the Americans believed they had proposed to him. The quotations are drawn from both Miles's and Geronimo's books. Miles's opinion of the Apaches is expressed on page 445, and Chapter XXXIX contains his account of the surrender. Geronimo's opening remarks appear in an account of the surrender written by Melton, which appears on page 172 of Geronimo's book.

Epilogue

In writing his autobiography, Miles's memory played him false, for his account of Mangas's capture is incorrect. Davis's book contains the right version. My figures for the sheep and cattle wars are taken from Frank Lockwood's report of what Lorenzo Hubbell said, as told by him in *Pioneer Portraits*. Hubbell was a sheriff at the time. The quotation from Geronimo was made during an interview that appeared in the Tucson *Daily Star* on December 6, 1908, a little more than a year before his death. Geronimo spoke in halting Spanish, and it is doubtful whether he actually referred to the President as the Great White Father. The Apaches used that term as little as they used "pale face," but it is what the newspaper reader would have expected. In the Gatewood Collection in the Arizona Pioneers' Historical Society are several references by contemporaries to Miles's action in assigning Gatewood to clerical duties so that he could not attend the dinner in Tucson. Davis also says this happened.

The other material in this epilogue is contained in most accounts of the Apache Wars. The opinions are obviously my own.

Bibliography

The following are some of the most important sources consulted in the preparation of this book.

Because they are more easily obtainable, I have listed reprints rather than the original editions when reprints are available. What cannot be listed—and yet are equally important—are hundreds of miles of travel in Arizona, New Mexico, Chihuahua, and Sonora, visiting battle sites and following Apache trails, travels I started many years ago. As Crook commented to Sheridan, no one can understand the Apache wars or the Indians' strategy without an understanding of the unusual terrain. Nor is it possible to list numerous conversations with Mexicans, Indians, and some of the people who still retained the spirit of the frontiersmen. Because memories fade and traditions change with the passing years, such conversations produce less direct information than the more formal sources, but they are significant in discovering attitudes and ways of life.

Arizona Pioneers' Historical Society, Tucson, Arizona, The Hayden, Hughes, and Gatewood Collections; issues of contemporary Arizona newspapers, including the *Weekly Arizonian,* the Tucson *Weekly Star,* the Arizona *Citizen,* and the Tombstone *Daily Nugget;* and other documents.

Baird, George W., "General Miles' Indian Campaign." *The Smoke Signal* (Spring, 1967), pp. 110–13.

Baldwin, Gordon C., *The Warrior Apaches.* Tucson, Arizona, Dale Stuart King, 1965.

Ball, Eve, *In the Days of Victorio.* Tucson, Arizona, University of Arizona Press, 1970.

Banning, William, with Banning, George Hugh, *Six Horses.* New York, Century Company, 1930.

Bartlett, John Russell, *Personal Narratives of Explorations and Incidents in Texas, New Mexico, California, Sonora, and Chihuahua.* New York, D. Appleton & Company, 1854.

Basso, Keith H., *Western Apache Witchcraft.* Tucson, Arizona, University of Arizona Press, 1969.

Betzinez, Jason, with Nye, Wilbur Sturtevant, *I Fought with Geronimo.* Harrisburg, Pennsylvania, Stackpole Company, 1960.

Bigelow, John, Jr., *On the Bloody Trail of Geronimo,* with a foreword, introduction, and notes by Arthur Woodward. Los Angeles, Westernlore Press, 1968.

Bourke, John G., *An Apache Campaign in the Sierra Madre,* introduction by J. Frank Dobie. New York, Charles Scribner's Sons, 1958.

———, "General Crook in Indian Country." *The Smoke Signal* (Spring, 1967), pp. 99–109.

———, *On the Border with Crook.* Glorieta, New Mexico, Río Grande Press, 1969.

Brandes, Ray, *Frontier Military Posts of Arizona.* Globe, Arizona, Dale Stuart King, 1960.

Brewerton, George Douglas, *Overland with Kit Carson,* Stallo Vinton, ed. New York, Coward-McCann, Inc., 1930.

Briggs, L. Vernon, *Arizona and New Mexico, 1882; California, 1886; Mexico, 1891.* Ann Arbor, Michigan, University Microfilms, Inc., 1966.

Carroll, John Alexander, "A Commentary of the Crooks-Miles Controversy." *The Smoke Signal* (Spring, 1967), pp. 114–15.

Casanega, T. D., Typescript of reminiscences in the Arizona Pioneers' Historical Society, Tucson, Arizona.

Chapel, Charles Edward, *Guns of the Old West.* New York, Coward-McCann, Inc., 1961.

Clark, Thomas D., *Frontier America; The Story of the Western Movement.* New York, Charles Scribner's Sons, 1969.

Clum, Woodworth, *Apache Agent: The Story of John P. Clum.* Boston, Houghton Mifflin Company, 1936.

Colyer, Vincent, *Peace with the Apaches of New Mexico and Arizona.* Washington, D.C., Government Printing Office, 1872.

Connor, Daniel Ellis, *Joseph Reddeford Walker and the Arizona Adventure,* Donald J. Berthrong and Odessa Davenport, eds. Norman, Oklahoma, University of Oklahoma Press, 1956.

Cremony, John Carey, *Life Among the Apaches.* Glorieta, New Mexico, Río Grande Press, 1969.

Crook, George, *Autobiography,* edited and annotated by Martin F. Schmitt. Norman, Oklahoma, University of Oklahoma Press, 1946.

Davis, Britton, *The Truth About Geronimo,* with a foreword by Robert M. Utley. New Haven, Connecticut, Yale University Press, 1963.

DeVoto, Bernard, *The Year of Decision: 1846.* Boston, Little Brown and Company, 1943.

Dobie, J. Frank. *See* Bourke, John G.

Dodge, Irving Richard, *Thirty-three Years Among Our Wild Indians.* New York, Archer House, Inc., 1959.

Dunn, J. P., Jr., *Massacres of the Mountains.* New York, Archer House, Inc., No date. (Originally published in 1886.)

Executive Documents, Second Session, Forty-ninth Congress, 1886–1887, Vol. II, Nos. 111–25. Washington, D.C., U.S. Government Printing Office, 1887.

Farwell, John V., *Some Recollections of John V. Farwell.* Chicago, R. R. Donnelley & Sons Company, 1911.

Faulk, Odie B., *Land of Many Frontiers: A History of the American Southwest.* New York, Oxford University Press, 1968.

———, *The Geronimo Campaign.* New York, Oxford University Press, 1969.

Fireman, Bert M. *See* Paré, Madeline Ferrin.

Forbes, Jack D., *Apache, Navajo, and Spaniard.* Norman, Oklahoma, University of Oklahoma Press, 1960.

Forsyth, George A., *The Story of the Soldier.* New York, D. Appleton and Company, 1900.

———, *Thrilling Days in Army Life.* New York, Harper and Brothers, 1900.

Frazer, Robert W., *Forts of the Old West.* Norman, Oklahoma, University of Oklahoma Press, 1966. *See also* McCall, George Archibald.

Gardiner, Dorothy, *West of the River: A History.* New York, Thomas Y. Crowell, 1963.

Gates, Paul W., *History of Public Land Law,* with a chapter by Robert W. Swenson. Washington, D.C., U.S. Government Printing Office, 1968.

Geronimo's Story of His Life, told to and edited by S. M. Barrett. New York, Garrett Press, Inc., 1969.

Goodwin, Grenville, *The Social Organization of the Western Apache.* Tucson, Arizona, University of Arizona Press, 1969.

Gregg, Josiah, *Commerce of the Prairies,* Max L. Moorhead, ed. Norman, Oklahoma, University of Oklahoma Press, 1954.

Haley, J. Evetts, *Jeff Milton: A Good Man with a Gun.* Norman, Oklahoma, University of Oklahoma Press, 1949.

Hawgood, John A., *America's Western Frontiers.* New York, Alfred K. Knopf, 1967.

Hollon, W. Eugene, *The Southwest: Old and New.* New York, Alfred K. Knopf, 1967.

Horn, Tom, *Life of Tom Horn.* Norman, Oklahoma, University of Oklahoma Press, 1964.

Howard, Oliver Otis, *Autobiography.* 2 vols. New York, Baker and Taylor Company, 1907.

———, *Famous Indian Chiefs I Have Known.* New York, Century Company, 1908.

Irwin, B. J. D., "The Chiricahua Apache Indians: A Thrilling Incident in the Early History of Arizona Territory." *Infantry Journal,* Vol. XXXII, No. 4 (April, 1928), pp. 368–73.

Jackson, Helen Hunt, *A Century of Dishonor.* New York, Harper and Row, 1965.

Keim, DeB. Randolph, *Sheridan's Troopers on the Border: A Winter Campaign on the Plains.* New York, George Routledge and Sons, 1885.

Larson, Robert W., *New Mexico's Quest for Statehood: 1846–1912.* Albuquerque, New Mexico, University of New Mexico Press, 1968.

Lockwood, Frank C., *Pioneer Portraits.* Tucson, Arizona, University of Arizona Press, 1968.

———, *The Apache Indians.* New York, The Macmillan Company, 1938.

Lowie, Robert H., *Indians of the Plains.* Garden City, New York, Natural History Press, 1954.

Lummis, Charles F., *General Crook and the Apache Wars.* Flagstaff, Arizona, Northland Press, 1966.

———, *Land of Poco Tiempo.* Albuquerque, New Mexico, University of New Mexico Press, 1969.

McCall, George Archibald, *New Mexico in 1850: A Military View,* edited and with an introduction by Robert W. Frazer. Norman, Oklahoma, University of Oklahoma Press, 1968.

McHenry, J. Patrick, *A Short History of Mexico.* Garden City, New York, Doubleday & Company, Inc., 1962.

Miles, Nelson A., *Personal Recollections,* introduction by Robert M. Utley. New York, Da Capo Press, 1969.

Miller, Joseph, ed., *Arizona Cavalcade: The Turbulent Times.* New York, Hastings House, 1962.

Mullane, William H., *Indian Raids as Reported in the Silver City Enterprise.* No city, William H. Mullane, 1968.

Mulligan, R. A., "Apache Pass and Old Fort Bowie." *The Smoke Signal* (Spring, 1965), pp. 1–24.

Nye, Wilbur Sturtevant. *See* Betzinez, Jason.

Ogle, Ralph Hedrick, *Federal Control of the Western Apaches: 1848–1886.* Albuquerque, New Mexico, University of New Mexico Press, 1970.

Opler, Morris E., *Apache Life-Way.* New York, Cooper Square Publishers, Inc., 1965.

———, *Apache Odyssey*. New York, Holt, Rinehart, and Winston, 1969.

Paré, Madeline Ferrin, *Arizona Pageant: A Short History of the 48th State,* with the collaboration of Bert M. Fireman. Phoenix, Arizona, Arizona Historical Foundation, 1965.

Petterson, Thomas H., Jr., "Fort Lowell, A. T., Army Post during the Apache Campaign." *The Smoke Signal* (Fall, 1963), pp. 1–19.

Robbins, Roy M., *Our Landed Heritage: The Public Domain, 1776–1936.* Lincoln, Nebraska, University of Nebraska Press, 1962.

Robinson, Will H., *Under Turquoise Skies.* New York, Macmillan Company, 1928.

Russell, Carl P., *Guns on the Early Frontier.* New York, Bonanza, 1957.

Russell, Don, "Chief Cochise vs. Lieutenant Bascom." *Winners of the West,* Vol. XIV (December, 1936), pp. 1–3, 7–8.

San Carlos Reservation, San Carlos, Arizona, Typewritten and handwritten documents: A chronology of events prepared in connection with the Indian Claims Commission; Summaries of reports of Apache scouts' patrols.

Schellie, Don, *Vast Domain of Blood: The Story of the Camp Grant Massacre.* Los Angeles, Westernlore Press, 1968.

Schmitt, Martin F. *See* Crook, George.

Scott, Hugh Lenox, *Some Memories of a Soldier.* New York, Century Company, 1928.

Spicer, Edward Holland, *Cycles of Conquest: The Impact of Spain, Mexico and the United States on the Indians of the Southwest, 1533–1960.* Tucson, Arizona, University of Arizona Press, 1962.

Spring, John A., *John Spring's Arizona,* A. M. Gustafson, ed. Tucson, Arizona, University of Arizona Press, 1966.

Swenson, Robert W. *See* Gates, Paul W.

Tebbel, John, *The Compact History of the Indian Wars.* New York, Hawthorn Books, Inc., 1966.

Thrapp, Dan L., *Al Sieber, Chief of Scouts.* Norman, Oklahoma, University of Oklahoma Press, 1964.

———, *The Conquest of Apacheria.* Norman, Oklahoma, University of Oklahoma Press, 1967.

Utley, Robert M., *Historical Report on Fort Bowie, Arizona.* Santa Fe, New Mexico, U.S. Department of the Interior, National Park Service, 1967. *See also* Miles, Nelson A.

Webb, Walter Prescott, *The Texas Rangers: A Century of Frontier Defense.* Boston, Houghton Mifflin Company, 1935.

Wellman, Paul I., *The Indian Wars of the West.* Garden City, New York, Doubleday & Company, Inc., 1947.

Welsh, Herbert, *The Apache Prisoners at Fort Marion.* Philadelphia, Office of the Indian Rights Association, 1887.

Whitney, E. C. and Whitney, T. H., *History and Capture of Geronimo and Apache Indians: Prisoners in Fort Marion*. St. Augustine, Florida, published by the authors, 1887.

Wilson, Edward, *Exciting Days of Early Arizona*. Santa Fe, New Mexico, Stagecoach Press, 1968.

Index

INDEX

Note: Because the Apaches had no written language, the spellings of their names are phonetic. This was also true of the spelling of their Spanish names, for many Americans were relatively unfamiliar with that language. As a consequence, numerous variations exist. Chato is often spelled with two *t*'s and Nana with two *n*'s. Mangas in "Mangas Coloradas" appears as Magnus or Mangus, both of them variations of the proper spelling for the Spanish word for sleeves, *mangas*. Victorio is sometimes written as Victori*a*, and Nachez appears in a number of forms, such as Natchez and Naichez. With the exception of Juh, which sometimes appears as Whoa, these variations are recognizable, and because there are so many of them, it is not practical to list them individually.

With the passage of time many of the individual tribes became intermingled and almost undistinguishable from each other. References to specific tribes are therefore limited to instances in which the identity of the tribe is both clear and pertinent.

UNIVERSITY LIBRARY
NOTTINGHAM

about 23

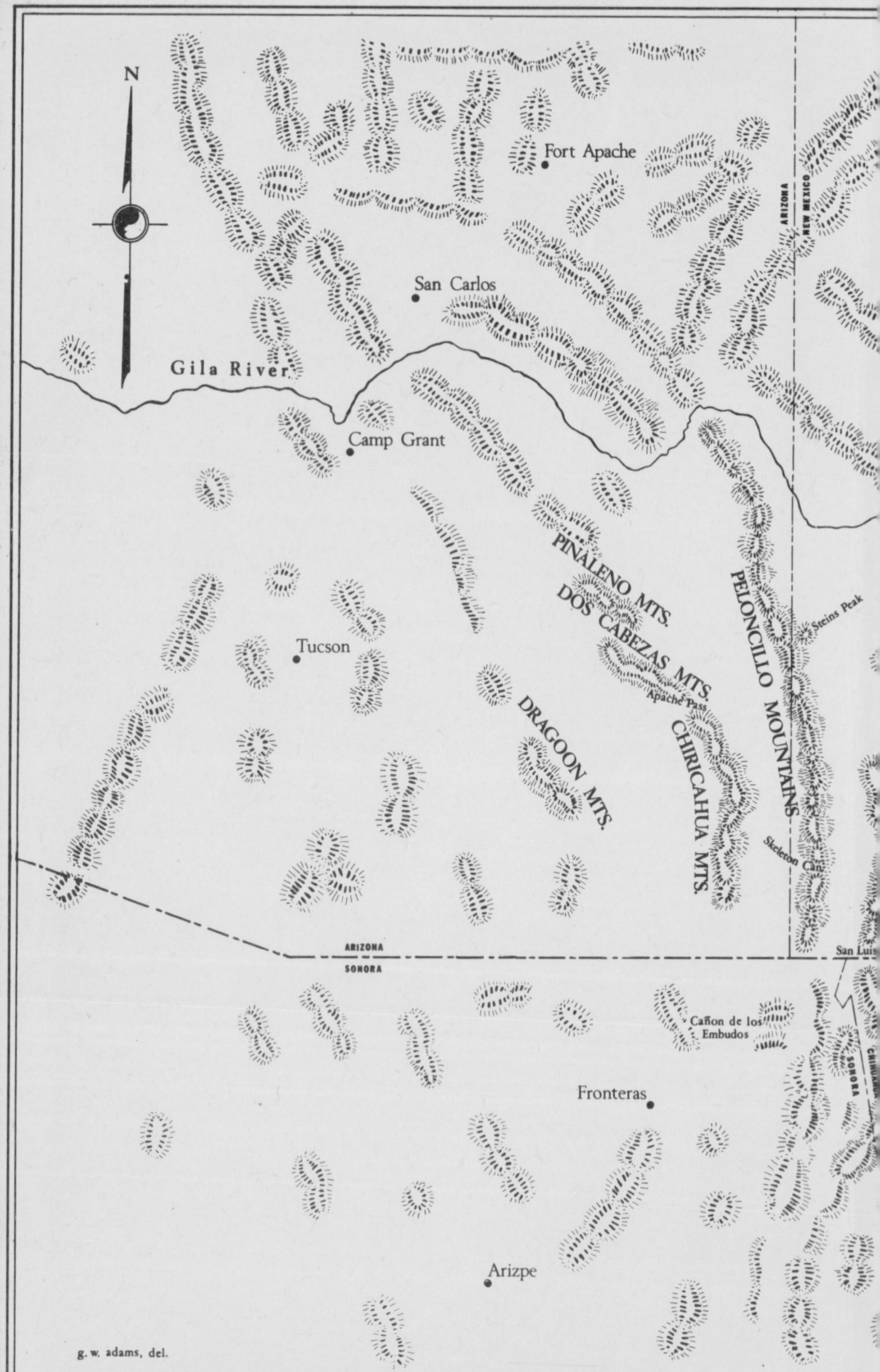

N
Fort Apache
San Carlos
Gila River
Camp Grant
ARIZONA
NEW MEXICO
PINALENO MTS.
DOS CABEZAS MTS.
PELONCILLO MOUNTAINS
Steins Peak
Tucson
Apache Pass
DRAGOON MTS.
CHIRICAHUA MTS.
Skeleton Can.
ARIZONA
SONORA
San Luis
Cañon de los Embudos
SONORA
Fronteras
Arizpe
g. w. adams, del.